MILITARY LEADERSHIP

bourboncolumbia
. com
1214 Main St.
Cola. S. 29063

SIXTH EDITION

★ ★ ★ ★ ★

MILITARY LEADERSHIP

In Pursuit of Excellence

EDITED BY

Robert L. Taylor
University of Louisville

AND

William E. Rosenbach
Emeritus, Gettysburg College

AND

Eric B. Rosenbach
Harvard Kennedy School

WITH A FOREWORD BY

Lieutenant General Gregory S. Newbold
(USMC Ret.)

Westview
PRESS
A Member of the Perseus Books Group

A CIP catalog record for this book is available from the Library of Congress
ISBN-13: 978-0-8133-4439-3
10 9 8 7 6 5 4 3 2 1

CONTENTS

PART ONE
LEADERSHIP
Perspectives and Context

PART TWO
CHARACTER
The Heart of Leadership

PART THREE
GENERAL OFFICERS
Leadership Challenges and Opportunities

PART FOUR
THE FUTURE OF MILITARY LEADERSHIP

About the Editors and Contributors

Editors

Lieutenant Colonel Robert L. Taylor (USAF Ret.) is professor of management, dean emeritus, and director of international programs at the College of Business, University of Louisville. During his twenty years in the US Air Force, he served as a combat defense operations officer, missile launch control officer, and professor and head of the Department of Management at the US Air Force Academy. He can be reached at bob.taylor@louisville.edu.

Colonel William E. Rosenbach (USAF Ret.) is the Evans professor of Eisenhower leadership studies and professor emeritus of management at Gettysburg College. Formerly professor and head of the Department of Behavioral Sciences and Leadership at the US Air Force Academy, he wrote or cowrote numerous articles and books on leadership topics. He is especially interested in the elements of effective followership and is the founding partner of the Gettysburg Leadership Experience. He can be reached at rosenbach@leadingandfollowing.com.

Eric B. Rosenbach is the executive director of the Belfer Center for International Affairs at Harvard University's John F. Kennedy School of Government. He formerly served as a professional staff member on the Senate Intelligence Committee and as national security adviser for Senator Chuck Hagel. As a commander in the Army, he earned the Meritorious Service Medal. He is a former Fulbright scholar and completed his bachelor's degree at Davidson College, master's degree at Harvard University, and juris doctor at Georgetown University. His e-mail is eric_rosenbach@ksg04.harvard.edu.

Contributors

PART ONE

Brigadier General Lincoln C. Andrews, a West Point graduate, was commander of the 86th Infantry Division during World War I. After retiring from the Army he served as the assistant secretary of the treasury in charge of prohibition enforcement.

General S. L. A. Marshall was chief US Army combat historian during World War II and the Korean War. He wrote some thirty books about warfare.

Daniel Goleman is founder of Emotional Intelligence Services, an affiliate of the Hay Group in Boston. A psychologist who for many years reported on the brain and behavioral sciences for the *New York Times,* Dr. Goleman previously was a visiting faculty member at Harvard. He attended Amherst College, where he was an Alfred P. Sloan scholar and graduated magna cum laude. His graduate education was at Harvard, where he was a Ford fellow, and he received his master's and doctoral degrees in clinical psychology and personality development.

James L. Stokesbury wrote *A Short History of World War I, A Short History of World War II, A Short History of the Korean War,* and *A Short History of the American Revolution.* Before his death in 1995, he was a professor of history at Acadia University in Nova Scotia, Canada.

John Charles Kunich is a professor of law at Appalachian School of Law, Grundy, Virginia, where he teaches courses in property, trial advocacy, and the First Amendment. In the Air Force, he served as both a prosecutor and a defense attorney in the Judge Advocate General (JAG) Corps, an instructor at the JAG School, chief counsel on constitutional torts and tax for Headquarters General Litigation Division, an environmental and labor attorney with Air Force Space Command, and senior legal counsel for Falcon Air Force Base, Colorado. The author of five books and numerous law-journal articles, Professor Kunich is a graduate of Squadron Officer School, Air Command and Staff College, and Air War College.

Dr. Richard I. Lester is dean of academic affairs at Ira C. Eaker College for Professional Development, Air University, Maxwell Air Force Base, Alabama.

He previously served as chief of social and behavioral sciences, US Armed Forces Institute; education officer with Strategic Air Command and US Air Forces in Europe; and faculty member at the University of Maryland. Dr. Lester frequently lectures at military institutions in the United States and abroad.

Earl H. Potter III is president of St. Cloud State University and former dean of the College of Business at Eastern Michigan University; Director of Organizational Development at Cornell University; and head of the Department of Management at the US Coast Guard Academy. He has a doctorate in organizational psychology from the University of Washington and over thirty-five years of experience in research and consulting on issues of leadership, team effectiveness, and organizational change. His leadership experience includes leading polar diving explorations, sailing a square-rigged ship with a crew of two hundred as executive officer, and chairing countless faculty meetings.

Lieutenant General Walter F. Ulmer Jr. is a graduate of West Point and a thirty-seven-year veteran of the US Army. For nine years he was president and CEO of the Center for Creative Leadership. His writing focuses on both the theory and practice of leadership and is grounded in his belief that there can be no true leadership without humanity.

Part Two

Jack Uldrich is a global futurist and author. His books include *Into the Unknown: Leadership Lessons from Lewis & Clark's Daring Westward Expedition.*

General Wesley Clark is a graduate of West Point and was a Rhodes scholar. During his thirty-four years in the Army, his assignments included commander of Operation Allied Force in the Kosovo War during his term as supreme allied commander Europe of NATO from 1997 to 2000.

James M. Kouzes is chairman emeritus of the Tom Peters Company and an executive fellow at the Center for Innovation and Entrepreneurship at the Leavey School of Business, Santa Clara University. He also cowrote *The Leadership Challenge.*

Sarah Sewall is director of the Carr Center and a lecturer in public policy at the Kennedy School of Government, Harvard University; she also directs the center's Program on National Security and Human Rights. During the Clinton administration, Sewall served in the Department of Defense as the first deputy assistant secretary for peacekeeping and humanitarian assistance. From 1987 to 1993, she served as senior foreign policy adviser to Senate Majority Leader George J. Mitchell, as delegate to the Senate Arms Control Observer Group, and on the Senate Democratic Policy Committee. Sewall has also worked at a variety of defense research organizations and as associate director of the Committee on International Security Studies at the American Academy of Arts and Sciences. She wrote the introduction to the University of Chicago edition of the US Army and Marine Corps Counterinsurgency Field Manual (2007). She was lead editor of *The United States and the International Criminal Court: National Security and International Law* (2000) and has written widely on US foreign policy, multilateralism, peace operations, and military intervention. Her current research focuses on the civilian in war and includes facilitating a dialogue between the military and human rights communities on the use of force.

Brian Friel covered management and human resources at *Government Executive* for six years and is now a *National Journal* staff correspondent.

Craig Chappelow is senior manager of assessment and development resources at the Center of Creative Leadership, where he focuses on 360-degree feedback and feedback-intensive training and leadership development programs.

PART THREE

Major General J. F. C. Fuller was a British army officer, military historian, and strategist, notable as an early theorist of modern armored warfare.

General Montgomery C. Meigs commanded the NATO Stabilization Force in Bosnia and Herzegovina from October 1998 to October 1999, concurrent with his command of US Army Europe/7th Army. He also served as a cavalry troop commander in the Vietnam War. Meigs graduated from the US Military Academy in 1967 and earned a PhD in history from the University of Wisconsin. He is currently a visiting professor of strategy and military operations at Georgetown University's School of Foreign Service.

Major Paula D. Broadwell most recently served as associate director of the Jebsen Center for Counter-Terrorism Studies at the Fletcher School, Tufts University. She is a major in the Army Reserves and has held counterterrorism assignments with the FBI Joint Terrorism Task Force, Defense Intelligence Agency, and US Special Operations Command. She is a graduate of West Point and has master's degrees from the University of Denver and Harvard University, and is a PhD candidate at King's College London War Studies Department. Broadwell also serves on the executive board of Women in International Security.

Lieutenant Colonel Paul Yingling is a battalion commander in the US Army. He has served two tours in the Iraq War, first as an executive officer and later as an effects coordinator.

Fred Kaplan is a journalist and contributor to *Slate* magazine. His "War Stories" column covers international relations, US foreign policy, and major related geopolitical issues.

Michael C. Desch is professor and Robert M. Gates chair in intelligence and national security decision-making at the George Bush School of Government and Public Service, Texas A&M University.

PART FOUR

Colonel John Tien served as the primary battalion commander for a unit of 1,100 personnel responsible for the city of Tal Afar, Iraq, from February to October 2006. He served a similar role in the northern portion of Ramadi from October 2006 to February 2007. Colonel Tien holds a bachelor's degree from the US Military Academy and a master's degree from Oxford University, where he was a Rhodes scholar. He has also been a White House fellow and a West Point political science professor, and he is a member of the Council on Foreign Relations. Colonel Tien was a national security fellow at the Harvard Kennedy School from 2007 to 2008. He currently serves as a director on the National Security Council staff in the White House.

Brigadier General Michael Flowers is a former commander of the Joint POW/MIA Accounting Command.

Ambassador Lawrence P. Taylor is a retired Foreign Service officer. He served in ten countries in a thirty-year diplomatic career, and his assignments included those of director of the Foreign Service Institute and US ambassador to Estonia. Since retiring he is active on several boards of directors, including those of the Baltic American Partnership Fund, the Lincoln Fellowship of Pennsylvania, and the Eisenhower Institute. He is a founding partner in the Gettysburg Leadership Experience and has served as senior adviser to three presidents of Gettysburg College.

Major General Robert H. Scales Jr. commanded two units in Vietnam, where he was awarded the Silver Star. He was commandant to the US Army War College before retiring from the Army. He is currently an independent consultant for defense matters.

Brigadier General Kevin Ryan served in the US Army for over twenty-nine years as an air defense and foreign area specialist. He commanded units up to the brigade level and was assigned as the US defense attaché in Moscow from 2001 to 2003. Now retired from the Army, he is a senior fellow at Harvard University's Belfer Center for Science and International Affairs.

Commandant Paul Whelan is an officer in the Irish Defense Forces. He has completed the Irish Military Staff Course and has earned a master's degree in leadership, management, and defense studies through the National University of Ireland.

Bernard M. Bass was director of the Center for Leadership Studies, Binghamton University New York; was principal investigator for the US Army Research Institute and served as a consultant to various Army and Navy personnel agencies. He received bachelor's, master's, and doctoral degrees from Ohio State University. He has served in a variety of staff positions, including professor and director, Management Research Center, University of Rochester; professor, University of Pittsburgh; professor, Louisiana State University; and visiting professor at the University of California, Berkeley; IESE, Barcelona, Spain; Massey University, Palmerton North, New Zealand; and University of Canterbury, Christchurch, New Zealand. He has written fifteen books, including *A New Paradigm of Leadership: An Inquiry into Transactional Leadership* and *Transformational Leadership: Industrial, Military and Educational Impact.*

FOREWORD

God grant that men of principle shall be our principal men.
—*Thomas Jefferson*

By good grace and fortune, we are citizens of the United States—the greatest country in the world and its sole superpower. As Americans, we are generally secure from the troubles, disease, poverty, and danger that trouble many other countries. We live in considerable comfort. For citizens living in such security, the most natural pathway would be to pursue a career free of stress and sacrifice. Some small percentage of Americans, though, are drawn to the opposite: a life that requires discipline, selfless sacrifice, restricted liberties, sometimes long separations, and low compensation. Those who voluntarily follow this path embrace its challenges and its commitment to protect others. For this, they are declared "in the service." It is an apt term. The Americans who accept this commitment do so willingly and recognize that danger, hardship, and low pay may be their due. They learn to put service before self and to subordinate their personal desires for the greater good of the organization. And make no mistake: America relies on these few citizens to a degree that is generally underappreciated.

The duty of these special citizens is so grave, and their obligations so important, that we make them swear an oath when they choose this path. The oath includes a pledge to "obey the orders" of those "appointed over them," even though it may put their lives at risk. What could be more significant? In return, they expect something intangible: good leadership.

What a daunting privilege and solemn obligation this is for military leaders. When we are entrusted with the privilege and responsibility of leading such individuals, how can we repay their faith and sworn obligation to us? The prospect is both exciting and intimidating. For those who are intrigued, this book is for you.

What is good leadership? How can we acquire the skills? The study of leadership is a lifelong effort, but you can achieve a solid beginning to the journey by reading, reflecting on, and absorbing the observations in this book. Don't start the book without a tool to highlight and annotate—you should enjoy the material, but also study it with some intensity. As you read, imagine how you would react in the challenging circumstances outlined in the book. Test yourself with the physical, mental, and ethical issues. My view is that the study of leadership, particularly coupled with actual examples, begins to create a personal set of principles and benchmarks that will serve you well. You'll find that your instincts—honed through study and self-examination—bring clarity to leadership challenges that vex others.

This book is organized in a way best designed to condition and then stimulate your thinking about leadership. You'll understand leadership in its various forms in Part One. Note that the fundamentals of leadership are nearly eternal, and that form, style, and requirements often change. Part Two is a wonderful reinforcement that the soul of leadership is character. Some of the events and thoughts in these chapters should provoke critical thinking, while others may inspire. Part Three elevates the discussion to those whose leadership domain often involves the strategic and engagements with the political—generals and admirals. This section of the book is deliberately and carefully crafted to ensure that the reader knows that increased rank involves increased consequences to actions, and that courage—a central tenet of leadership—takes on a meaning beyond the physical. Finally, you will note that Part Four stimulates the reader to think about how future military leadership will shift the importance of several leadership traits (agile and independent thinking, for example) without losing the necessity of the others.

And what of my own thoughts on leadership? Although it's been over thirty years since I first faced the daunting challenges of leading a unit, I still remember the traits and actions that seemed to gain the respect of the platoon of sixty-five Marines. I also remember vividly where I erred. Though much has changed in the intervening years (except my propensity for errors), I believe that many of the tenets of good leadership are eternal. You'll find them in the counsel of the ancients and repeated through the crucibles those in today's military face. My reflections may contain no great wisdom, but perhaps if they are repeated elsewhere they will at least gain weight through the lessons of experience.

Mission.   The first responsibility of a leader is to the task at hand. If you are competent in all other attributes but fall short in this one, you will fail overall.

Loyalty.   Traditional notions of loyalty envision the loyalty of a subordinate to a senior. In military leadership, they must apply equally. If the balance is skewed, those who are expected to follow you will do so only out of obligation, or you'll devote too little emphasis on the mission and will fail to accomplish it.

Listen.   No leader can have all the insights needed to make decisions, so the good ones listen to the counsel of their subordinates. This not only is smart but also encourages those in your organization to contribute more fully.

Act. After listening to others, decide quickly. Indecisiveness will quickly dissipate others' confidence in your leadership.

> An army of deer led by a lion is more to be feared
> than an army of lions led by a deer.
> —*Chabrias 410–375 BC*

Fairness.   Leadership frequently involves making decisions or taking actions in which someone loses or is perceived to have suffered. The pain of losing is made acceptable only by an impression that the action was taken with a sense of fairness.

Knowledge.   Though you can't know all that is essential in performing your duties, your organization will note how diligently you study and absorb the essential ingredients of the job. If you can apply this knowledge to improving the organization and its people, all the better.

Example.   Those in your charge expect you to embody the essential traits and ethos of your organization. "Standards" are not sufficient for a leader— the two terms are distinct and different. As a leader, you are expected to exceed standards. You are expected to lead by example.

Presence.   The mantle of leadership invariably entails instances in which you will be obliged to rule against one person or the other or make a decision that may cause hardship. Although your goal is to gain the respect— even the affection—of those in your charge, friendship is in neither their interest nor yours.

Honor.   A leader's moral compass is her or his sense of honor. Just as a journey without a compass can lead to a wrong destination, a compromise of honor will surely lead your organization—and your credibility as a leader—astray. The shorthand among those you will be charged to lead is revealing—"not only doing it right, but doing the right thing." A special note on honesty: Nothing is more injurious to the credibility of a leader than a perception that someone is less than honest. This trait is binary. You are honest, or you are dishonest. If you are perceived as dishonest, you'll probably never recover your subordinates' full confidence.

> **Leadership is a potent combination of strategy and character. But if you must be without one, be without the strategy.**
> —*General H. Norman Schwarzkopf*

Seek no credit. Those in your charge will observe closely who takes credit for actions. We've all known individuals who were quick to take credit and equally agile in avoiding responsibility. This trait is closely tied to how loyal your individuals perceive you to be, and how loyal they are to you.

> **A good leader inspires others with confidence in him; a great leader inspires them with confidence in themselves.**
> —*Unknown*

Praise in public; counsel in private. Almost without exception, this advice should be heeded studiously. Remember that those who berate in public probably lose esteem to the same degree as those berated.

Now . . . it's time to start the book and learn the lessons from distinguished authors. But before you do, establish an objective in mind. When you close the final page in the chapter on the Future of Military Leadership, what would you like the result to be? If the answer is to take an incremental step in becoming a better person and a more effective leader, then you'd better be ready to highlight and scribble notes. It's that important.

> **You can assign someone to a leadership position, but no one will ever really be a leader until their appointment is ratified in the hearts and minds of their soldiers.**
> —*Anonymous*

—Lieutenant General Gregory S. Newbold (USMC Ret.)

Lieutenant General Gregory S. Newbold previously served as the Director of Operations for the Joint Chiefs of Staff and as the Commanding General of the 1st Marine Division.

PREFACE

This book is substantially different from prior editions in that we have included only six articles from previous editions. Four of the new selections are original pieces written for this book. We also discovered two very interesting books from the archives at Harvard University that provide comparative perspectives of military leadership from different eras. Contrasted with our choices for the fifth edition, we had a rich array of articles to review for this edition. We expanded our searches and uncovered nearly 160 articles written since the last edition in 2005 and selected what we believe to be the best articles to complement the important classics. Ultimately, we found that the decision of what to include came easily.

We continue to mix classic and contemporary articles, authors, and settings in an attempt to reflect all the armed services. Either because of the wars in Iraq and Afghanistan or interest in writing about leadership, we found that most of the writing came from or was published by the Army. Our focus is leadership and our choices reflect articles that are relevant beyond a single military service. We wanted to include articles that will be attractive to students and practitioners as well as scholars. Fewer of our selections come from outside the military journals, which makes us wonder about who will independently examine military leadership perspectives in the future.

We added a third editor to begin the transition to a new generation. Eric Rosenbach joins us to provide a contemporary perspective. His political science background and experience in the military and government yielded a new network for us that links writings about the military to the issues of today. His experience of living and working abroad increases our range of international approaches so we can look at military leadership with more breadth.

There are four parts to this edition: leadership perspectives and context; character as the heart of leadership; general officers' leadership challenges and opportunities; and the question of the future of leadership. Because of increasing scrutiny of the performance of our senior military leaders over the past several years, we do concentrate a bit on flag officers. Some may question the emphasis, but clearly the leadership lessons apply to everyone. In many respects, it is the same attention that has been given to corporate and organizational executives in recent times. No matter where the successes and failures occur, the people at the top are, and ultimately should be, held accountable.

This book is designed to stimulate an intellectual, as well as practical, understanding of leadership development. Traditional leadership studies explore the various theories and research findings. Our companion text, *Contemporary Issues in Leadership,* provides theoretical perspectives as well as current thinking from business and politics. This volume presents a specific military perspective with the purpose of identifying factors and issues that define the domain of military leadership. We provide selected articles and essays we believe will help our readers understand and appreciate the complexities of leadership in today's world.

In the quest to find the best possible material, we discovered two books: one written in 1918 and the other written in 1936. We enjoyed reading about leadership and leadership development in earlier times because it gave us context as we explored the current literature. You will not be surprised that not much is really "new." Much of what people describe as the characteristics and behaviors for effective military leadership has not changed. What is different is our understanding of transactional and transformational leadership. Thus, this edition gives us the opportunity to structure leader effectiveness in terms of transformational leadership theory.

We trust that you will discover a logic and order to the book. At the same time, we recognize that readers may want to select articles without a specific rationale or context. Whatever the format may be, we propose this book to those who continue their leadership development and those who are responsible for training the military leaders of the future.

In Part One, we explore the perspectives and context of leadership as seen by leaders and by careful observers. Leaders and scholars give perspectives on what they believe leadership is or should be. The military has always provided a forum for the study of leadership because the concept is critical to individual and organizational success. Since the consequences of leadership failure are severe, understanding the historical perspectives as well as a context for today's environment are critical to personal leadership development.

Part Two examines character associated with effective leadership. Candor, persuasion, loyalty, language and values, presence, and influence are addressed as essential character traits for the transformational (note that you have a choice: you may be "transformational" or "transforming") leader. All of these appear to be common traits of successful leaders. How they are developed and nurtured becomes the issue for leadership development.

In Part Three, we address the leadership opportunities and challenges our senior leaders face. A novel perspective is presented from 1936 that is, in part, humorous but generally a template for the leadership to which many aspire. Research about women and their success in achieving senior leadership positions provides a contemporary view of challenges and opportunities. How commanders can be held accountable to multiple, sometimes contradictory expectations is highlighted with the caveat that many of the short-term criticisms were later proved to be incorrect. The conflicts over meeting political and strategic expectations are brought to the forefront for the reader to consider.

Part Four inquires about the future of leadership. The substance and process of leadership development are discussed with the idea that what we teach will be different for the future. Two international perspectives clarify the issues important to training military leaders of tomorrow. A process for developing transformational leadership skills in emerging leaders provides one model for how we must think about leadership development in the future.

The clash between personal and organizational values is a paradox of leadership that often leads to disappointment and loss for both the individual and the unit. Leaders identify and give meaning to core values, building ownership with the followers to embrace and live those values. Ultimately, this is the basis upon which we deal with paradoxes and hard choices as well as our day-to-day actions.

Both individual and organizational values influence a leader's style. Introspection, self-awareness, and an understanding of the consequences of our actions are necessary for a leader to choose the most appropriate style. Finally, character, the individual value important to our effectiveness as both leaders and followers, turns out to be not only our own responsibility but also our responsibility to each other.

We continue to be most grateful to colleagues and friends in the armed services who have encouraged us over the years. Their feedback on our work has been helpful. Senior officers and retired colleagues have unselfishly given of their time and talent as we have developed each of the book's six editions. Of course, we accept responsibility for the form and substance of this edition, but it would not have happened without the assistance from those who serve.

Our sincere thanks to Roz Sterner, who cheerfully took on the task of assembling the material and creating the manuscript. We also thank Laura Stine at Westview Press for her careful management of the production process. We have enjoyed the continuing relationship with Westview Press as our publisher for more than twenty-five years. Finally, without the personal support of our spouses, Linda, Colleen, and Alexa, the friendship and book we share would not be possible.

—ROBERT L. TAYLOR, WILLIAM E. ROSENBACH,
AND ERIC B. ROSENBACH

PART ONE

LEADERSHIP

Perspectives and Context

ALTHOUGH LEADERSHIP IS A WIDELY discussed and often-studied discipline, little agreement exists among scholars or practitioners about what defines it. Concepts of leadership are either disarmingly simple or awesomely complex. In fact, there are almost as many definitions of leadership as there are people attempting to define it. Yet, we know good leadership when we experience or observe it. In 1978, Pulitzer Prize winner James MacGregor Burns wrote that we know a lot about leaders, yet very little about leadership. Lieutenant General Walter F. Ulmer Jr., former president and CEO of the Center for Creative Leadership, believes that we know more than we used to about leaders but that much of our knowledge is superficial and fails to examine the deeper realms of character and motivation that drive leaders, particularly in difficult times.

Understanding leadership begins with examining what leadership is not. Leadership is not hierarchical, top-down, or based on positional power and authority. Although effective commanders must practice good leadership and effective leaders must possess command skills, leadership is not command or some part or principle of it. To understand leadership, one must understand its essential nature: the process of the leader and followers engaging in reciprocal influence to achieve a shared purpose. Leadership is all about getting people to work together to make things happen that might not otherwise occur or to prevent things from happening that would ordinarily take place.

Looking through the history of the study of leadership, we find that the earliest coherent thrust centered on an approach now referred to as the Great Man or Great Person Theory. For a full generation, leadership scholars concentrated on identifying the traits associated with great leaders. At first it seemed obvious: Are not great leaders exceptionally intelligent, unusually energetic, far above the norm in their ability to communicate, and so on? However, when these "obvious" propositions were subjected to test, they all proved false. Yes, leaders were a bit more intelligent than the average person, but not much more. And yes, they were more energetic and dynamic—but not significantly so. True, they were better-than-average public speakers with some charm, but again their overall advantage was not very great. And so it went: Each of these and other leadership myths evaporated under the glare of scientific scrutiny.

What followed was a focus on the behavior of leaders. If the key was not *who* they were, perhaps the crux of leadership could be found in *what* they did. In fact, researchers identified two crucial types of leader behavior: behavior centered on task accomplishment and behavior directed toward interpersonal relations. Their peers typically reported individuals who consistently exhibited high levels of both of these types of behaviors as leaders. Those who engaged in a high level of task-related behavior but only an average level of relationship-centered behavior sometimes still were designated leaders. Peers rarely designated those who engaged only in a high level of relationship behavior as leaders. Finally, those who did little in the way of either task or relationship-centered activity were never seen as leaders.

Some took a new path, suggesting that leadership effectiveness might require different combinations of task and relationship behavior in different situations. Theoretically, the most effective combination would depend upon certain situational factors, such as the nature of the task and the ability of employees reporting to a certain supervisor. Another somewhat different path was to combine the situational hypothesis with some variation of the personal-characteristics approach. Like earlier attempts, however, those efforts to explain effective leadership met with limited results.

Interestingly, the theme of focusing on relationship and task behaviors is common to the many theories developed over the past decades. The attempts to develop predictive and prescriptive models led to serious research and popular fads as scholars worked to solve the leadership puzzle. As popular literature focused on leadership tools and techniques, we noted that most people remained skeptical about leaders and leadership. Thus, we ask, what have we really learned?

In this book we distinguish between two basic types of leadership. *Transactional* leadership clarifies the role followers must play both to attain the organization's desired outcomes and to receive valued personal rewards for satisfactory performance, giving them the confidence necessary to achieve those outcomes and rewards. Transactional leadership is the equitable transaction or exchange between the leader and followers whereby the leader influences the followers by focusing on the self-interests of both. The leader's self-interest is satisfactory performance, and the followers' self-interests are the valued rewards for good performance. Used well, and in appropriate situations, transactional leadership is simply good management and might be considered managerial leadership.

Transformational or *transforming* leadership involves strong personal identification of followers with the leader. The transformational leader motivates followers to perform beyond expectations by creating an awareness of the importance of the mission and the vision in such a way that followers share beliefs and values and can transcend self-interests to tie the vision to self-esteem and self-actualization, both higher-order needs. Transformational leaders create a mental picture of the shared vision in the minds of the followers through the use of language that has deep meaning from shared experiences. In addition, they are role models: In their daily actions they set an example and give meaning to shared assumptions, beliefs, and values. Transformational leaders empower or, better yet, enable followers to perform beyond expectations by sharing power and authority and ensuring that followers understand how to use them. These leaders are committed to developing the followers into partners. In the end, transformational leaders enable followers to transform purpose into action.

In "Leadership" (Chapter 1), Brigadier General Lincoln C. Andrews's 1918 answer to the question "What then is your first consideration, if you wish to succeed in the military service?" is summed up by his declaration that in all dealings with one's "men," the team captain must have their respect, unhesitating obedience, and, if one is man enough to win it, their enthusiastic loyalty. This opening chapter is included to demonstrate how expectations and perspectives of military leaders have and have not changed over a period of almost one hundred years.

General S. L. A. Marshall writes in "Leaders and Leadership" (Chapter 2) that great military leaders of the past possessed a set of inner qualities rather than outward marks of greatness. Relatively few leaders were acclaimed for leadership in their early years; Marshall's thesis is that most successful leaders are molded by the influences around them and that they have the average person's faults and vices. Leaders have a common desire for substantial recognition (ego) and the will to earn it fairly. Too often, people with great inner strength hold in contempt those who are less well endowed by nature than they are and, hence, fail as leaders. He cites courage, humor, presence, and integrity as the ingredients for successful military leadership.

In "What Makes a Leader?" (Chapter 3), Daniel Goleman, the premier expert on emotional intelligence, describes why emotional intelligence is the crucial component of leadership and how it is displayed in leaders. Superb leaders have very different ways of leading, and each situation calls for a different style of leadership. The author has found, however, that effective leaders are alike in one crucial way: They all have a high degree of what has come to be known as emotional intelligence. Goleman discusses each component of emotional intelligence and shows how to recognize it in potential leaders and how it can be learned. The concept is one with great relevance to military leaders.

Unlike many writers, James L. Stokesbury uniquely differentiates leadership from headship or command in "Leadership as an Art" (Chapter 4). He focuses on the leader as a person and does not address those who merely serve (as "heads") in leadership positions. In an attempt to define leadership, he says we are trapped by the inadequacies of the language and often wind up with a tautological definition. Stokesbury deals with this dilemma by defining leadership as an art and by suggesting that the best method for learning about leadership is to study the examples provided by history. He chose four historic leaders: the Marquis of Montrose, Alexander Suvorov, Robert E. Lee, and Philippe Pétain, all of whom had little in common other than attributes Stokesbury believes constitute the art of leadership. He concludes by observing that the highest elements of leadership remain an art, whereas the lesser elements can be learned scientifically and can be treated by artifice. He ironically observes that the better the times, the less artifice works, and the more art is needed.

In "Reality Leadership" (Chapter 5), John Charles Kunich and Dr. Richard I. Lester argue that despite myriad opinions, leadership is neither mystical nor mysterious. They examine the reality of leadership by attempting to explain that the core of leadership makes a difference, creates positive change, moves people to get things accomplished, and gets rid of everything else that does not contribute to the mission.

Earl H. Potter III and William E. Rosenbach present their conceptual model of followership in "Followers as Partners: Ready When the Time Comes" (Chapter 6). They describe effective followers as partners who are committed to taking the initiative for high performance and healthy relationships with their leaders. The authors argue that leaders who encourage partnerships as well as followers who seek to be partners characterize leaders whose organizations thrive in the rapidly changing global environment.

In "Leaders, Managers, and Command Climate" (Chapter 7), Lieutenant General Walter F. Ulmer Jr. defines climate in terms of the leader's example and the performance standards expected in a group or organization. How well people adapt to the climate can be changed by altering leadership and managerial habits of senior officers, for they set the standards of performance. It is still the combination of leadership and management that moves from routine good intentions to routine best practices that will make a difference. He advocates credible standardized methods for evaluating command climate and leader development.

As mysterious as leadership remains, the American military has somehow sustained momentum for systematic leadership development throughout the ranks that few institutions in the world have equaled.

★ ★ ★ **1** ★ ★ ★

Leadership

Brigadier General Lincoln C. Andrews

Wʜᴀᴛ ᴛʜᴇɴ ɪs ʏᴏᴜʀ ꜰɪʀsᴛ consideration, if you wish to succeed in the military service? *To fit yourself to be team captain of your group, be it squad, platoon, or company.* To be a good team captain requires first that you be a good disciplinarian, next that you acquire and use those qualities that characterize natural leaders of men. In all dealings with your men you must have their respect, unhesitating obedience, and, if you are man enough to win it, their enthusiastic loyalty.

To attain the confidence and respect of your men, the first requisite is *superior knowledge.* That will give you the self-confidence to appear as a leader, and will justify your men in following you. Therefore never appear before them unprepared to play your part in the game. You are a sorry object pretending to lead when there are men in ranks who know your part better than you do.

There are many circumstances in which a leader may advise with his subordinates, but it must be clear in the end that the final judgment is his own. It is possible, too, for the best men to make mistakes—these should always be frankly acknowledged as such, and no attempt made to bluff them through. Apologies and explanations why are but harmful. The men appreciate manliness; you cannot fool them long, and found out as a bluffer, your leadership is hopeless.

It is proper that you should aspire to popularity, to be beloved of your men, to be one of those leaders of whom it is boasted that their men would follow them anywhere. And remember that while history speaks of such leaders generally in the higher grades, their success was made possible only by the fact that their armies were made up of many small groups, in which the men were following their leaders with equal loyalty.

But do not be deluded into thinking that this popularity is attained by easygoing methods, by favoritism, by winking at delinquencies and overlooking failures in strict performance of duty. Such popularity fades when the real test comes, and changes to disrespect, insubordination, and contempt, when real men are at the fore, leading through hardships and dangers. Build then your popularity on the firmer qualities of justice and fairness to all, inflexibility in demanding obedience and faithful performance of duty, and constant vigilance for the welfare and interests of your men, and above all, by forethought and preparation, on such conduct of your office as will inspire respect and even admiration for your ability as a leader.

The popular noncommissioned officer is the one whose squad is the most snappy and efficient. His men admire him and they have the habit of jumping when he speaks. He does not waste their time through lack of forethought, nor make them do unnecessary work through lack of headwork. His brain is active, and in each case alert to such management as is easiest for his men. He does not uselessly march them around three sides of a square when a direct movement would have accomplished the purpose. He demands strict compliance with his orders, and close attention from all whenever he is giving general instructions; and sees that all work, hardship, or privilege is fairly apportioned among them.

It is psychologically true that every group of men, working together for a common purpose, soon comes to have a soul of its own. It is true of a company, it is true of a squad, and equally true of a gang of workmen on a job. The good leader learns to know that soul, and deal intelligently with it—knows its aspirations, its limits of endurance, how to inspire it to increased endeavor, how to inspirit it when discouraged in fatigue or hardship, how to arouse its interest in the work at hand. Let him always consider this in planning the work for his men, in controlling them in their work. There are many means of appeal to this spirit; you must learn and use them. You can make lagging footsteps quicken and fatigue-dulled minds brighten, just as martial music will make a jaded column spring to life; the men are no less tired, but new nerve-forces have supervened and made them forget the fatigue. This soul is as susceptible to bad influences as to good. How disastrous if the leader offends it. How important that he be in touch with it and treat it intelligently.

It is *spirit* that makes the soldier endure and dare. Especially among men of quality, spirit will carry through where cold-blooded training alone must fail. Watch the good troop leader; on the march, in camp, at drill, in the school room, by word and even more by thoughtful conduct of the work in hand, he is always fostering spirit. His men know that what he requires is reasonable, they feel that he is regarding their welfare in every move, making their work as interesting as possible, and conducive to future success. It is even possible to attain such a group spirit that the failure or delinquency of one man will so hurt the feelings of the group that his punishment may rest on that alone.

Every man delights in work well done, in actually doing well what he puts his hand to. The farmer boy takes pride in hoeing a row of corn expeditiously, the carpenter delights in his clever handiwork. Remember this when you direct the drill or work of your men. It must control your manner and tone when you criticize them. They enjoy being snappy, being efficient, doing the right thing at the right time, avoiding wasted time or energy—and they are disgusted with the reverse of these. Appreciation of this principle will cause a helpful chagrin when you see failure result from your own inability or inefficient leadership. You are applying it when you commend some man for particularly good performance, when you call out "Good!" as the men execute a movement properly at drill. The leader who truly appreciates this phase of human nature, and intelligently uses it in his work, has taken a long step toward success.

The state of discipline, a mental status, is attained more by a system of rewards than of punishment—yet both are necessary and potent factors. And do not imagine that there is a class to be controlled by punishments alone. For in our service there is no class of men in which you may not appeal successfully to the men's better qualities. If such individuals arrive, the spirit of the group should force them into such uncomfortable isolation that they will either strive to emulate the good or else soon withdraw.

In the system of rewards the leader finds the most powerful ally in building up that discipline which leads to *esprit* and morale. He must be on the lookout for opportunities to use it. A word or even a look of approbation is often sufficient. In every group will be found natural leaders, men who, when hardships bear down the spirits of the majority, are found doing more than their share, and not only by example, but often by cheerful word or quip, are unconsciously inspiriting the whole to better endurance. The leader must find every opportunity to show public recognition of merit of these men, thus strengthening their influence with their fellows. Give them the important missions; be sure it is such a one who is detailed to any conspicuous or daring duty; if favor must be shown, be sure it goes to such a man. Again, there are generally found would-be leaders of the opposite temperament, chronic pessimists and kickers, who, by example and frequently by grumblings, lower the average of endurance and performance. It is equally important that the leader undermine the influence of these men, quietly giving them the disagreeable details that often must be performed, and never making the vital mistake of appearing to approve by selecting such a man for a conspicuous detail. How absolutely important then that a leader truly know the personalities of his men. Not only must he pick the man best qualified for the task at hand, but he must consider the effect of his selection on the morale of his group. And this demands constant observation of his men at their work. What supreme confidence in divine guidance must inspire that captain, who, at the end of a hard, hot march, has the first detail pitch his tent, roll the walls, arrange the cot and fly net, and then passes quietly to repose, while the soldiers perform their arduous duties unobserved. If this captain were required to detail an orderly to the colonel the next day, he might easily pick some man who, through indifference or meanness, had been a humiliation to his squad the day before.

Commanders are better paid and better mounted that they may endure more than those under them; greater and greater grow the demands for tireless vigilance as the grade of the officer increases. In this truth lies one of the main reasons why as war continues we find the younger and more virile men attaining the superior commands. An ambitious troop leader will avoid dissipation, conserving his energies in peace that he may draw on them unsparingly in war, and that he may not need then to rest when by vigilance he might be guarding the welfare of his men and building up their morale for the supreme test to come.

Punishments cannot be administered in accordance with any set standard. Every offense contains the elements of the personal equation of the offender, the attending circumstances, the motive, and always the effect on the discipline of the group. Your decision must be the voice of calm, impartial justice. A troop leader is ever a judge, guarding the tone of his group as a good judge guards the tone of his civil community. Remember there are two sides to every question. Be sure the accused has a fair hearing, and always look for the motive. A soldier rarely commits a serious offense gratuitously.

The authority in you to reward and punish the acts of individual men is a greater power for good or for evil—not alone to the individual, but through your treatment of his case to the whole group. It is in your power to ruin a man's career, if you will, as it is to take a weakling and, by proper treatment, make a man and soldier of him. A sense of this should give the leader pause when he is about to emit some hasty judgment formed in passion—the very passion often the result of an inner consciousness of his own failure or knowledge of human nature and of "cause and effect." It is of the greatest value, too, to be able to see from the man's viewpoint, as well as from your own. Could that always be done, it would be the controlling factor in most correct decisions.

Since both punishments and rewards are given for their effect on the discipline and morale of the whole group, they should always follow the act as closely as possible, thus giving full effect. Where the reward is a word of commendation, or the punishment one of reprimand, this may always be done. In any case, the first steps toward punishment, where punishment is necessary, should be promptly taken to avoid discussions and argument among the men and the growth among them of the feeling that perhaps the "old man hasn't the nerve" to back up his authority.

Be calm in emergency; unruffled, even sardonic if you have it in you, in the face of hardships; unperturbed and even casual in the face of danger. The psychological power of mental suggestion is now well understood, and accepted as one of the surest means of controlling men. If you are a real leader, your men will take their mental attitude from what yours appears to be. In danger they will watch your movements, even facial expression, for reassurance. It is then that you drop some casual remark, "borrow the makings" and roll a cigarette, do any simple thing naturally, showing that you are at ease and confident in these abnormal circumstances, and your men regain their wavering confidence, feeling that you are not afraid. So, in time of unavoidable hardship, you must avoid showing annoyance or impatience. Your sardonic acceptance of necessary conditions will unconsciously lead to theirs, and save the nerve strain and damage to *esprit* which result from grumbling, and bucking, and cursing out everything in general. And in emergency you must show perfect self-control. Remember that your conduct will determine that of your men. If you are excited, they will be more so. The emergency will call for perhaps the most accurate, determined, self-controlled work, and if your heart has jumped into your throat and made your voice quaver and your ideas confused (and this will happen to the best of men), nothing but disaster can result if you communicate this to your men. You will gain time and success in the end, if you take time now to swallow your heart, and regain perfect self-control, before you say one word to betray your perturbation. Then with calm self-assured demeanor give your directions as becomes a real leader. Directions so given are a great comfort to the men, and assure steady intelligent execution. We are now considering one of the most characteristic failures in inexperienced troop leadership. Try to train yourself so that you will be one of the exceptions, by acquiring the habit in any given situation, of being first sure of yourself, and then calmly giving directions to your men.

It is the genius of war to seize the fleeting opportunity. Train yourself to make quick decisions, carried out with calm self-confidence. In the hesitation which surprise causes lies its great advantage. Hence the danger of ambuscade. The enemy gets the jump while you are trying to decide what to do. It is not so important what you do, as that you do something and do it quickly. Make a quick decision and then calmly carry it out. Do not change to another plan that may look better an instant later. Vacillation destroys all confidence in a leader. Take a simple plan, a bold one, and then unquestioningly bend every energy to its accomplishment. You may train yourself for this in peace time. Often, in civil life, you are present at some accident or emergency. There is generally someone in the crowd whose mind has acted instantaneously, who has jumped in and done the right thing. Question your mental processes, why were not you the man? In the small affairs of daily life, experiment with making quick decisions, till you get the habit of deciding quickly, and acquire confidence in your ability to do so correctly. This will be of the greatest value to you, to your men, and to your superiors—and if opportunity comes, you may grasp it to your great honor and that of your cause.

"Soldiers are like children." There is one relation to the leader in which this is true. He is a father to them. On the battlefield at Santiago I saw a young second lieutenant put his hand on the shoulder of a grey-haired old soldier and call him his boy, and there was confidence in the face of the old man as he started alone on his mission. This feeling of mutual sympathy and confidence will spring from thoughtful leadership, and you should aspire to it, and make yourself worthy of it.

History records many daring deeds where an intrepid leader has led his men to victory against seemingly overwhelming odds, and all credit is given to his courage. A mistake. There may be hundreds who would have dared lead the charge, but their men were not prepared. Credit must be given not alone to courage, but even more to the intelligent leadership that had brought the men to this opportunity prepared to meet it successfully; confident in the ability of their leader, disciplined and buoyed up by *esprit,* in the best possible condition of mind and body through their leader's constant exercise of vigilance for their daily welfare on the march and in the camp. The making of the heroic leader who will win laurels on the battlefield begins surely in the drill hall at home, and follows throughout the conduct of each day's work in camp and on campaign. He must be not only a disciplinarian and a psychologist, but something of a doctor, a cook, a tailor, a saddler and cobbler, a veterinarian, and a blacksmith. He must know the army "Rules for Health" and see that his men observe them. He must follow up his men like children, and see that they are properly clothed, fed, rested, entertained, kept in health and spirits, giving freely of his vitality that he may reasonably demand tremendous exertion from them when the opportunity offers.

The fundamental principle for the conduct of a successful march, camp, or bivouac is to *reduce to a minimum the hardships for the men.* In former wars the casualties of the march and camp have exceeded those of battle. We are too advanced for that today, and demand an intelligence in leaders which will prevent it. "Careful preparation," "march discipline and sanitation" are matters of Field Service Regulations and proper training. Even then it is surprising in how many ways a thoughtful leader may add to the comfort and *esprit* of his command, which an ignorant or careless leader will overlook, to the detriment of both.

Men will not take care of themselves without the direction of someone in authority; they will wade through mud to get water from a spring where five minutes of work would place stepping stones or rails to keep their feet dry. The leader must see to such things, considering each new camp an interesting problem for him to solve to the very best interests of his men. Often brush shelters can be quickly erected for protection from winds or storms. It is easy to cut brush and make artificial shade where natural shade does not exist. It should be arranged artificially in hot weather for at least one assembly place where the men may eat and sit about after meals. A few minutes' work will often clean out a spring, and add 100 percent to its value. A quickly built dam will often make a comfortable pool from a shallow stream. The men soon learn that these things are for their own comfort, and while they will not do them undirected, they are easily interested in doing them under enthusiastic leadership. It is impossible even to suggest all that may be done—it is up to the ingenuity of the leader and it is no time for him to rest in the shade and let the men shift for themselves.

A leader who wants his men to do good work will give every consideration to their physical and mental well being—they will be well fed, keep reasonable hours, have proper relaxation; then they are ready and glad to give splendid service. How often civil contractors fail in this—and lose profits accordingly. Even worse, by ill feeding and mean shelter, by offending the laborer's manliness and self-respect, they arouse actual disloyalty and a spirit of deadbeating.

Every war has had its famous brigades, famous regiments, and famous batteries. They had made a reputation for success and easily maintained it. Their appearance on the battlefield was heralded with acclaim by other organizations. Their personnel was easily kept up because good men were anxious to join them. This may be equally true in handling any organization in peacetime. Let it get a reputation for excellence and it will be more excellent, and its personnel will be easily maintained from the best men. This is one of the surest means of attaining organization spirit—to excel in something, it may be in shooting or in shoveling, in close-order drill, or in having the best mess. The men begin to take pride in their organization, in their leaders, and good men begin to seek admission to its membership. This may be as true of a squad as of a company, and should be the proper object of attainment for the squad leader. Men take delight in doing those things in which they are displaying skill and efficiency. With the bodily and mental training that come from doing things well come self-respect, laudable pride, and an assurance that strengthen the individual character and weld the whole organization into a potent force for accomplishment.

A good leader is as one with his men, he speaks their language, he shares their blessings and their hardships, he is jealous of their name, he defends their sensibilities and their rights in the larger organization; in fact, he is the recognized guardian of their welfare, physical and mental, as individuals and as a group. He becomes their hero and is affectionately nicknamed. Making camp after a hard march, he will not accept an invitation to lunch while his men go hungry awaiting a delayed wagon; he would not take shelter while his men lay out in a storm. He would be the first to question the fairness of the action of an outsider that seemed to work injustice to his group, or to one of them. If supplies are short, he goes and learns why, and remedies it if possible. He sends an ailing man to the doctor and follows up the case with interest, as would a football captain follow up the treatment of a member of his team during the season. In short, he is looking out for their interests, not his own selfish comfort. It is incidentally true that when hardships come he will be more than repaid by their devotion to him and care for his comfort.

As a thorough example of a great cavalry leader's appreciation of the value of considering the human element in dealing with soldiers, and as an interesting illustration for you of the seeming trifles to which a successful leader gives his personal attention, the following is quoted from General de Brack's instructions to his officers:

The Pipe—Every trooper should be encouraged to smoke a pipe. Why? Because it will keep him awake. The pipe is a means of diversion which, far from interfering with the trooper's performing his duty, attaches him to it and renders it less burdensome. It soothes him, kills time, banishes unpleasant thoughts, and keeps the trooper in bivouac and near his horse. While the trooper, seated upon a pile of hay or grass, smokes his pipe, no one will venture to steal the forage from his horse to give it to another; he is certain that his horse is eating his food, and that he is not getting kicked; the provisions are not stolen from his wallet; he has time to discover the repairs which should be made to his saddlery, clothing, etc.

On outpost, all sleep is forbidden. What a comfort you will then find the pipe, which drives away drowsiness, speeds the weary hours, renders the rain less chilly, and makes hunger and thirst more easy to endure. If you have to make long night marches after the fatigues of the day, when sleep overpowering you is a veritable torture and cause of numerous injuries to the horse, nothing will keep you awake like smoking your pipe.

In a campaign, where men's resources are so limited, there is nothing so trifling as to be devoid of value. The pipe is a medium of exchange, of pleasure, and of duty in the fraternal associations of our military life; in certain cases, when loaned, it becomes a veritable means of relieving distress.

Therefore, whatever Aristotle and his learned cabal may say, smoke, and make your troopers smoke.

Do not delude yourself that you are all right because the men recognize your constituted authority in ordinary conditions and good-naturedly obey your commands. That is easy. Consider this question: Will they follow you in an emergency? Be sure of that. The corporal's plaintive "Follow me," heard so often on the drill field, will be lost in battle. Those inspiring words must then boom out in no uncertain tone, and carry conviction. When the stress comes, the best men will be at the fore, and unless you have trained yourself and are of the best, you will find, to your own great humiliation, the men looking to some other man for leadership. How much better that this other, who had the real stuff, should have had charge of the training. I have seen a sergeant, when the test came, actually fade into the ranks; while a private, who had it in him, naturally took the leadership of the squad through the emergency. It is not to quit when this is true, but to get down to bedrock and train yourself to lead. Acquire superior knowledge, and the power to command. You can do it if you care enough. Next to a coward, the most dangerous man to attempt leadership is one who is ignorant or lazy, or both. If you are not prepared to learn to lead, retire and let another have the chance. If you will stop to realize what your failure on the battlefield might mean of disaster and even disgrace, and not alone to your organization but perhaps through it to the whole cause— you will decide now either to take yourself seriously in hand to learn the game, or else to move down and let another try.

How important is your ability to give orders properly? I have had to reduce many noncommissioned officers because they were reporting this man and that for disobedience of orders. They were unfitted to give orders. Disobedience is almost always the fault primarily either of the order or of the way in which it is given. It is a safe rule that your men originally intend to do right. Assume that first. Then be sure that your order is right and that it is something that should be done. It is demoralizing to discipline to give an order, and then have to change it. And above all be sure there is no suspicion of a question in your own breast but that the order will be obeyed. So often a man has disobeyed because you have shown by voice or manner that you were not sure he would obey. You were not sure of yourself or of your authority. You simply invited disobedience.

There are circumstances in which it is often possible, and even advisable, to add the reason for an order given, thus enlisting the man's intelligent interest in its execution. But in doing this, great care must be taken to avoid any appearance of apologizing for giving the order, and to avoid the possibility of creating a habit that might lead the soldier to stop and ask why on the battlefield.

Give your orders in a quiet, decent tone—just as a baseball captain would tell a player to cover second base. There is no question of insult, nor of disobedience, nor of argument. Your tone has not made his manhood rebel, tempting him to tell you to go to the devil. He is a member of the team, helping toward ultimate success by obeying you as a leader. That is the attitude for both you and him.

But too often there are those placed in authority who so far miss the true situation as to treat their subordinates somewhat as though they were dogs. By word, tone, or manner, they wantonly insult their manliness and thus sacrifice loyalty and cheerful subordination. They thus show themselves unfit for command of men. Furthermore, such treatment of subordinates is now a violation of orders. It is the clear intention of government that American officers and men shall work together in an intelligent appreciation of the manliness of their mutual service. Let them remember that military courtesy goes as much from the superior to the inferior as from the inferior to the superior. You want to command a team of men, not of dogs. And you will never get discipline or loyal service from men by outraging their manliness.

To bring this home—I have actually been in camp with two different troops of militia cavalry in which the noncommissioned officers were constantly heard cursing the men, shouting profanity and vulgarity in a vain effort to exercise authority. A pathetic spectacle. They could not command the respect of the meanest man in the organization. Open disregard of their orders was a common occurrence, and to be expected. And what of the troop commander who allowed any human being to curse one of his men without himself jumping in and resenting it! The whole situation showed an absolute lack of appreciation of the true spirit of discipline and leadership. These men meant right, but had somewhere picked up that silly tradition of the brutality of army discipline, and were floundering along, outraging every sense of decency and loyalty, hopeless of ever attaining organized efficiency. In each outfit there is just one individual who may do any cursing—the "Old Man." He will do it for all; and if he wants them to be his men, he will not only exercise this prerogative judiciously, but will be extremely jealous that none other ever infringe upon it ever so slightly.

He who can make his men jump with a low firm tone of voice has an enviable force of character. The man who has to raise his voice, scream and roar and curse in order to get action is pathetic. He will be an even sorrier figure when trying to lead in an emergency. He has probably missed the first essential, self-control, and is too likely conscious of his own inherent weakness or inability.

Avoid giving too many orders, or indefinite halfhearted orders. Your order must be so expressed as to leave no question whatever as to your intentions. Be sure it is understood, but avoid the atrocious habit of repeating yourself, and generally of talking too much. Pride yourself on giving your order so clearly and concisely that it may be understood; and conversely when receiving an order concentrate your attention and try to get the whole idea without questions and repetitions. But never go away with the order half understood or misunderstood. This is vital.

When you do give an order see that it is carried out to the letter. It is so easy, especially in the beginning of your career as a leader, for you to overlook the slight deviations and omissions. The men may be trying you out. If you overlook slight omissions they will grow until some man is found in a serious disobedience of orders. And it will be all your fault. If you wish to go slowly at first in enforcing your orders inflexibly, go slowly in giving them, not in demanding execution. Willful disobedience of orders is one of the gravest military offenses, a violation of the man's oath at enlistment, a slur on the ability of the troop leadership, and a blot on the *esprit* of the organization. Do not let it be true that you led to this through your shiftless squad leadership, whether due to your laziness, ignorance, or moral weakness.

It may happen, though rarely, that a combination of circumstances has goaded a man into positive insubordination on some certain point. Considered psychologically he has concentrated his faculties to oppose some order—forcing them from the normal easier channels of obedience, he is stubbornly holding them directed solely on breaking out this new channel of disobedience. It will be exactly wrong to oppose him directly on this one point, for that will assist in keeping his faculties concentrated in opposition, and will but increase the evil. If such a case must be dealt with at once, you will do well first to divert his faculties by quietly requiring of him some simple thing, like adjusting his uniform, or correcting his position, in which he will obey through force of habit. And thus through easy stages you may develop a state of feeling in which he can discuss the situation reasonably, thus regaining control and saving him from grave consequences. This is illustrated by a principle in horse training. Often where you persist in attempting some one movement the horse becomes stubborn and refuses to move at all. It then becomes necessary to change absolutely to some simple thing, that you are sure he will do at your command—perhaps to walk, halt, and walk again. Thus you reestablish control, and then, through steps that he will perform, return to the first test of obedience and find him tractable.

If in any particular case the above methods have failed, there still remain the sterner methods of enforcing military control. Your authority must be respected. It is backed by the entire military force of the nation.

"Actions speak louder than words." A military leader does not preach. Generally it will be by brief expressions, by holding to a standard of performance, by your own invariable conduct and your example, that you will attain the desired results. You do not keep your men "on their toes" by telling them that you want them there, but rather by making the work so interesting, by putting so much snap and vitality and intelligent direction into it yourself, you bring them and hold them there unconsciously. Then, after the work is over, they do the talking about how snappy it was, and you get the credit.

Whenever you do address remarks to a group of men, first see to it that all of them are giving you attention. It is ridiculous for you to be talking to them, and they wandering about, interested in their own affairs of conversation. Always call them to attention first, and see that they have all obeyed it; when they are all quiet and attentive, then you may talk, and may properly hold them responsible for having heard what you said. They may be "at ease," but they must be attentive. If the men be in ranks at attention, direct them "look to me," as eyes to the front is part of their military position, and generally you want their eyes on you if your remarks are of any moment.

The leader is held responsible for the appearance, conduct, and performance of duty of his men. He accomplishes this first by being an example; in neatness of dress, care of arms and equipment, punctuality at formations, cheerfulness in performance of all duties, unvarying observance of regulations, military courtesy, etc. And then he must follow up the delinquents, to see that they also conform. If wise, he will do this by arousing the men's interest in keeping up—in any case he must so do it as to avoid nagging. In insisting upon an exact observance of regulations in all small matters, dress, police, stable duty, etc., he is requiring his men to form habits of obedience that will make discipline easy and be of great value later in the service. Why not explain this to the men? It will add to their interest in all their work.

You expect loyalty, so show it yourself to your superiors. If you receive an order for your command to perform a disagreeable duty, go to its execution loyally; do not try to purchase cheap popularity with your men by saying that "so and so has ordered this and we've got to do it." This is too cheap, and your men will know that you are not playing your part in the teamwork. Nor may you even listen quietly while your men curse the order. Remember that your team is part of the next higher organization and that you are working to make that the best in the service, to make your men proud to belong to it and proud of its leader. Seek to learn the spirit of an order, then execute it loyally. That is the example you want to give, and the service you owe your superiors. Do not be so petty as to spend time criticizing the form or wording of an order, or so unmindful of your part as a soldier.

It seems as though every organization has to have at least one man who is always "agin the government." His mentality and force may have made him a leader, but he has the curse of pessimism, and his lifting force in any proposition toward progress has generally a negative sign before it. If you are this unhappy individual, lay violent hands on your temperament, and the next time enthusiasm begins to stir a conference, curb your impulse to kick, and see how it feels to get behind and push.

One of the essential qualities of a good soldier is cheerfulness. That squad is indeed unfortunate which does not count among its members at least one indomitable soul (generally Irish) to jolly it through the endurance of hardships. This quality may be cultivated in the "squad spirit," and should be. Some swinging song, peculiar to your outfit, will bring it happily into camp, when others are barely dragging along the dusty road. In any event, growling at hardships is only demoralizing to *esprit*, and weakening to the powers of endurance. It must not be tolerated. Ability to endure hardship must characterize a successful army. It is claimed that modern Americans lack it. We are to disprove that statement.

In performing work assigned his command the leader must not actually work with his hands, any more than an officer would enter the firing line with a rifle in battle, not because it is beneath his dignity, but because he is in charge and must give his attention to control and direction, and to observation of his men in the work. How often we see an inexperienced noncommissioned officer in the ditch with the shovel while a wise private smokes at ease on the bank. There is no one thing more conducive to dissatisfaction than for the leader to allow certain smooth "deadbeats" continually to put it over on the others who must do their share of the work. No, you had better be in observation, and using your faculties to see that the "smooth ones" get their full share. This will add to *esprit*. Where the task is unfamiliar or difficult, conditions might easily arise in which you would do best to jump in and set the pace for a minute. But you are not to put yourself in as an equal in sharing the work.

And how easy it is always to call upon the willing ones to do the task. Smith is full of good spirits, a willing worker. So a careless squad leader, or one lacking confidence in his own authority over his men, will always send Smith to this and that. Instead of always putting the work on the cheerful ones, on the capable ones, thus putting a premium on worthlessness and sullenness, a good leader will see that the lazy and sullen get at least their full share of the hard work, thus showing himself just, and capable of handling his team.

If you could only appreciate the value of arousing the men's interest in the work at hand. Imagine a detail of recruits digging their first kitchen incinerator. They may be shoveling dirt to kill time for all they know. But first let the corporal tell them what they are going to make, what an incinerator is and what it is for, and that each company kitchen has to have one. He may thus arouse their interest in it, and their pride in making theirs the best in camp—and now see them work. So, with each task, the men should know at least what they are about and why it is necessary; and so be allowed to participate with you in the pleasure and credit of doing well.

Most tasks require especial forethought and planning on the part of the leader. You have got to sit down and study it ahead of time, foresee every detail, and plan to meet it with system and the least friction and lost motion for the men. Then only will you be able to conduct the work as a real leader should. Failure in this is far too common. You see regular officers conducting the work, detraining a command, breaking a camp, what you will, everything working smoothly, and seem to think that the officer does this by inspiration. In reality, if he does it smoothly, it is only because he has anticipated each step and planned ahead for it.

Do not assume that in putting on your uniform you have clothed yourself with any peculiar omniscience that will enable you to guess right as the situations arise. The best-trained lawyer would not appear in court without specially preparing himself to meet the conditions of the case in hand. It is equally necessary for you to plan ahead your line of action; and those who appear such successful leaders have thus prepared themselves. If a foreman on a job employed his men without intelligent direction, in the shiftless time-killing way most noncommissioned officers go about a piece of work, he would be properly fired by the superintendent. The men themselves would be disgusted with him. When you are detailed to do a piece of work, size up the situation and plan it so that when the men are at it they will work with the highest degree of efficiency. Do not have men standing about idle. Get the work done and let the men go. If you have eight men to do two men's work, divide it into four reliefs, and make each two hum while their shift is on. Anticipate what tools you will need, get everything in hand, allot the work to the men, and then go to it. They will like it any amount better than dragging around for twice the length of time.

In the military service certain rules are always observed governing the relations and intercourse of military men. Long experience has proven them most conducive to discipline, and essential to control on the battlefield. They are the growth of centuries of experience, and are much the same in all the armies of the world. They forbid improper familiarity between the noncommissioned officer and his men, or between officers and enlisted men. They prescribe the military salute, the military forms of address, the position of attention, etc.—all are visible signs of discipline and characterize the organization that has a fine *esprit*.

The observance of this relation between leader and men is difficult for both if beginners. It will help if both have a clear understanding of its necessity to preclude the possibility of questioning an order from the superior. Experience, bringing respect for authority, soon makes this come easily. For the chief still treats his subordinate as a fellow human being, when occasion warrants shows an interest in his personal affairs, and, while they enjoy a fellowship in common service, the chief still holds back that something of intimacy which keeps clearly defined the line of subordination. This is done without patronizing, for the subordinate must not sacrifice self-respect, but rather feel pride in his work, developing self-confidence and initiative.

Even more difficult is the not infrequent situation of the subordinate, keen on his job, ambitious for himself and his organization, who feels sure he could suggest changes for the better—and too often he could. Good leadership should make this possible—for it is a rare man whose management is beyond improvement. But be sure the suggestion is good, choose carefully the occasion, and most carefully the words in which you make it. You can thus avoid offending the rights of superior command, and often attain the improvement to your credit and that of your superior.

And how shall the ambitious man gain the attention of his superior? By smartness of appearance, and cheerful performance of every duty. If the captain himself does not mark you, his attention will be called to you by others. You can never win by talking, and above all avoid anything that smacks of "freshness." Learn your job. Your chance will come some day, quite unexpectedly. Go to it coolly, with quiet confidence, even if you feel rattled.

A soldier's career may depend largely on how he is started in the service. The noncommissioned officer must consider this in dealing with recruits. They have no clear conception of what it is all about, you must explain the why of many things, and arouse an intelligent interest in the drill and all forms of work. Recall how stupid and unreasonable much of it seemed to you in your early experience. The recruit soon learns to look to you for instruction and advice. Keep that relation in use. Later you may have opportunity to advise him about his conduct, and thus keep him out of some trouble into which his own thoughtlessness or shiftlessness or even viciousness might lead him. Men are going to have grievances. Encourage them to come to their corporal freely with their troubles, and let him use his tact in setting these matters for the best good of the organization spirit.

And how important that you seize the recruit and, from the first step, exact the most rigid accuracy and observance of military regulations. He will then commence forming habits of exact obedience. He will be military and glory in it. Civilians generally admire the military; and in their eyes you are a wonder of perfection and precision. How disastrous then if you appear before them uncertain or indifferent. You first disappoint them and soon deaden or disgust their keen appreciation and ambition. You inculcate habits of indifference rather than of smartness. Think of that, you leaders, and do not disappoint your men by being easygoing, indifferent soldiers. Be military to a degree, and make them the same. They will admire you for it, and your captain bless you.

You must have imagination, or acquire it. The cold prosaic matter-of-fact brain makes a poor leader in a battle exercise at drill. Imagination and spirit must make him see the enemy when there is no enemy, feel his coming through those distant woods, see him break into the open, see his column form for defense as you launch your attack. You must not only be able to see this yourself, but have the power of expression to make your men see and feel it.

And in war, you must have imagination, to enable you to anticipate the moves of the enemy. As you advance you will constantly consider the situation from his point of view, foresee how he may use the terrain to meet you coming as you are, and prepare to act quickly to meet him. Then surprise will not benumb you. In fact, you are anticipating him and there is no surprise.

Competition and rivalry are good among equals. They are an application of the principle that men take pleasure in excelling, and in having their excellence recognized. You will use this in building up *esprit* in your squads, your platoons, and your troops.

But it is a narrow-minded policy to arouse *esprit* in your arm of the service at the expense of other arms by invidious comparison or by holding them up to scorn or ridicule. He who does this has missed the vital spirit of teamwork so essential to the success of the army. He has failed to appreciate the interdependence of the arms, and how each must have confidence in the other and give it loyal encouragement and support in the time of battle. He is ignorant of the "Brotherhood of Arms," and not only is he thus showing himself unworthy of leadership therein but he is lending his influence toward weakening that so important bond.

The proudest characteristic of the service, and the one most jealously guarded, is the nicety of its honor. The plain statement of an officer, "I do so and so," is as good as his "I certify on honor." Practices that might be accepted in civil life would be intolerable in this knightly brotherhood. An officer is a gentleman, and if he fails of that standard, the law knows but the one sentence of dismissal. Truthfulness of statement is absolutely necessary to military intercourse. The machine cannot work on any other basis. The liar has to get out. Measure yourself by this standard, and your relations with your fellows, and with the men under you, cannot go far wrong.

★ ★ ★ **2** ★ ★ ★

Leaders and Leadership

General S. L. A. Marshall

IN THAT GALLERY OF GREAT Americans whose names are conspicuously identified with the prospering of the national arms in peace and war, there are almost as many types as there are men.

There were a certain few qualities they had to possess in common or their names would never have become known beyond the county line.

But these were inner qualities, often deeply buried, rather than outward marks of greatness that men recognized immediately upon beholding them.

Some almost missed the roll call, either because in early life their weaknesses were more apparent than their strengths, or because of an outward seeming of insignificance, which at first fooled their contemporaries.

In the minority are the few who seemed marked for greatness almost from the cradle, and were acclaimed for leadership while still of tender years.

Winfield Scott, a brigadier in the War of 1812 when brigadiers were few, and Chief of Staff when the Civil War began, is a unique figure in the national history.

George Washington, Adjutant of the State of Virginia at twenty-one, is one other military infant prodigy who never later belied his early fame.

The majority in the gallery are not like these. No two of them are strikingly alike in mien and manner. Their personalities are as different, for the most part, as their names. Their characters also ran the length of the spectrum, or nearly, if we are talking of moral habit rather than of conscientious perform-ance of military duty. Some drank their whiskey neat and frequently; others loathed it and took a harsh line with any subordinate who used it.

One of the greatest generals in American history, celebrated for his fight-ing scarcely more than for his tippling, would walk from the room if any man tried to tell an off-color story in his presence. One of the most celebrated and successful of our World War II admirals endeared himself to millions of men in all ranks by his trick of gathering his chief subordinates together just before battle, issuing his orders sternly and surely, and then relaxing long enough to tell them his latest parlor story, knowing that finally it would trickle down through the whole command.

In Korea, one infantry division commander was a skilled banjo player. Up at the front, he formed a small orchestra of enlisted men and fitted into it. Be-tween fire fights, they played for troops. The men loved him for it. Later, he became one of the Army's ranking generals and was named to one of its top posts. His name: Arthur G. Trudeau.

Among the warriors in this gallery are men who would bet a month's pay on a horse race. There are duelists and brawlers, athletes and aesthetes, men who lived almost saintly lives and scholars who lived more for learning than for fame.

Some tended to be so over-reclusive that they almost missed recognition; others were hail-fellow-well-met in any company.

Their methods of work reflected these extreme variations in personal type, as did the means they used to draw other men to them, thereby setting a foun-dation for real success.

Part of their number commanded mainly through the sheer force of ideas; others owed their leadership more to the magnetism of dynamic personality.

In the very few there was the spark of genius. All things seemed to come right with them at all times. Fate was kind, the openings occurred, and they were prepared to take advantage of them.

But the greater number moved up the hill one slow step at a time, not always sure of their footing, buffeted by mischance, owning no exalted opinion of their own merits, reacting to discouragement much as other men do, but finally accumulating power as they learned how to organize the work of other men.

While a young lieutenant, Admiral William S. Sims became so incensed when the United States would not take his word on a voucher that he offered to resign.

General Ulysses S. Grant signally failed to organize his life as an individual before a turn of the wheel gave him his chance to organize the military power of the United States in war.

General W. T. Sherman, who commanded the Army for almost fifteen years, was considered by many of his close friends to be a fit subject for confinement as a mental case just before the Civil War.

General George Meade, one of the calmest and most devoted of men in his family relationships, lacked confidence in his own merits and was very abusive of his associates during battle.

Admiral David Farragut, whose tenderness as an individual was demonstrated during the sixteen years in which he personally nursed an invalid wife, was so independent in his professional thought and action that both in and out of the Navy he was discredited as a "climber." He got into wretched quarrels with his superiors mainly because he felt his assignments afforded him no distinction. The Civil War gave him his opportunity.

General Winfield Scott, as firm a commander as any in our history, plagued the Army with his petty bickering over rank, seniority, and precedent.

Being human, they had their points of personal weakness. A newly appointed ensign or second lieutenant also has chinks in his armor, and sometimes views them in such false proportion that he doubts his own potential for high responsibility.

There is not one perfect life in the gallery of the great. All were molded by the mortal influences surrounding them. They reacted in their own feelings, and toward other men, according to the rise and fall of their personal fortunes. They sought help where it could be found. When disappointed, they chilled like anyone else. But along with their professional talents, they possessed in common a desire for substantial recognition, accompanied by the will to earn it fairly, or else the nation would never have heard their names.

All in all it is a much mixed gallery. If we were to pass it in review and then inspect it carefully, it would still be impossible to say: "This is the composite of character. This is the prototype of military success. Model upon it and you have the pinnacle within reach."

The same thing would no doubt hold true of a majority of the better men who commanded ships, squadrons, regiments, and companies under these commanders, and at their own level were as superior in leadership as the relatively few who rose to national prominence because of the achievements of the general body.

The same rule will apply tomorrow. Those who come forward to fill these places, and to command them with equal or greater authority and competence, will not be plaster saints, laden with all human virtue, spotless in character, and fit to be anointed with a superman legend by some future Parson Weems. They will be men with ambition and a strong belief in the United States and the goodness of a free society. They will have some of the average man's faults and maybe a few of his vices. But certainly they will possess the qualities of courage, creative intelligence, and physical robustness in more than average measure.

What we know of our great leaders in the current age should discourage the idea that only a genius may scale the heights. Trained observers have noted in their personalities and careers many of the plain characteristics each man feels in himself and mistakenly regards as a bar to preferment.

Drew Middleton, the American correspondent, wrote of General Carl "Tooey" Spaatz: "This man, who may be a heroic figure to our grandchildren, is essentially an unheroic figure to his contemporaries. He is, in fact, such a friendly, human person that observers tend to minimize his stature as a war leader. He is not temperamental. He makes no rousing speeches, writes no inspirational orders. Spaatz, in issuing orders for a major operation involving 1,500 airplanes, is about as inspiring as a groceryman ordering another five cases of canned peas."

An interviewer who called on General Ira C. Eaker when he was leading the 8th Air Force against Germany found "a strikingly soft-spoken, sober, compact man who has the mild manner of a conservative minister and the judicial outlook of a member of the Supreme Court. But he is always about two steps ahead of everybody on the score, and there is a quiet, inexorable logic about everything he does." Of his own choice, Eaker would have separated from military service after World War I. He wanted to be a lawyer, and he also toyed with the idea of running a country newspaper. In his off hours, he wrote books on aviation for junior readers. On the side, he studied civil law and found it "valuable mental training."

On the eve of the Guadalcanal landing, General A. A. Vandegrift's final order to his command ended with the stirring and now celebrated phrase "God favors the bold and strong of heart." Yet in the afterglow of later years, the nation read a character sketch of him that included this: "He is so polite and so soft-spoken that he is continually disappointing the people whom he meets. They find him lacking in the fire-eating traits they like to expect of all Marines, and they find it difficult to believe that such a mild-mannered man could really have led and won the bloody fight." When another officer spoke warmly of Vandegrift's coolness under fire, his "grace under pressure," to quote Hemingway's phrase, he replied, "I shouldn't be given any credit. I'm built that way."

The point is beautifully taken. Too often the man with great inner strength holds in contempt those less well endowed by nature than himself.

Brilliance of intellect and high achievement in scholarship are an advantage, though in the end they have little or no payoff if character and courage are lacking. Thousands of officers who served in Vietnam, some dubious about the wisdom of the national policy, questioning whether the tight rein on operations made military sense, still believed that "My country right or wrong" is the only course possible for one who has taken the oath.

No, brain trusting and whiz kidding are not what it takes. Of 105 major generals who served in World War I, 56 had failed to score above the middle of their class in mathematics. Of 275 in World War II, 158, or 58 percent, were in the middle group or among the dubs in the same subject. General William C. Westmoreland, who commanded in Vietnam and was later Army Chief of Staff, had punched practically none of the buttons. As for military schooling, for over thirty years after graduating from West Point, he attended only Cooks and Bakers School and the Airborne School. One of his outstanding subordinates, a two-star general, respected and loved by all who served under him, had joined the service at the age of fifteen out of reform school to straighten himself out. By sweat and study, he won his sergeant's stripes at eighteen and his commission at twenty-one. He made his resolve and stayed with it, which was the main thing. The solution of every problem, every achievement is, as Justice Oliver Wendell Holmes said, a bird on the wing; and he added, one must have one's whole will on one's eye on that bird. One cannot be thinking of one's image, or one's place in history—only of that bird.

While there are no perfect men, there are those who become relatively perfect leaders of men because something in their makeup brings out in strength the highest virtues of all who follow them. That is the way of human nature. Minor shortcomings do not impair the loyalty or growth of the follower who has found someone whose strengths he deems worth emulating. On the other hand, to recognize merit, you must yourself have it. The act of recognizing the worthwhile traits in another person is both the test and the making of character. The man who scorns all others and thinks no one else worth following parades his own inferiority before the world. He puts his own character into bankruptcy just as surely as does that other sad sack of whom Thomas Carlyle wrote: "To recognize false merit, and crown it as true, because a long trail runs after it, is the saddest operation under the sun."

William Sherman, John A. Logan, John A. Rawlins, and the many others hitched their wagons to Grant's star because they saw in him a man who had a way with other men, and who commanded them not less by personal courage than by patient work in their interest. Had Grant spent time brooding over his own civilian failures, he would have been struck with a disorderly camp and would never have gotten out of Illinois. He was not dismayed by his own shortcomings. Later he said: "I doubt that any of my officers ever discovered that I hadn't bothered to study tactics."

The nobility of the private life and influence of General Robert E. Lee and the grandeur of his military character are known to every American schoolboy. His peerless gifts as a battle leader have won the tribute of celebrated soldiers and historians throughout the world. Likewise, the deep religiosity of his great lieutenant, Stonewall Jackson, the fiery zeal and almost evangelical power with which he lifted the hearts of all men who followed him, are hallmarks of character that are vividly present in whatever context his name happens to be mentioned.

If we turn for a somewhat closer look at Grant, it is because he, more than any other American soldier, left us a full, clear narrative of his own growth, and of the inner thoughts and doubts pertaining to himself which attended his life experience. There was a great deal of the average man in Grant. He was beset by human failings. He could not look impressive. He had no sense of destiny. In his great hours, it was sweat, rather than inspiration, dogged perseverance, rather than the aura of power, that made the hour great.

Average though he was in many things, there was nothing average about the strong way in which he took hold, applying massive common sense to the complex problems of the field. That is why he is worth close regard. His virtues as a military leader were of the simpler sort that plain men may understand and hope to emulate. He was direct in manner. He never intrigued. His speech was homely. He was approachable. His mind never deviated from the object. Though a stubborn man, he was always willing to listen to his subordinates. He never adhered to a plan obstinately, but nothing could induce him to forsake the idea behind the plan.

History has left us a clear view of how he attained to greatness in leadership by holding steadfastly to a few main principles.

At Belmont, his first small action, he showed nothing to indicate that he was competent as a tactician and strategist. But the closing scene reveals him as the last man to leave the field of action, risking his life to see that none of his men had been left behind.

At Fort Donelson, where he had initiated an amphibious campaign of highly original daring, he was not on the battlefield when his army was suddenly attacked. He arrived to find his right wing crushed and his whole force on the verge of defeat. He blamed no one. Without more than a fleeting hesitation, he said quietly to his chief subordinates: "Gentlemen, the position on the right must be retaken." Then he mounted his horse and galloped along the line shouting to his men: "Fill your cartridge cases quick; the enemy is trying to escape and he must not be permitted to do so." Control and order were immediately reestablished by his presence.

At Shiloh the same thing happened, only this time it was worse; the whole Union Army was on the verge of rout. Grant, hobbling on crutches from a recent leg injury, met the mob of panic-stricken stragglers as he left the boat at Pittsburgh Landing. Calling on them to turn back, he mounted and rode toward the battle, shouting encouragement and giving orders to all he met. Confidence flowed from him back into an already beaten Army, and in this way a field nearly lost was soon regained, with decisive help provided by Buell's Army.

The last and best picture of Grant is on the evening after he had taken his first beating from General Lee in the campaign against Richmond. He was new with the Army of the Potomac. His predecessors, after being whipped by Lee, had invariably retreated to a safe distance. But this time, as the defeated army took the road of retreat out of the wilderness, its columns got only as far as the Chancellorsville House crossroad. There the soldiers saw a squat, bearded man sitting horseback, and drawing on a cigar. As the head of each regiment came abreast of him, he silently motioned it to take the right-hand fork—back toward Lee's flank and deeper than ever into the wilderness. That night, for the first time, the Army sensed an electric change in the air over Virginia. It had a man.

"I intend to fight it out on this line" is more revealing of the one supreme quality that put the seal on all of U. S. Grant's great gifts for military leading than everything else that the historians have written of him. He was the essence of the spirit that moderns call "seeing the show through." He was sensitive to a fault in his early years, and carried to his tomb a dislike for military uniform, caused by his being made the butt of ridicule the first time he ever donned a soldier suit. As a junior officer in the Mexican War, he sensed no particular aptitude in himself. But he had participated in every engagement possible for a member of his regiment, and had executed every small duty well, with particular attention to conserving the lives of his men. This was the school and the course that later enabled him to march to Richmond, when men's lives had to be spent for the good of the nation.

In more recent times, one of the great statesmen and soldiers of the United States, Henry L. Stimson, has added his witness to the value of this force in all enterprise: "I know the withering effect of limited commitments and I know the regenerative effect of full action." Though he was speaking particularly of the larger affairs of war and national policy, his words apply with full weight to the personal life. The truth seen only halfway is missed wholly; the thing done only halfway had best not be attempted at all. Men can't be fooled on this score. They will know every time when the arrow falls short for lack of a worthwhile effort. And when that happens, confidence in the leader is corroded, even among those who themselves were unwilling to try.

There have been great and distinguished leaders in our military services at all levels who had no particular gifts for administration and little for organizing the detail of decisive action either within battle or without. They excelled because of a superior ability to make use of the brains and command the loyalty of well-chosen subordinates. Their particular function was to judge the goal according to their resources and audacity, and then to hold the team steady until the goal was gained. So doing, they complemented the power of the faithful lieutenants who might have put them in the shade in any IQ test. Wrote Grant: "I never knew what to do with a paper except to put it in a side pocket or pass it to a clerk who understood it better than I did." There was nothing unfair or irregular about this; it was as it should be. All military achievement develops out of unity of action. The laurel goes to the man whose powers can most surely be directed toward the end purposes of organization. The winning of battles is the product of the winning of men. That aptitude is not an endowment of formal education, though the man who has led a football team, a class, a fraternity, or a debating society is the stronger for the experience he has gained. It is not unusual for those who have excelled in scholarship to despise those who have excelled merely in sympathetic understanding of the human race. But in the military services, though there are niches for the pedant, character is at all times at least as vital as intellect, and the main rewards go to him who can make other men feel toughened as well as elevated:

- Quiet resolution.
- The hardihood to take risks.

- The will to take full responsibility for decision.
- The readiness to share its rewards with subordinates.
- An equal readiness to take the blame when things go adversely.
- The nerve to survive storm and disappointment and to face toward each new day with the scoresheet wiped clean, neither dwelling on one's successes nor accepting discouragement from one's failures.

In these things lie a great part of the essence of leadership, for they are the constituents of that kind of moral courage that has enabled one man to draw many others to him in any age.

It is good, also, to look the part, not only because of its effect on others, but because, from out of the effort made to look it, one may in time come to be it. One of the kindliest and most penetrating philosophers of our age, Abbe Ernest Dimnet, has assured us that this is true. He says that by trying to look and act like a socially distinguished person, one may in fact attain to the inner disposition of a gentleman. That, almost needless to say, is the real mark of the officer who takes great pains about the manner of his dress and address, for as Walt Whitman said: "All changes of appearances without a change in that which underlies appearances are without avail." All depends upon the spirit in which one makes the effort. By his own account, U. S. Grant, as a West Point cadet, was more stirred by the commanding appearance of General Winfield Scott than by any man he had ever seen, including the President. He wrote that at that moment there flashed across his mind the thought that some day he would stand in Scott's place. Grant was unkempt of dress. His physical endowments were such that he could never achieve the commanding air of Scott. But he left us his witness that Scott's military bearing helped kindle his own desire for command, even though he knew that he could not be like Scott. Much is said in favor of modesty as an asset in leadership. It is remarked that the man who wishes to hold the respect of others will mention himself not more frequently than a born aristocrat mentions his ancestor. However, the point can be labored too hard. Some of the ablest of the nation's military commanders have been anything but shrinking violets; we have had now and then a hero who could boast with such gusto that this very characteristic somehow endeared him to his men. But that would be a dangerous tack for all save the most exceptional individual. Instead of speaking of modesty as a charm that will win all hearts, thereby risking that through excessive modesty a man will become tiresome to others and rated as too timid for high responsibility, it would be better to dwell upon the importance of being natural, which means neither concealing nor making a vulgar display of one's ideals and motives, but acting directly according to his dictates.

This leads to another point. In several of the most celebrated commentaries written by higher commanders on the nature of generalship, the statement is made rather carelessly that to be capable of great military leadership a man must be something of an actor. If that were unqualifiedly true, then it would be a desirable technique likewise for any junior officer; he, too, should learn how to wear a false face and play a part that cloaks his real self. The hollowness of the idea is proved by the lives of such men as Robert E. Lee, W. T. Sherman, George C. Marshall, Omar N. Bradley, Carl A. Spaatz, William H. Simpson, Chester A. Nimitz, Harold K. Johnson, Matthew B. Ridgway, Lew Walt, Creighton W. Abrams, and John S. McCain, Jr., to mention only a few. As commanders, they were all as natural as children, though some had great natural reserve, and others were warm and much more outgoing. They expressed themselves straightforwardly rather than by artful striving for effect. There was no studied attempt to appear only in a certain light. To use the common word for it, their people did not regard them as "characters." This naturalness had much to do with their hold on other men.

Such a result will always come. He who concentrates on the object at hand has little need to worry about the impression he is making on others. Even though they detect the chinks in the armor, they will know that the armor will hold.

On the other hand, a sense of the dramatic values, coupled with the intelligence to play upon them skillfully, is an invaluable quality in any military leader. Though there was nothing of the "actor" in Grant, he understood the value of pointing things up. To put a bold or inspiring emphasis where it belongs is not stagecraft but an integral part of the military fine art of communicating. System that is only system is injurious to the mind and spirit of any normal person. One can play a superior part well and maintain prestige and dignity without being under the compulsion to think, speak, and act in a monotone. In fact, when any military commander becomes overinhibited along these lines because of the illusion that this is the way to build a reputation for strength, he but doubles the necessity for his subordinates to act at all times like human beings rather than robots.

Coupled with self-control, consideration and thoughtfulness will carry a man far. Men will warm toward a leader when they come to believe that all the energy he stores up by living somewhat within himself is at their service.

But when they feel that this is not the case, and that his reserve is simply the outward sign of a spiritual miserliness and concentration on purely personal goals, no amount of restraint will ever win their favor. This is as true of him who commands a whole Service as of the leader of a squad.

To speak of the importance of a sense of humor would be futile, if it were not that what cramps so many men isn't that they are by nature humorless as that they are hesitant to exercise what humor they possess. Within the military profession, this is as unwise as to let the muscles go soft or to spare the mind the strain of original thinking. Great humor has always been in the military tradition. The need of it is nowhere more delicately expressed than in Kipling's lines:

> My son was killed while laughing at some jest,
> I would I knew
> What it was, and it might serve me in a time
> When jests are few.

Marcus Aurelius, Rome's soldier philosopher, spoke of his love for the man who "could be humorous in an agreeable way." No reader of Grant's *Memoirs* (one of the few truly great autobiographies ever written by a soldier) could fail to be impressed by his light touch. A delicate sense of the incongruous seems to have pervaded him; he is at his whimsical best when he sees himself in a ridiculous light. Lord Kitchener, one of the grimmest warriors ever to serve the British Empire, warmed to the man who made him the butt of a practical joke. There is the unforgettable picture of Admiral Beatty at Jutland. The *Indefatigable* had disappeared beneath the waves. The *Queen Mary* had exploded. The *Lion* was in flames. Then word came that the *Princess Royal* was blown up. Said Beatty to his Flag Captain, "Chatfield, there seems to be something wrong with our [expletive] ships today. Turn two points nearer the enemy." Admiral Nimitz, surveying the terrible landscape of the Kwajalein battlefield for the first time, said gravely to his staff: "It's the worst devastation I've ever seen except for that last Texas picnic in Honolulu." There is a characteristic anecdote of General Patton. He had just been worsted by higher headquarters in an argument over strategy. So he sat talking to his own staff about it, his dog curled up beside him. Suddenly he said to the animal, "The trouble with you, too, Willy, is that you don't understand the big picture." General Eisenhower, probably more than any other modern American commander, had the art of winning with his humor. He would have qualified under the English essayist Sydney Smith's definition: "The meaning of an extraordinary man is that he is eight men in one man; that he has as much wit as if he had no sense, and as much sense as if he had no wit; that his conduct is as judicious as if he were the dullest of human beings, and his imagination as brilliant as if he were irretrievably ruined."

In Korea, just before the first battle of Pork Chop Hill began, Lieutenant Thomas V. Harrold heard a loud wailing from the Communist trench and asked his company its meaning.

"They're prayer singing," said an interpreter. "They're getting ready to die."

Said Harrold: "Then I guess we ought to be singing too."

And not a bad idea. The 1st Marine Division, fighting its way back from the Chosin Reservoir in December 1950, was embattled amid the snows from the moment the column struck its camp at Hagaru. By midnight, after heavy loss through the day, it had bivouacked at Kotori, still surrounded, still far from the sea. Major General Oliver P. Smith was alone in his tent. It was his bad moment. The task ahead seemed hopeless. Suddenly he heard music. Outside some truckers were singing the Marine Hymn. "All doubt left me," said Smith. "I knew then we had it made."

Concerning leadership within the terms here set forth, the final thought is that there is a radical difference between training and combat conditions.

In training the commander may be arbitrary, demanding, and a hard disciplinarian. But so long as his sense of fair play in handling his men becomes evident to them, and provided they become aware that what he is doing is making them more efficient than their competition, they will approve him, if grudgingly, stay loyal to him, and even possibly come to believe in his lucky star.

They are more likely to do it, however, if he takes a fatherly interest in their personal welfare. But that feeling doesn't have to come naturally to a man for him to win the respect of troops. If he knows his business, they're on his team.

When it comes to combat, something new is added. Even if they have previously looked on him as a father and believed absolutely that being with him is their best assurance of successful survival, should he then show himself to be timid and too cautious about his own safety, he will lose hold of them no less absolutely. His lieutenant, who up till then under training conditions has been regarded as a mean creature or a sniveler, but on the field suddenly reveals himself as a man of high courage, can take moral leadership of the company away from him, and do it in one day.

On the field there is no substitute for courage, no other binding influence toward unity of action. Troops will excuse almost any stupidity; excessive timidity is simply unforgivable. This was the epitome of Captain Queeg's failure in *The Caine Mutiny.* Screwball that he was, and an oppressor of men, his other vices would have been tolerable had he, under fire, proved himself somewhat better than a coward.

3

What Makes a Leader?

Daniel Goleman

EVERY BUSINESSPERSON KNOWS A STORY about a highly intelligent, highly skilled executive who was promoted into a leadership position only to fail at the job. And they also know a story about someone with solid—but not extraordinary—intellectual abilities and technical skills who was promoted into a similar position and then soared.

Such anecdotes support the widespread belief that identifying individuals with the "right stuff" to be leaders is more art than science. After all, the personal styles of superb leaders vary: Some leaders are subdued and analytical; others shout their manifestos from the mountaintops. And just as important, different situations call for different types of leadership. Most mergers need a sensitive negotiator at the helm, whereas many turnarounds require a more forceful authority.

I have found, however, that the most effective leaders are alike in one crucial way: They all have a high degree of what has come to be known as emotional intelligence. It's not that IQ and technical skills are irrelevant. They do matter, but mainly as "threshold capabilities"; that is, they are the entry-level requirements for executive positions. But my research, along with other recent studies, clearly shows that emotional intelligence is the sine qua non of leadership. Without it, a person can have the best training in the world, an incisive, analytical mind, and an endless supply of smart ideas, but he still won't make a great leader.

In the course of the past year, my colleagues and I have focused on how emotional intelligence operates at work. We have examined the relationship between emotional intelligence and effective performance, especially in leaders. And we have observed how emotional intelligence shows itself on the job. How can you tell if someone has high emotional intelligence, for example, and how can you recognize it in yourself? In the following pages, we'll explore these questions, taking each of the components of emotional intelligence—self-awareness, self-regulation, motivation, empathy, and social skill—in turn.

Evaluating Emotional Intelligence

Most large companies today have employed trained psychologists to develop what are known as "competency models" to aid them in identifying, training, and promoting likely stars in the leadership firmament. The psychologists have also developed such models for lower-level positions. And in recent years, I have analyzed competency models from eighty-eight companies, most of which were large and global and included the likes of Lucent Technologies, British Airways, and Credit Suisse.

In carrying out this work, my objective was to determine which personal capabilities drove outstanding performance within these organizations, and to what degree they did so. I grouped capabilities into three categories: purely technical skills like accounting and business planning; cognitive abilities like analytical reasoning; and competencies demonstrating emotional intelligence such as the ability to work with others and effectiveness in leading change.

To create some of the competency models, psychologists asked senior managers at the companies to identify the capabilities that typified the organization's most outstanding leaders. To create other models, the psychologists used objective criteria such as a division's profitability to differentiate the star performers at senior levels within their organizations from the average ones. Those individuals were then extensively interviewed and tested, and their capabilities were compared. This process resulted in the creation of lists of ingredients for highly effective leaders. The lists ranged in length from seven to fifteen items and included such ingredients as initiative and strategic vision.

When I analyzed all this data, I found dramatic results. To be sure, intellect was a driver of outstanding performance. Cognitive skills such as big-picture thinking and long-term vision were particularly important. But when I calculated the ratio of technical skills, IQ, and emotional intelligence as ingredients of excellent performance, emotional intelligence proved to be twice as important as the others for jobs at all levels.

Moreover, my analysis showed that emotional intelligence played an increasingly important role at the highest levels of the company, where differences in technical skills are of negligible importance. In other words, the higher the rank of a person considered to be a star performer, the more emotional intelligence capabilities showed up as the reason for his or her effectiveness. When I compared star performers with average ones in senior leadership positions, nearly 90 percent of the difference in their profiles was attributable to emotional intelligence factors rather than cognitive abilities.

Other researchers have confirmed that emotional intelligence not only distinguishes outstanding leaders but can also be linked to strong performance. The findings of the late David McClelland, the renowned researcher in human and organizational behavior, are a good example. In a 1996 study of a global food and beverage company, McClelland found that when senior managers had a critical mass of emotional intelligence capabilities, their divisions outperformed yearly earnings goals by 20 percent. Meanwhile, division leaders without that critical mass underperformed by almost the same amount. McClelland's findings, interestingly, held as true in the company's US divisions as in its divisions in Asia and Europe.

In short, the numbers are beginning to tell us a persuasive story about the link between a company's success and the emotional intelligence of its leaders. And just as important, research is also demonstrating that people can, if they take the right approach, develop their emotional intelligence. (See Table 3.1.)

Self-Awareness

Self-awareness is the first component of emotional intelligence—which makes sense when one considers that the Delphic oracle gave the advice to "know thyself" thousands of years ago. Self-awareness means having a deep understanding of one's emotions, strengths, weaknesses, needs, and drives. People with strong self-awareness are neither overly critical nor unrealistically hopeful. Rather, they are honest—with themselves and with others.

People who have a high degree of self-awareness recognize how their feelings affect them, other people, and their job performance. Thus a self-aware person who knows that tight deadlines bring out the worst in him plans his time carefully and gets his work done well in advance. Another person with

TABLE 3.1   FIVE COMPONENTS OF EMOTIONAL INTELLIGENCE AT WORK

	Definition	**Hallmarks**
Self-Awareness	The ability to recognize and understand your moods, emotions, and drives, as well as their effect on others	Self-confidence Realistic self-assessment Self-deprecating sense of humor
Self-Regulation	The ability to control or redirect disruptive impulses and moods The propensity to suspend judgment—to think before acting	Trustworthiness and integrity Comfort with ambiguity Openness to change
Motivation	A passion to work for reasons that go beyond money or status A propensity to pursue goals with energy and persistence	Strong drive to achieve Optimism, even in the face of failure Organizational commitment
Empathy	The ability to understand the emotional makeup of other people Skill in treating people according to their emotional reactions	Expertise in building and retaining talent Crosscultural sensitivity Service to clients and customers
Social Skill	Proficiency in managing relationships and building networks An ability to find common ground and build rapport	Effectiveness in leading change Persuasiveness Expertise in building and leading teams

high self-awareness will be able to work with a demanding client. She will understand the client's impact on her moods and the deeper reasons for her frustration. "Their trivial demands take us away from the real work that needs to be done," she might explain. And she will go one step further and turn her anger into something constructive.

Self-awareness extends to a person's understanding of his or her values and goals. Someone who is highly self-aware knows where he is headed and why; so, for example, he will be able to be firm in turning down a job offer that is tempting financially but does not fit with his principles or long-term goals. A person who lacks self-awareness is apt to make decisions that bring on inner turmoil by treading on buried values. "The money looked good so I signed on," someone might say two years into a job, "but the work means so little to me that I'm constantly bored." The decisions of self-aware people mesh with their values; consequently, they often find work to be energizing.

How can one recognize self-awareness? First and foremost, it shows itself as candor and an ability to assess oneself realistically. People with high self-awareness are able to speak accurately and openly—although not necessarily effusively or confessionally—about their emotions and the impact they have on their work. For instance, one manager I know of was skeptical about a new personal-shopper service that her company, a major department store chain, was about to introduce. Without prompting from her team or her boss, she offered them an explanation: "It's hard for me to get behind the rollout of this service," she admitted, "because I really wanted to run the project but I wasn't selected. Bear with me while I deal with that." The manager did indeed examine her feelings; a week later, she was supporting the project fully.

Such self-knowledge often shows itself in the hiring process. Ask a candidate to describe a time he got carried away by his feelings and did something he later regretted. Self-aware candidates will be frank in admitting to failure—and will often tell their tales with a smile. One of the hallmarks of self-awareness is a self-deprecating sense of humor.

Self-awareness can also be identified during performance reviews. Self-aware people know—and are comfortable talking about—their limitations and strengths, and they often demonstrate a thirst for constructive criticism. By contrast, people with low self-awareness interpret the message that they need to improve as a threat or a sign of failure.

Self-aware people can also be recognized by their self-confidence. They have a firm grasp of their capabilities and are less likely to set themselves up to fail by, for example, overstretching on assignments. They know, too, when to ask for help. And the risks they take on the job are calculated. They won't ask for a challenge that they know they can't handle alone. They'll play to their strengths.

Consider the actions of a midlevel employee who was invited to sit in on a strategy meeting with her company's top executives. Although she was the most junior person in the room, she did not sit there quietly, listening in awestruck or fearful silence. She knew she had a head for clear logic and the skill to present ideas persuasively, and she offered cogent suggestions about the company's strategy. At the same time, her self-awareness stopped her from wandering into territory where she knew she was weak.

Despite the value of having self-aware people in the workplace, my research indicates that senior executives don't often give self-awareness the credit it deserves when they look for potential leaders. Many executives mistake candor about feelings for "wimpiness" and fail to give due respect to employees who openly acknowledge their shortcomings. Such people are too readily dismissed as "not tough enough" to lead others.

In fact, the opposite is true. In the first place, people generally admire and respect candor. Further, leaders are constantly required to make judgment calls that require a candid assessment of capabilities—their own and those of others. Do we have the management expertise to acquire a competitor? Can we launch a new product within six months? People who assess themselves honestly—that is, self-aware people—are well suited to do the same for the organizations they run.

Self-Regulation

Biological impulses drive our emotions. We cannot do away with them—but we do much to manage them. Self-regulation, which is like an ongoing inner conversation, is the component of emotional intelligence that frees us from being prisoners of our feelings. People engaged in such a conversation feel bad moods and emotional impulses just as everyone else does, but they find ways to control them and even to channel them in useful ways.

Imagine an executive who has just watched a team of his employees present a botched analysis to the company's board of directors. In the gloom that follows, the executive might find himself tempted to pound on the table in anger or kick over a chair. He could leap up and scream at the group. Or he might maintain a grim silence, glaring at everyone before stalking off.

But if he had a gift for self-regulation, he would choose a different approach. He would pick his words carefully, acknowledging the team's poor performance without rushing to any hasty judgment. He would then step back to consider the reasons for the failure. Are they personal—a lack of effort? Are there any mitigating factors? What was his role in the debacle? After considering these questions, he would call the team together, lay out the incident's consequences, and offer his feelings about it. He would then present his analysis of the problem and a well-considered solution.

Why does self-regulation matter so much for leaders? First of all, people who are in control of their feelings and impulses—that is, people who are reasonable—are able to create an environment of trust and fairness. In such an environment, politics and infighting are sharply reduced and productivity is high. Talented people flock to the organization and aren't tempted to leave. And self-regulation has a trickle-down effect. No one wants to be known as a hothead when the boss is known for her calm approach. Fewer bad moods at the top mean fewer throughout the organization.

Second, self-regulation is important for competitive reasons. Everyone knows that business today is rife with ambiguity and change. Companies merge and break apart regularly. Technology transforms work at a dizzying pace. People who have mastered their emotions are able to roll with the changes. When a new change program is announced, they don't panic; instead, they are able to suspend judgment, seek out information, and listen to executives explain the new program. As the initiative moves forward, they are able to move with it.

Sometimes they even lead the way. Consider the case of a manager at a large manufacturing company. Like her colleagues, she had used a certain software program for five years. The program drove how she collected and reported data and how she thought about the company's strategy. One day, senior executives announced that a new program was to be installed that would radically change how information was gathered and assessed within the organization. While many people in the company complained bitterly about how disruptive the change would be, the manager mulled over the reasons for the new program and was convinced of its potential to improve performance. She eagerly attended training sessions—some of her colleagues refused to do so—and was eventually promoted to run several divisions, in part because she used the new technology so effectively.

I want to push the importance of self-regulation to leadership even further and make the case that it enhances integrity, which is not only a personal virtue but also an organizational strength. Many of the bad things that happen in companies are a function of impulsive behavior. People rarely plan to exaggerate profits, pad expense accounts, dip into the till, or abuse power for selfish ends. Instead, an opportunity presents itself, and people with low impulse control just say yes.

By contrast, consider the behavior of the senior executive at a large food company. The executive was scrupulously honest in his negotiations with local distributors. He would routinely lay out his cost structure in detail, thereby giving the distributors a realistic understanding of the company's pricing. This approach meant the executive couldn't always drive a hard bargain. Now, on occasion, he felt the urge to increase profits by withholding information about the company's costs. But he challenged that impulse—he saw that it made more sense in the long run to counteract it. His emotional self-regulation paid off in strong, lasting relationships with distributors that benefited the company more than any short-term financial gains would have.

The signs of emotional self-regulation, therefore, are not hard to miss; a propensity for reflection and thoughtfulness; comfort with ambiguity and change; and integrity—an ability to say no to impulsive urges.

Like self-awareness, self-regulation often does not get its due. People who can master their emotions are sometimes seen as cold fish—their considered responses are taken as a lack of passion. People with fiery temperaments are frequently thought of as "classic" leaders—their outbursts are considered hallmarks of charisma and power. But when such people make it to the top, their impulsiveness often works against them. In my research, extreme displays of negative emotion have never emerged as a driver of good leadership.

Motivation

If there is one trait that virtually all effective leaders have, it is motivation. They are driven to achieve beyond expectations—their own and everyone else's. The key word here is *achieve*. Plenty of people are motivated by external factors such as a big salary or the status that comes from having an impressive title or being part of a prestigious company. By contrast, those with leadership potential are motivated by a deeply embedded desire to achieve for the sake of achievement.

If you are looking for leaders, how can you identify people who are motivated by the drive to achieve rather than by external rewards? The first sign is a passion for the work itself—such people seek out creative challenges, love to learn, and take great pride in a job well done. They also display an unflagging energy to do things better. People with such energy often seem restless with the status quo. They are persistent with their questions about why things are done one way rather than another; they are eager to explore new approaches to their work.

A cosmetics company manager, for example, was frustrated that he had to wait two weeks to get sales results from people in the field. He finally tracked down an automated phone system that would beep each of his salespeople at 5 PM every day. An automated message then prompted them to punch in their numbers—how many calls and sales they had made that day. The system shortened the feedback time on sales results from weeks to hours.

That story illustrates two other common traits of people who are driven to achieve. They are forever raising the performance bar, and they like to keep score. Take the performance bar first. During performance reviews, people with high levels of motivation might ask to be "stretched" by their supervisors. Of course, an employee who combines self-awareness with internal motivation will recognize her limits—but she won't settle for objectives that seem too easy to fulfill.

And it follows naturally that people who are driven to do better also want a way of tracking progress—their own, their team's, and their company's. Whereas people with low achievement motivation are often fuzzy about results, those with high achievement motivation often keep score by tracking such hard measures as profitability or market share. I know of a money manager who starts and ends his day on the Internet, gauging the performance of his stock fund against four industries—set benchmarks.

Interestingly, people with high motivation remain optimistic even when the score is against them. In such cases, self-regulation combines with achievement motivation to overcome the frustration and depression that come after a setback or failure. Take the case of another portfolio manager at a large investment company. After several successful years, her fund tumbled for three consecutive quarters, leading three large institutional clients to shift their business elsewhere.

Some executives would have blamed the nosedive on circumstances outside their control; others might have seen the setback as evidence of personal failure. This portfolio manager, however, saw an opportunity to prove she could lead a turnaround. Two years later, when she was promoted to a very senior level in the company, she described the experience as "the best thing that ever happened to me; I learned so much from it."

Executives trying to recognize high levels of achievement motivation in their people can look for one last piece of evidence: commitment to the organization. When people love their jobs for the work itself, they often feel committed to the organizations that make that work possible. Committed employees are likely to stay with an organization even when they are pursued by headhunters waving money.

It's not difficult to understand how and why a motivation to achieve translates into strong leadership. If you set the performance bar high for yourself, you will do the same for the organization when you are in a position to do so. Likewise, a drive to surpass goals and an interest in keeping score can be contagious. Leaders with these traits can often build a team of managers around them with the same traits. And, of course, optimism and organizational commitment are fundamental to leadership—just try to imagine running a company without them.

Empathy

Of all the dimensions of emotional intelligence, empathy is the most easily recognized. We have all felt the empathy of a sensitive teacher or friend; we have all been struck by its absence in an unfeeling coach or boss. But when it comes to business, we rarely hear people praised, let alone rewarded, for their empathy. The very word seems unbusinesslike, out of place amid the tough realities of the marketplace.

But empathy doesn't mean a kind of "I'm okay, you're okay" mushiness. For a leader, that is, it doesn't mean adopting other people's emotions as one's own and trying to please everybody. That would be a nightmare—it would make action impossible. Rather, empathy means thoughtfully considering employees' feelings—along with other factors—in the process of making intelligent decisions.

For an example of empathy in action, consider what happened when two giant brokerage companies merged, creating redundant jobs in all their divisions. One division manager called his people together and gave a gloomy speech that emphasized the number of people who would soon be fired. The manager of another division gave his people a different kind of speech. He was upfront about his own worry and confusion, and he promised to keep people informed and to treat everyone fairly.

The difference between these two managers was empathy. The first manager was too worried about his own fate to consider the feelings of his anxiety-stricken colleagues. The second knew intuitively what his people were feeling, and he acknowledged their fears with his words. Is it any surprise that the first manager saw his division sink as many demoralized people, especially the most talented, departed? By contrast, the second manager continued to be a strong leader, his best people stayed, and his division remained as productive as ever.

Empathy is particularly important today as a component of leadership for at least three reasons: the increasing use of teams; the rapid pace of globalization; and the growing need to retain talent.

Consider the challenge of leading a team. As anyone who has even been a part of one can attest, teams are cauldrons of bubbling emotions. They are often charged with reaching a consensus—hard enough with two people and much more difficult as the numbers increase. Even in groups with as few as four or five members, alliances form and clashing agendas get set. A team's leader must be able to sense and understand the viewpoints of everyone around the table.

That's exactly what a marketing manager at a large information technology company was able to do when she was appointed to lead a troubled team. The group was in turmoil, overloaded by work and missing deadlines. Tensions were high among the members. Tinkering with procedures was not enough to bring the group together and make it an effective part of the company.

So the manager took several steps. In a series of one-on-one sessions, she took the time to listen to everyone in the group—what was frustrating them, how they rated their colleagues, whether they felt they had been ignored. And then she directed the team in a way that brought it together: She encouraged people to speak more openly about their frustrations, and she helped people raise constructive complaints during meetings. In short, her empathy allowed her to understand her team's emotional makeup. The result was not just heightened collaboration among the members but also added business, as the team was called on for help by a wider range of internal clients.

Globalization is another reason for the rising importance of empathy for business leaders. Cross-cultural dialogue can easily lead to miscues and misunderstandings. Empathy is an antidote. People who have it are attuned to subtleties in body language; they can hear the message beneath the words being spoken. Beyond that, they have a deep understanding of the existence and importance of cultural and ethnic differences.

Consider the case of an American consultant whose team had just pitched a project to a potential Japanese client. In its dealings with Americans, the team was accustomed to being bombarded with questions after such a proposal, but this time it was greeted with a long silence. Other members of the team, taking the silence as disapproval, were ready to pack and leave. The lead consultant gestured them to stop. Although he was not particularly familiar with Japanese culture, he read the client's face and posture and sensed not rejection but interest—even deep consideration. He was right: When the client finally spoke, it was to give the consulting firm the job.

Finally, empathy plays a key role in the retention of talent, particularly in today's information economy. Leaders have always needed empathy to develop and keep good people, but today the stakes are higher. When good people leave, they take the company's knowledge with them.

That's where coaching and mentoring come in. It has repeatedly been shown that coaching and mentoring pay off not just in better performance but also in increased job satisfaction and decreased turnover. But what makes coaching and mentoring work best is the nature of the relationship. Outstanding coaches and mentors get inside the heads of the people they are helping. They sense how to give effective feedback. They know when to push for better performance and when to hold back. In the way they motivate their protégés, they demonstrate empathy in action.

In what is probably sounding like a refrain, let me repeat that empathy doesn't get much respect in business. People wonder how leaders can make hard decisions if they are "feeling" for all the people who will be affected. But leaders with empathy do more than sympathize with people around them: They use their knowledge to improve their companies in subtle but important ways.

Social Skill

The first three components of emotional intelligence are all self-management skills. The last two, empathy and social skill, concern a person's ability to manage relationships with others. As a component of emotional intelligence, social skill is not as simple as it sounds. It's not just a matter of friendliness, although people with high levels of social skill are rarely mean-spirited. Social skill, rather, is friendliness with a purpose: moving people in the direction you desire, whether that's agreement on a new marketing strategy or enthusiasm about a new product.

Socially skilled people tend to have a wide circle of acquaintances, and they have a knack for finding common ground with people of all kinds—a knack for building rapport. That doesn't mean they socialize continually; it means they work according to the assumption that nothing important gets done alone. Such people have a network in place when the time for action comes.

Social skill is the culmination of the other dimensions of emotional intelligence. People tend to be very effective at managing relationships when they can understand and control their own emotions and can empathize with the feelings of others. Even motivation contributes to social skill. Remember that people who are driven to achieve tend to be optimistic, even in the face of set-backs or failure. When people are upbeat, their "glow" is cast upon conversations and other social encounters. They are popular, and for good reason.

Because it is the outcome of the other dimensions of emotional intelligence, social skill is recognizable on the job in many ways that will by now sound familiar. Socially skilled people, for instance, are adept at managing teams—that's their empathy at work. Likewise, they are expert persuaders—a manifestation of self-awareness, self-regulation, and empathy combined. Given those skills, good persuaders know when to make an emotional plea, for instance, and when an appeal to reason will work better. And motivation, when publicly visible, makes such people excellent collaborators; their passion for the work spreads to others and they are driven to find solutions.

But sometimes social skill shows itself in ways the other emotional intelligence components do not. For instance, socially skilled people may at times appear not to be working while at work. They seem to be idly schmoozing—chatting in the hallways with colleagues or joking around with people who are not even connected to their "real" jobs. Socially skilled people, however, don't think it makes sense to arbitrarily limit the scope of their relationships. They build bonds widely because they know that, in these fluid times, they may need help someday from people they are just getting to know today.

For example, consider the case of an executive in the strategy department of a global computer manufacturer. By 1993, he was convinced that the company's future lay with the Internet. Over the course of the next year, he found kindred spirits and used his social skill to stitch together a virtual community that cut across levels, divisions, and nations. He then used this de facto team to put up a corporate Web site, among the first by a major company. And, on his own initiative, with no budget or formal status, he signed up the company to participate in an annual Internet industry convention. Calling on his allies and persuading various divisions to donate funds, he recruited more than fifty people from a dozen different units to represent the company at the convention.

Management took notice: Within a year of the conference, the executive's team formed the basis for the company's first Internet division, and he was formally put in charge of it. To get there, the executive had ignored conventional boundaries, forging and maintaining connections with people in every corner of the organization.

Is social skill considered a key leadership capability in most companies? The answer is yes, especially when compared with the other components of emotional intelligence. People seem to know intuitively that leaders need to manage relationships effectively; no leader is an island. After all, the leader's task is to get work done through other people, and social skill makes that possible. A leader who cannot express her empathy may as well not have it at all. And a leader's motivation will be useless if he cannot communicate his passion to the organization. Social skill allows leaders to put their emotional intelligence to work.

It would be foolish to assert that good old-fashioned IQ and technical ability are not important ingredients in strong leadership. But the recipe would not be complete without emotional intelligence. It was once thought that the components of emotional intelligence were "nice to have" in business leaders. But now we know that, for the sake of performance, these are ingredients that leaders "need to have."

It is fortunate, then, that emotional intelligence can be learned. The process is not easy. It takes time and, most of all, commitment. But the benefits that come from having a well-developed emotional intelligence, both for the individual and for the organization, make it worth the effort.

4

Leadership as an Art

James L. Stokesbury

THERE IS A CERTAIN SENSE of paradox, almost of impudence, in choosing as the opening title for a social science annual the topic "Leadership as an Art." If one is thrown off balance by this, it is because society's perceptions have changed so radically over the past century. A hundred years ago, no one would have suspected that leadership might be anything other than an art, and impudence would have lain in asserting that there were scientific aspects to it.

Indeed, as late as fifty years ago the social sciences had still not come of age, and the most popular British historian of his time, Philip Guedalla (1923: 149), could dismiss them quite offhandedly as "light-minded young things like Psychology, with too many data and no conclusions, and Sociology, with too many conclusions and no data." In the 1960s, a distinguished American military historian used to tell his classes that the social sciences and statistical method were capable of telling us "all those things that are not worth knowing," a remark which the disgruntled humanist, pushed ever farther back behind the shrinking perimeter of his defenses, teaching Latin in his office or lecturing on Napoleon to an audience that confuses the Weimar with the Roman Republic, is likely to cherish lovingly.

Now the development of computer technology has finally given the social scientist the tools he needs to amass data as never before and to extract from it conclusions that are necessarily changing our ways of approaching problems.

53

Social science has come of age, and the humanistic protest that "there is more to it than that" sounds increasingly plaintive. Students who used to read the classics now study executive management, and where they once learned how Caesar addressed his men or Napoleon tweaked his grenadiers' earlobes when he was pleased with them, they now absorb graphs and mathematical formulas that are supposed to magically guarantee results. It is a sort of acupuncture of the mind: If you put the needle in here, the object will respond by doing whatever it is supposed to do.

There remains, however, a place for art. The essence of science is in mathematics and predictability. It has become more and more feasible to forecast how more and more of any given group will respond to certain stimuli. If the president looks forthright on television, public confidence will strengthen; if he looks tired or if his makeup is the wrong shade, the stock market will drop so many points. Elections, we are confidently told, depend on that falling number of mavericks whose reactions simply cannot be predicted.

History is repeating itself, as it always does, with twists and quirks. In the eighteenth century, at the height of the Enlightenment, critics of society thought that if only they could be rid of the few remaining irrationalities, they would then achieve the perfect society. Old anomalous institutions like the monarchy (and especially the Church), founded on emotion and faith rather than on the dictates of pure reason, had to be swept away; once they were, all would be for the best in the best of all possible worlds, as Voltaire wrote in his jibe at Leibnitz. Unhappily, when people destroyed the old institutions, they got the Terror and the Napoleonic Wars, and reason turned out to be little better a guide than tradition, emotion, or history. One suspects a tendency now on the part of the computer analysts to feel much as the philosophers did in their day: If only we could reduce everything to quantifiable factors, then we should have perfection.

Happily, we cannot, and though a great many of the things that matter in life have been shown to be more amenable to quantitative analysis and scientific predictability than was previously thought to be the case, there still remains the province of art. We still respond to the leader; we hear more and more desperate cries for the emergence of one. The leader, to bridge that last gap between corporate management and true leadership, still depends on unmeasurables, that is, on art rather than on science. The elements of his gift, or his skill and how he develops it, are qualitative rather than quantitative, and the problem for the humanist describing the leader is that he is trapped by the inadequacies of the language to describe qualities that defy precise definition. A leader, he may say, needs courage, resolution, self-reliance, and on and on. But he can only define any one of these terms by reference to others of them, and in the end he has produced a tautology: The leader is a leader because he can exercise leadership. One can hardly blame the social scientist for finding this less than adequate and for preferring to work with something he can pin down (i.e., can measure).

One way out of this dilemma is that history does teach by example. If it is no more than vicarious experience, it is also no less than that. It is useful to look at men whose place in history, large or small, has been guaranteed by the passage of time, and to try to extract from their careers, or episodes in them, elements that epitomize the qualities of leadership that men have most prized. In a not-quite-random sampling, consider the careers of the Marquis of Montrose, Suvorov, Robert E. Lee, and Henri Philippe Pétain. These four all achieved pinnacles of leadership, but they are useful examples in that the external details of their careers had little in common. Each was from a different country in a different century. Two were losers—most of the time; two were winners—most of the time; two fought in civil wars and two in external wars; two fought more or less unconventional wars, and two conventional. Two were in the pre-, and two in the postindustrial period. Though all are admittedly in the European tradition, that is after all our own, and it is legitimate to suggest in the aftermath of Shogun that some of the elements of leadership in other traditions may be so significantly different from ours as to be safely disregarded here.

The Marquis of Montrose

If the Stuart dynasty had been worthy of the devotion it inspired, there would still be a Stuart on the throne of England, and Elizabeth II would be just Mrs. Battenburg. James Graham, Marquis of Montrose, was born in 1612 and educated in Scotland and abroad. As a leading member of the Scottish nobility, he took part in the risings against the introduction of the Anglican prayer book in Scotland in the 1630s, and was one of the foremost signers of the Solemn League and Covenant. When the Scottish Presbyterians became ever more insistent on their own interpretations of salvation and politics, Montrose drifted openly into the Royalist cause, and in 1644 he came out for Charles I. For the next two years, he routed army after army of Scottish troops, relying on his own brilliance as a tactician and a leader of men. His ultimate inability to hold Scotland for King Charles lay more in Charles's failure (or unwillingness) to support him fully and Montrose's own lack of resources to overcome the tremendous power of the Campbells, the strongest of the western clans and the most determinedly anti-Stuart, than in any personal failing of his own.

Montrose's tiny army was finally routed in 1646; he himself got away to the Continent, where he remained until after the execution of Charles I. In a last chivalrous gesture, the Marquis returned to Scotland with a forlorn hope; most of his little band was shipwrecked; he himself was betrayed and sold to the Covenanters, and he was hanged in chains in Edinburgh in 1650.

It was a short but glorious career, and ever since its end the story of Montrose has seemed to epitomize all that courage and daring might achieve in the face of great odds. It is the more remarkable in that Montrose had no formal military training, though of course every gentleman of the day, and especially every great lord, was expected to know something of war. Nor did he ever have much in the way of troops. For the most part his army was made up of Irish peasants, often brought over with their families and following their own chiefs, or Scots of the Highland clans who came out for the love of fighting and the hope of booty.

Yet Montrose knew how to get the most from such men; he never asked for more than they could perform, though he asked much indeed of them. He took them into the Great Glen in the midst of winter and harried the Campbell lands when others said it could not be done, and he held his little army together in spite of reverses and the general sinking of the Royalist cause. Nothing typifies the spirit of his leadership more than his performance in his first battle, at Tippermuir. Here, with but 3,000 men, no cavalry and his musketeers down to one round per man, he met a well-equipped army of 5,000 horse and foot. The Covenanters spent several hours in prayers and exhortations, but Montrose's speech to his men was short and to the point, and set precisely the right tone:

> Gentlemen! It is true you have no arms; your enemy, however, to all appearance have plenty. My advice therefore is, that as there happens to be a great abundance of stones upon this moor, every man should provide himself in the first place with as stout a one as he can well manage, rush up to the first covenanter he meets, beat out his brains, take his sword, and then I believe, he will be at no loss how to proceed! (Williams, 1975: 155)

The Irish and the Highlanders did exactly that, and when the survivors of the Covenanters fled back to Perth they had lost over 3,000 men; one of Montrose's men was killed, and a second later died of his wounds.

Such disproportionate figures as that would tend to the conclusion that Montrose's lopsided victory was no more than a fluke and that any reasonably resolute force would have defeated the Covenanters. However, Montrose did it again, at Kilsyth in August 1645. Once more outnumbered, by three to two this time, he attacked the overconfident Covenanters as they marched across his front. He lost three men; his enemy something more than 6,000. The clansmen and Irish slaughtered their fleeing foes for eighteen miles before they finally stopped from exhaustion.

Yet Montrose himself was not a bloody-minded man. He did his best to avoid the excesses of seventeenth-century warfare, and gave quarter where he could manage to do so. He remained a high-minded gentleman, courteous to his adversaries when he was not actively engaged in killing them, and was the very archetype of all that later Romantics saw as the virtues of the Cavalier party. He was something of a minor poet too and spent the night before his execution composing some appropriate lines. Probably best known are the lines from "I'll Never Love Thee More" that have been attributed to him; they sum up his career and his character as a leader:

> He either fears his fate too much,
> Or his deserts are small,
> That puts it not unto the touch,
> To win or lose it all.
> (Williams, 1975: 395–396)

Montrose had the conventional upbringing and education of the nobility of his day. His knowledge of warfare was instinctive and intuitive rather than studied, and that indeed remained the norm in the British service until well into the nineteenth century. Except for the scientific arms, engineers, and artillery, the function of British officers was to lead their men and, if necessary, to die well; the bulldog spirit was more important than technical expertise.

This was true of most armies of the eighteenth century, and most soldiers who studied war did so because they were interested in it, rather than because such study was a prerequisite for advancement. Knowledge could be an actual impediment in some cases; it was practically that in the career of Alexander Suvorov.

Alexander Suvorov

Born in 1729, the weak and sickly son of a former military officer who transferred into the civil service side of the Russian bureaucracy, Suvorov never
wanted to be anything but a soldier. He read voraciously, and pushed his frail
body to and beyond its limits. His father, much against his will, enrolled him
as a cadet in the Semenovosky Regiment when he was thirteen. That was late
for a Russian noble to start his military career (officers were often put on a
regiment's list at birth), and Suvorov's rise was extraordinarily slow. He spent
years in staff and routine work, and the ordinary chores of garrison duty.
Even through the early years of the Seven Years' War he saw no action, though
he was present at Kunersdorf in 1759, where Austro-Russians slaughtered half
of Frederick the Great's army.

Not until 1761 did Suvorov see independent action, and from that point on
he never stopped. His many years of dull service had given him a great contempt for the scheming courtier-soldiers he saw constantly promoted ahead
of him, but an even greater love for the Russian soldier, conscripted for life,
punished by the knout and the gauntlet, and consistently abused by his superiors. Suvorov understood such men, and empathized with them. He started
making his name as a leader of Cossack irregulars, and his commander noted
he was "swift in reconnaissance, daring in battle and cold-blooded in danger"
(Longworth, 1965: 26).

After the war, as commander of the Suzdal regiment, he rewrote the drill
and tactical manuals, and spent his time working up a unit that in spirit and
performance resembled Sir John Moore's light infantry more than it did other
Russian formations. There was active service in Poland against the armies that
tried to reverse the Polish slide toward oblivion and Suvorov enhanced his
growing fame particularly by the siege and taking of the fortress of Cracow.

Real glory came to him over the next twenty years as he was almost inces-
santly campaigning against the Turks in Catherine the Great's wars to expand
Russia southward. His success is the more amazing in view of his constant ill
health, and before one of his greatest battles, Rymnik, he was too weak to
carry his own sword but not too weak to lead his men personally on an all-
night march that set up the victory.

His brilliance lay not only in intensive study allied to native military genius, but in his leadership qualities. More than any Russian before or perhaps
since, he had the touch that appealed to his soldiers. On campaign he ate and

slept with them, and was more than content with a pile of straw for a bed. This was a period when many Russian officers could not even address their men, having been brought up speaking French, and often those who could would not deign to do so. Suvorov, by contrast, was the common Russian writ large. In a gathering of officers, he looked like a tough weed among a bed of lilies. Regrettably, his popularity with his soldiers cost him both advancement and patronage, for just as he despised most of his fellow generals, he was hated by them. While Catherine lived he was protected, for she had learned to value his deeds more than his manners, but when she died in 1796, he was dismissed abruptly, and not recalled until Russia joined the Second Coalition against France in 1799. After a brilliant campaign in northern Italy, in which he again showed all the qualities that had made him a great soldier, he was caught up in the general Allied defeat in Switzerland, and forced to lead his starving army over the Alps and back to the Danube. Tsar Paul fired him a second time, refused to see him, and he died in disgrace in 1800.

His spirit lived on in the Russian army, however, and the great *Encyclopedia Britannica* edition of 1911 (26: 173) compared the Russian army to him in its "spirit of self-sacrifice, resolution, and indifference to losses," adding a remark which we would do well to remember in our own time: "In an age when war had become an act of diplomacy, he restored its true significance as an act of force." In 1941 and 1942, when war was universally recognized as being an act of force, Russian patriotic posters showed the ghostly figure of Suvorov, still leading Holy Mother Russia's sons into battle.

Robert E. Lee

Probably no American soldier has ever epitomized the art of leadership more fully than Robert E. Lee. Washington was often aloof, Jackson erratic for all his brilliance. MacArthur and Patton were both perhaps a little too overtly propagandistic to win the unreserved loyalties of their men, but it is safe to say of Lee that he was truly loved. On the Federal side only George H. Thomas approached Lee in this. McClellan came close for a while, until his men found out he was so solicitous of them that he refused to risk their lives in battle, an apparently ironic fault that soldiers are quicker to perceive as such than members of less dangerous professions.

Where Suvorov was a fierce old warhorse, and a looter and slaughterer of civilians as well, Lee was every inch a gentleman. Few soldiers have ever fought a civil war more chivalrously; Lee was in the peculiar position of having been offered the command of the army against which he was fighting, and he studiously referred to the Federals as "those people," never as "the enemy."

In spite of a brilliant record in the Mexican War and being offered the command of the Union forces, Lee did not do anything outstanding in the Confederate service until after his appointment to command the Army of Northern Virginia in June 1862. But the new posting proved a happy mating of leader and material. Both still had much to learn, as the following campaigns showed, but they had less to learn than their opponents, and they learned it faster. The result was to produce as nearly perfect a fighting force as the world is ever likely to see again. Consider the battle of Chancellorsville, universally regarded as Lee's masterpiece. Outnumbered by better than two to one and virtually surrounded at the outset of the battle, he ended it by nearly surrounding his foes and driving them off the field in full retreat. And that against an army that was itself one of the great ones of military history!

Lee's brilliance as a commander was matched and sustained by his leadership of his men, and the love they bore him. Even in, perhaps especially in, defeat this relationship shone forth. After Pickett's immortal failure at Gettysburg, there was little sense that Lee had been wrong in sending the Confederates against the steady Union center. The famous diorama at West Point that shows the Rebels straggling back from their charge, and their officers reporting to Lee, reflects both his anguish at having sent them on such a mission and theirs at having failed to do what he asked of them, even if flesh and blood could not do it.

Perhaps the most revealing of all episodes of Lee's career, however, is the fight at the Bloody Angle at Spottsylvania Court House. That was nearly a year after Gettysburg, and the shadows were gathering around the Confederacy. U. S. Grant had come out of the West to command the Union armies, and he was, as Lincoln said of him, "a man who knew his arithmetic." It was just before Spottsylvania that he wired back to Washington, "Our losses have been heavy, but so have those of the enemy. I propose to fight it out on this line if it takes all summer." Here was no McClellan, husbanding and pampering his troops to no purpose; here was a man who knew that if you killed enough men in gray and butternut brown, eventually there would be no Confederacy, and that was precisely what he intended to do. While that terrible litany of battles went on through the summer, Lee too came to recognize what fate held in store. As Grant slid south toward Richmond, Lee stopped him in the

Wilderness, and entrenched next around Spottsylvania Court House, with his line forming an acute angle.

On the morning of 12 May soldiers of Hancock's II Corps swept like a blue tidal wave over the point of that angle, and the life of the Confederacy hung on a single thread. That morning Lee rode among his soldiers, his sword uplifted, and proposed personally to lead the counterattack. His men would not have it, and shouting "General Lee to the rear" they went forward weeping, screaming, and cursing, to die in his place. For the rest of the day Confederates and Union soldiers fought as bitterly as men have ever done over a rotten little abatis. Lee lost one-fifth of his army, and Grant more than a tenth of his, and students who think that war is a matter of computers or that Americans do not "know their arithmetic" would do well to study the Civil War.

Later, one day when it was all winding down to its sad finish, Lee lamented what might become of his country, and one of his aides interrupted, "General, for the last two years, these men have had no country; you are their country, and what they have fought for."

In the twenty-first century, the tasks of leadership at the highest levels of authority have become strangely complicated. On the one hand, the simple growth of the population has made it increasingly difficult for a leader to touch all his potential followers; on the other, the development of modern communications methods has made it easier for a leader to project at least an image of himself to vast numbers of people. That, we may all agree, has been a mixed blessing. We have moved rapidly from the era of the newspaper image, early in the century, when the public followed with bated breath the reports of royalty and nobility visiting this fair or launching that battleship, to the era of the radio, when men as diverse as Franklin Roosevelt and Adolf Hitler discovered the uses of the ether for informing or misinforming their constituencies. And we have moved even more rapidly still to the era of the television set, the all-seeing, all-telling eye that dominates our contemporary scene. If, in the age of mass man, the leader has to reach more people than ever before, he has in the instrument of mass communication an unprecedented means of doing so.

Such problems were in their infancy, and but imperfectly perceived, at the time of World War I. Until 1914 men were convinced that modern masses could meet and overcome any challenge by the application of modern technology. There was then what now looks like a charmingly naive confidence that anything might be achieved. Had not man recently learned to fly? A few years earlier, when the machine gun was developed, writers had praised the new tool as a means by which the savages and natives of backward territories might be civilized and Christianized the more rapidly. That was the era of Samuel Smiles and self-help, and if you believed you could do better, then by golly you could do better.

That complacent confidence had evaporated by 1917. It had been slaughtered on the "corpsefield of Loos," blown apart on the slopes of Vimy Ridge, and ground into the mud on the Somme and Verdun. In April, when General Robert Nivelle led the French armies once more to defeat in the Second Battle of the Aisne, they finally broke and mutinied. It was for France the greatest crisis of the war, and the government resolved it by the appointment of the one man who typified the army's ideal of leadership, General Philippe Pétain.

Philippe Pétain

Pétain had already made his mark several times over the years, and until fairly recently that mark had always been a black one. As a junior officer he had thoroughly identified with his men in the *Chasseurs alpins,* much as Suvorov had done in an earlier time. Like his famous predecessor, he was as unpopular with his superiors as he was popular with his men, and one of his fitness reports contained the always-quoted remark, "If this officer rises above the rank of major it will be a disaster for France." His chief problem was not his personality, though; it was his studying of modern tactics which led him to fly in the face of accepted French military dogma. In the late nineteenth century the French, falling behind Germany in all the statistics of great power status, convinced themselves that such statistics meant nothing, and that French spirit was irresistible. They adopted the idea of the all-conquering offensive as an article of religious faith, and Ferdinand Foch became its high priest. Pétain was the heretic in the congregation. He believed in the superior power of the defensive, and to all paeans on the attack at all costs he replied with a laconic "Fire kills." By 1914 he was a disgruntled colonel on the verge of retirement.

The outbreak of the war changed all that, and Pétain, twelve years a captain, went from colonel to lieutenant general in three months. He did well at the Marne, got command of the Second Army in mid-1915, and a year later his name was a household word, for when the Germans launched the great Verdun offensive, Pétain was sent to stop it.

He did so at enormous cost in men and material. He instituted a rotation system, and it is estimated that 60 percent of the French army passed through the fighting at Verdun at one phase or another of the battle. He organized the supply system, sending an endless chain of men and materials up the *voie sacrée*. When the battle finally ended, the French had lost more than a quarter of a million men, but they had held Verdun, and Pétain's name, whatever it might become in another war, was irrevocably linked with this greatest of the Third Republic's victories.

So it was that when the army at last refused duty after Nivelle's vainglorious Aisne offensive—a sort of Fredericksburg writ [at] large—Pétain was appointed to the supreme command, and set about to restore order and morale. He did so by the simplest of measures: He showed the soldiers that someone in authority was interested in them. That does not seem like much, but it was far more than most French soldiers had received so far in the war.

British writers charge that after Pétain the French army was relatively inactive, and took little offensive part in the war. That is certainly true, but the fact derived more from the enormous wastage of the army before Pétain took it over; in terms of generalship he did little but recognize reality. That, indeed, had always been his specialty, and accounted for his prewar unpopularity. As a leader, however, as a restorer of morale, a man who empathized with his troops and won their loyalty and respect, he had few equals in the twentieth century. That accounts in large part for the way in which he was greeted as a savior when he assumed power in 1940. His ultimate tragedy was that he lived too long, and the sad later years of his career should not obscure the enormous impact of his leadership on the soldiers of France in 1916, 1917, and 1918.

A Common Thread

All four of these men, in their own time and since, have been acknowledged as masters of the art of leadership. Do these cursory examinations of their careers reveal any general characteristics, from which it is possible to extract some of the essence of leadership? The answer is both yes and no. No, because there tends to be relatively little in common between them except that they were all soldiers, and, of course, great leaders. But the conditions of war under which Pétain labored were not very similar to those of Montrose's day, and the personality of Robert E. Lee was not very much like that of Suvorov. There are, however, some elements that can be isolated.

Each of these leaders believed in his men, in their power to rise to the heights of endeavor to which he called them. It is often preached that loyalty is a two-way street; unhappily it is less often practiced. The potential leader cannot demand the unswerving loyalty of his followers unless he is willing to return it. If he sees his men only as instruments to further his own career, he is not going to be very successful. Napoleon once remarked to Metternich that he could use up a million men a month, "for what does a man like me care for such as these," but that was after the legend was established, indeed, that was when Napoleon was already on the way down, and events were to prove he could not use up a million men a month. The leader who says, "You must be loyal to me, but I need think only of my next fitness report" will not go far.

These men also believed in a cause which transcended themselves and their own desires or ambitions. Those causes may in our own day be difficult to discern, but that is more our problem than theirs. Montrose believed both in the right of the Stuarts to rule Britain and in his own concept of freedom of religion. Suvorov served the dynastic state in the person of Catherine the Great. Robert E. Lee believed in the Confederacy, in fact epitomized what was best in it. Pétain was similarly the embodiment of France, the real France of small villages and infinitely tenacious peasantry (in spite of a reputation for frivolity, the French are among the most dour nations on earth), and he inspired the same attitudes in his men.

It is probable that their followers believed less in these causes than they did in the men who led them. Montrose's Irish and Highlanders followed their own lords to war and were but dimly aware of the constitutional principles involved in the English Civil War. Suvorov's peasant soldiers were not asked if they cared to aggrandize Russia when they were dragged off to the army for life. It was the humane treatment, the fact that he was actually interested in them, that made them follow Suvorov, and that made him subsequently a Russian legend, for surely there has not been much of that sort of leadership in Russian history since then. For the most part, leadership as practiced in Russia has been of the remote and awe-inspiring (or fear-inspiring) variety.

Charles de Gaulle (1960: 65), who had considerable professional interest in the problem, commented on this facet of leadership. He wrote between the wars,

It is, indeed, an observable fact that all leaders of men, whether as political figures, prophets, or soldiers, all those who can get the best out of others, have always identified themselves with high ideals. Followed in their lifetime because they stand for greatness of mind rather than self-interest, they are later remembered less for the usefulness of what they have achieved than for the sweep of their endeavors.

It is safe to say that de Gaulle and Bernard Montgomery agreed on little, but they both agreed on that. Montgomery (1961: 17) thought that one of the prime requisites for leadership was "selflessness, by which I mean absolute devotion to the cause he serves with no thought of personal reward or aggrandizement."

The student is apt to retort that neither de Gaulle nor Montgomery, both of whom were acknowledged as great leaders, particularly lived up to this requirement. Both of them would insist, in rebuttal, that indeed they had. Both saw themselves, however historians have seen them, as essentially selfless men. Here is de Gaulle (1960: 64) again: "Every man of action has a strong dose of egotism, pride, hardness, and cunning. But all those things will be forgiven him, indeed they will be regarded as high qualities, if he can make of them the means to achieve great ends." He would therefore argue that selflessness does not mean self-abnegation; one may be ruthlessly thrusting and ambitious, provided that ambition is directed in the service of something that is perceived as a greater good, and equally provided that the leader has the ability to convey to his followers the importance of that greater good, and not just his own ambition.

Military history is littered with the names of great and good men who were not quite hard enough, and whose disinclination to get their men killed caused only more suffering in the long run; consider again McClellan's solicitousness for his men, which may well have prolonged the Civil War by years, or Ian Hamilton's reluctance to interfere with his subordinate commanders at Gallipoli, which threw away a campaign that might well have been won on the first day. Some writers maintain that one of the few deficiencies of Sir Harold Alexander as a field commander was his preference for the soft word, and it may have cost him the capture of most of the German army south of Rome in May 1944. Napoleon summed it up when he sent Brune down to clean up the Vendée in 1800; he told his general it was better to kill 10,000 now than to be too soft and have to kill 100,000 later on.

The leader therefore not only has to believe in his men, and have that belief reciprocated; he has to be able to inspire them to risk their lives for some greater end which they may only very dimly perceive, and he has to have himself the courage to demand that they do so. It is of course in this particular that military leadership differs from other kinds.

As we are now once again engaged in an active war, there is a tendency, unfortunate but perhaps inevitable in such periods, to regard military leadership as little different from directing, for example, a large company or a
political entity. If a man can run a railroad, he ought to be able to run the
United States Army, so we say. This, as it happens, is not the case, though
the example of Montrose, moving smoothly from civilian to military leadership in his society, might seem to suggest that it was. In such times as these,
we try to repress the knowledge that the military obligation, the "profession
of arms," in Sir John Hackett's phrase, demands a greater commitment: It demands, in the last analysis, that men agree to die if necessary in fulfilling their
tasks. That is rather a different affair from the possibility of losing one's job if
one does not do well. The man who raises his right hand and dons a uniform
is saying, in so many words, "I shall perform a certain task, and if necessary I
shall put my life on the line to succeed in it." Not many trade unions and not
many managerial staff would be willing to make that sort of statement
(though if they were required to do so, Chrysler might have started making
small cars several years ago). If the military leader has the advantage of
trained and disciplined followers, he also has the disadvantages of the much
higher risks of their profession.

This is not, it appears, an unnecessary laboring of the obvious. In recent
years, in spite of having the television bring war into our front rooms, there
has been a very real sense of suppression of this basic fact. People are not
"killed," they are "wasted" or "terminated" in common parlance, and statisti-
cians succumb to the same impulse that makes undertakers describe people
as having "passed away"; bodies at the funeral home are "resting" rather than
"dead." This is a most unfortunate attitude. If there were clearer recognition
that someone who is "killed" is "dead," there would be fewer temptations to
resort to war as "an extension of politics," a mistaken definition that Clausewitz only belatedly recognized.

The Problem of War

The problem of war, and of leadership, is that if your soldiers are brought to
acknowledge the necessity of achieving their objective or dying in the effort,
so are the enemy's. It is that which calls forth the leader's ability to deal with
the unforeseen, "the contingent element inseparable from the waging of war
[which] gives to that activity both its difficulty and its grandeur" (de Gaulle,
1960: 16). "Whimsy, the irrational or unpredictable event or circumstance,

Fortuna" (Record, 1980: 19), these are the things that are not susceptible to computer analysis, these are what makes war an art, and therefore leadership an art as well.

There are of course those parts of the trade, or art, which can be studied, and therefore learned. There have been few great leaders who were not knowledgeable about the mechanics of the business; you cannot be an inspiring leader if you neglect the logistics that feed your men. They will not give you their confidence if you forget to bring up the reserve ammunition, or if you leave them with no way out of an ambush, or even if you consistently schedule two columns to use the same crossroads at the same time. All of that level of operation is subject to scientific principles, and can be taught. Any reasonably intelligent person can learn the routine of siting a battery, or even of administering a battalion. One can go very far on basic managerial skills, and one cannot do much without them. One of the difficulties, in fact, of dealing with the question of leadership is the tendency not to distinguish between the aspects of it that relate to making sound military decisions, and the aspects that relate to leading men in battle. The last people to insist that science was nothing, art and spirit were all, were the French military advocates of *l'attaque à l'outrance*, the *furia francese*, before World War I, and all they managed to do was kill off the better part of their army in the first couple of weeks of the war, as Pétain had all too accurately foreseen. It has been pointed out that if Waterloo was won on the playing fields of Eton, Gallipoli and Singapore were also lost there.

It would therefore again be a mistake to insist on too wide a cleavage between science and art, and to say that either one was all, the other nothing. Every aspect of life has elements of both in it. To repeat the example above, there is an art to siting a battery, but it must be done on scientific principles, as the British discovered when they tried to unlimber within range of the Boer rifle pits at Colenso; they lost 1,100 men, and ten out of twelve of their guns, for a Boer loss of less than 50. The higher elements of leadership remain an art, though the lesser ones can be learned scientifically, can be treated, as it were, by artifice.

Ironically, the better times are, the less artifice works, and the more art is needed. We live in what is undeniably the most prosperous society that has ever existed, with better conditions for more people than has so far been possible in human history. Artifice does not work, because our servicemen are for the most part sufficiently intelligent and sophisticated to see through it. Our society has become so free that preoccupation with freedom as an end in itself has led us to neglect the responsibilities and the obligations that have always been thought to accompany it. No state in history has been able to say to its citizens that they need not, if they do not choose, take any part in defending the unit against the outside world. Most states resorted to conscription of a sort; even Britain, if for two centuries it had no obligatory service, had the press gang when necessary, which was a type of lottery conscription: If you happened to be in the wrong place at the wrong time, you got caught. The United States, however, only rarely in its history has had to resort to a form of conscription that was always far more selective than it was universal. In recent years we have based our security forces on the thesis that enough money will answer our needs, and that if we pay our servicemen sufficiently, they will continue to be servicemen in spite of the siren song of civilian life, a thesis that does not seem, by and large, to be proving correct. The nature of the obligation, once again, and the constraints of military life, are such that even our society does not produce sufficient to pay enough men enough money to fulfill our needs.

To this fact that prosperity breeds a disinclination for the military life must be added the further one that our recent experience has not been such as to enhance the prestige and morale of the military forces. Our position in this respect is summed up, oddly enough, by de Gaulle (1960: 71–72) writing about France after World War I:

> The aversion felt for war in general has crystallized around the army. This is an anthropomorphic phenomenon of the same kind as that which makes us dread the dentist even more than the toothache. . . . But the mystique of our times must not be allowed to discourage or to humiliate those who wield the sword of France. What better guarantee can be offered to a people gorged with good things, looked at from abroad with embittered resentment, and whose frontiers are so drawn that a single lost battle may put its very capital in jeopardy, than the efficiency of its armed forces.

It is perfectly normal that after a period of unhappy foreign adventuring Americans should prefer to remain at home, that after a long wasting war that was actively opposed by a substantial portion of the population the military services, the most visible target for both fiscal retrenchment and public resentment, should be unpopular. But such attitudes, now hopefully diminishing in the face of returning awareness that there still is a world out there, and that it is not a very friendly one, make the task of leadership, and the exercise of it, all the more difficult.

The more difficult such leadership becomes, the more it requires skill approaching art. One is still left with the problem of precisely what that is, or how to inculcate it into potential leaders. But this is by no means a new problem. Ever since society departed, somewhere in the nineteenth century, from a stratified system in which certain persons were thought by right of birth to be capable of exercising leadership, men have attempted to grapple with it. Lord Palmerston, when pressed to support the idea of examinations for the civil and military service, wrote to a friend: "Success at an examination is certainly not a decisive proof of Fitness for official employment, because after all, examination is chiefly a test of memory acting upon previous Study, and there are other qualities besides Memory and Studious Habits required to make a Good official Man."

How to produce the good official man, or how to recognize him, has remained one of the besetting problems of our time. If we believe, as our whole history attests we do, in the career open to talent, then talent must be recognizable and rewarded as such. But how to recognize it, and how to cut through the "media hype" that tries to convince us today that a man can walk on water, and the day after he is elected or put in command that he cannot walk at all?

De Gaulle (1960: 127), again, groped for a solution. "Enlightened views and supreme wisdom," he said,

> . . . are all a matter of intuition and character which no decree can compel, no instruction can impart. Only flair, intelligence and above all, the latent eagerness to play a part which alone enables a man to develop ability and strength of character, can be of service. It all comes to this, that nothing great will ever be achieved without great men, and men are great only if they are determined to be so.

"Intuition," "character," "flair," "greatness through determination to be great," all these are unsatisfactory to the social scientist as explanations of why men do the things they do. They are, in other words, in the province of art. Leadership remains the most baffling of the arts, and in spite of all the tricks that supposedly make it manageable, it will remain that way. As long as we do not know exactly what makes men get up out of a hole in the ground and go forward in the face of death at a word from another man, then leadership will remain one of the highest and most elusive of qualities. It will remain an art.

References

De Gaulle, C. *The Edge of the Sword*. Translated by G. Hopkins. New York: Criterion, 1960.

Guedalla, P. *Men of War*. London: Hodder & Stoughton, 1923.

Longworth, P. *The Art of Victory*. New York: Holt, Rinehart & Winston, 1965.

Montgomery, B. *The Path to Leadership*. London: Collins, 1961.

Record, J. "The Fortunes of War." *Harper's*, April 1980, pp. 19–23.

Ridley, J. *Lord Palmerston*. London: Panther, 1972.

"Suvorov." In *Encyclopedia Britannica*, 26: 172–173. Cambridge: Cambridge University Press, 1911.

Williams, R. *Montrose: Cavalier in Mourning*. London: Barrie & Jenkins, 1975.

5

Reality Leadership

John Charles Kunich and Dr. Richard I. Lester

> There is such a difference between the way we really live and the way we ought to live that the man who neglects the real to study the ideal will learn how to accomplish his ruin, not his salvation.
>
> —*Machiavelli,* The Prince

LEADERSHIP MEANS DIFFERENT THINGS TO different people in different contexts, which accounts for the baffling spectrum of theories, models, and methods, all jockeying for the leadership vanguard. Every serious student of the subject has a personal opinion about leadership, even if he or she has not (yet) offered us a written record of it. But leadership is neither mystical nor mysterious, at least in the abstract, where theorists remain unencumbered with the messy chores of implementation and execution. That's why people have written so much about it—everyone wants a quick solution, and it's not hard to write some ideas that make sense on paper and that even sound rather scientific. But after we peel away all the layers of wrapping paper and wade through the packaging popcorn, leadership involves nothing more than making a difference, creating positive change, moving people to get things done, and getting rid of everything else that does not contribute to the mission. This means reinforcing core values, articulating a clear and powerful vision, and then setting people free to develop better ways and better ideas. Yes, most of the clichés are true: Leadership entails trusting and giving authority back where it belongs—to the human beings who actually perform the great bulk of what we call work. Trust is the glue that holds organizations together, and empowerment is the fruit of trust. True—and far easier to say than to do.[1]

Leadership by cliché will not work unless personal strength, character, skills, and performance lie behind the phalanx of platitudes. The sad truth is that it is never easy to be a leader—to cope with the myriad intractable challenges that come bundled with the territory. If it were easy, many more people would do it. We do not learn most of the useful leadership lessons from reading. As much as we might crave the swift, effortless, and low-impact fix from books and articles, that passive and painless process rarely can substitute for little things like ability, talent, upbringing, diligence, creativity, opportunity, personality, experience, courage, vision, drive, values, perseverance, and luck. If only we could squeeze the essence of those sweet secrets into words on a page and enable readers instantly to make up for decades of error, wasted time, poor habits, inaction, bad advice, ill fortune, and laziness! Maybe if we could conceive a catchy and sophisticated-sounding new name to disguise our refried old bromides—perhaps Eight Omega Leadership or the One-Second Ruler—it would suddenly become a panacea for our power outage. Alas, instant leadership remains only a fantasy, even in this age of perpetual gratification, high-speed Internet, and no-fault living. No extreme makeover of the superficial trappings of musty, rusty, and medieval management methods will trick reality for us. The virtual reality of the self-help cult is a poor understudy for no-kidding reality, as numberless frustrated managers discover to their dismay when they fail to wring miracles out of all those gleaming formulas. A wise person understands that leadership success is a process and not an event.

Assuming a leadership role in the real world today guarantees us a mixed bag—more accurately a perverse piñata, loaded with both good and bad surprises as our reward for all that effort to crack open the shell of success. Along with the obvious satisfaction and benefits come tough pressures and responsibilities. Leaders are expected to inspire lethargic people to do their best, handle problem personnel and bad attitudes with ease, make difficult or unpopular decisions before breakfast, maintain high credibility, fend off cutthroat competition from all over the planet, explain senior management's inexplicable positions to staff members, and keep cool in the face of contentious disagreement and unfair criticism.[2] No wonder leaders would like a little help. Based on our experience, we will pass along some lessons we have learned about specific strategies, techniques, and ideas to help leaders live with the challenges unique to their role. These tips will probably not work overnight magic, morphing someone from Homer Simpson into Alexander the Great as he or she sleeps. Anyone looking for that type of happy-news leadership liposuction can put this article down now. Remember, this is reality leadership—not something in the fantasy section.

What Leaders Really Do

The best leaders do not start out with the question "What's best for me?" Rather, they ask, "What can and should I do to make a positive difference?" These leaders constantly ask themselves and their followers, "What are the organization's mission and goals? Do they need to be modified? What surprises might lie ahead that we need to anticipate? What constitutes winning performance in this fluid environment?" In these challenging times, leaders prepare organizations for change and help them adjust as they struggle through it. Leaders never fake it, and there are no shortcuts they can take, as they first learn all they can about the situation, including resources and obstacles, trends and unmet needs, as well as hidden potential and ossified misconceptions. Still, the all-knowing person does not make the best leader—the all-understanding one does. Now more than in the past, a leader cannot often act like a dictator/tyrant. The leader's people have human needs, and in the modern era, in many quarters, they are accustomed to being treated with dignity, respect, and maybe even kid gloves.

People today need to know—demand to know—that the leader cares and will do his or her utmost to help them get the job done. An old-school General Patton wannabe who tries to shove a "my way or the highway" leadership model past the gritted teeth of today's personnel will soon find himself discredited. Flexibility, sensitivity to individual circumstances, and a determination to empathize are more suited to the twenty-first-century workplace than the old leadership-through-intimidation paradigm. Just as people cannot lead from behind, they cannot lead solely by applying their soles to their workers' behinds—not anymore, at least. And that is a hard lesson. Techniques that might have worked a few decades or centuries or millennia before are not guaranteed to work as well next week. They probably require serious adjustment before we can graft them onto a contemporary leadership style. After all, leadership is not arithmetic or Newtonian physics—closer analogues are chaos math and the quantum-mechanics world of the uncertainty principle. It is all about people, and people are ever-changing. The leader who does not know that, or who does not want to know that, is apt to find no one following his or her lead. Why not? Did not it work for Attila the Hun?[3]

The tried-and-true (and trite) old tricks often don't work on the new dogs in this year's workplace. The reason for that lies at the center of what reality leaders really do—and really need to do—to succeed now. People currently entering the workforce are different from the entry-level employees of even a couple of decades ago in ways that present a leader with a jumbled grab bag of adversities and advantages. They may have shorter attention spans, less acquaintance with strict standards, and lower experience with long, arduous tasks. Today's young employees—even those with college diplomas and advanced degrees—may lack some basic skills and background knowledge once taken for granted. As our educational system has transformed—with much less emphasis on fact learning, rote memorization, and what used to be the fundamentals of reading, writing, mathematics, spelling, grammar, logic, and other disciplines—our graduates require much more critical thinking, remedial education, and training before they can perform at an acceptable level in many jobs. The leader has to provide that education and training. A progressive intellectual environment becomes possible only when critical thinking serves as the foundation of education. Why? Because when students learn to think through the core competencies they are learning, they are in a better position to apply this learning to their lives and daily work. In a world characterized by constant change and increasing complexity, people need critical thinking for economic, social, political, military, and educational survival.

Young graduates today have far more technological sophistication than the previous generation of new employees and usually can teach their leaders a thing or sixty about computer-aided research, software, hardware, and a host of powerful, modern tools. They can handle all manner of telecommunication and high-speed computerized methods with a facility that will astound many old-timer leaders who climb on a chair if someone mentions a mouse in the office. The wise leader is humble enough to use this digital edge to the fullest, even while filling in the young associates on some basic writing and sociocultural fundamentals.

Teacher-leaders cannot safely assume anything about new recruits in terms of knowledge, skill, or attitude—only that they are human and will surprise them in ways that range from delightful to dreadful. If entry-level employees (or even senior ones) appear to have a work-ethic deficit or seem disrespectful or ill mannered, no contemporary Attila can change all that by merely barking a few orders. People have a deep-seated and ineradicable need to achieve and succeed, but a modern leader must find the right way to access that latent potential within each individual, and this often entails considerable teaching and back-to-basics skill training in the workplace. Screams, threats, and periodic exclamations of "You're fired" or "You just don't fit in" will not compensate for decades of acculturation and educational priorities that are a bit (or a lot) off track from what the leader wants from his or her people. Teaching and learning remain central to what today's leaders really do, and that continues throughout the life cycle of their relationship with their people. (That is why we touch on the concept of perpetual learning later in this article.) If a person ignores either teaching or learning for long, the leader's office will soon house someone new who better "fits in" the twenty-first-century boss's chair.

Healing an Achilles Heel

Primarily, leaders fail or fall short of their potential because they have an undiscovered and/or unhealed Achilles heel—a weakness serious enough to negate all of the many positive attributes they may be blessed with. It follows that perhaps one of the most important actions a leader can take is to find and rectify whatever hidden flaw threatens his or her future. This is unpleasant, painful, and arduous work; thus, most people never do it. No off-the-shelf text on liposuction leadership can swiftly suck out our latent and long-festering vulnerability while we recline and rest. Unless we face our flaws, we gamble that one day they will face us—at a moment when a single, unaddressed issue jeopardizes everything we have achieved, and one big "Oh, no" upends a career overflowing with "Attaboys."

The metaphor of an Achilles heel is potent because legendary Achilles himself was a demigod and the greatest warrior who ever lived, virtually a one-man army capable of winning wars with his unmatched abilities for whatever side he favored. He could slay the enemy's premier hero, even Hector of Troy, and conquer the mightiest of obstacles. Yet his famous heel was ever present throughout his astonishing string of marvelous triumphs, and at the climax of his crowning victory over Troy, it allowed a far inferior enemy to kill him. If a lowly heel can fell the ultimate military genius at the pinnacle of his power, all leaders would do well to check carefully for whatever vulnerability threatens their own success.

That does not mean that such self-inspection is fun or easy. No one, from Achilles on down, likes to confront his or her own imperfections—especially ones deep and deadly enough to provoke utter failure. Sometimes we have no awareness of our own worst weaknesses, at least on a conscious level, simply because it is far more comfortable to avoid them and pretend that all is fine than to wrestle with such pernicious internal perils. Moreover, some character defects manifest themselves only when a particular, specific combination of unusual circumstances coalesces, which might not happen more than once or twice in a lifetime—if at all. Staring long and closely at ourselves in a starkly lit mirror to identify those often well-concealed weaknesses can be challenging and repugnant work. It involves methodical analysis of often horrible memories of incidents in which things went very wrong. When and why did this happen? Has it recurred? Could it recur?

All of us could also effortlessly critique many leaders—great and not-so-great, ancient and modern—and catalogue the flaw or cluster of flaws that undermined them. From Julius Caesar, Hannibal, and Alexander the Great to Ronald Reagan, Bill Clinton, and George W. Bush, it is so easy for us to play "Name That Heel" that one wonders why these prominent individuals did not do it themselves and proactively root out all those inimical defects. How could they not see their glaring blind spots? Why would such successful and eminently experienced leaders make colossal blunders—even make them repeatedly—when the consequences seem so obvious and predictable to us in our retrospection recliners? We can help ourselves to a few cheap laughs at the Big Boys' expense. But then, when it is our turn to literally help ourselves by putting our own character under the microscope, the game jumps suddenly to a much more challenging and decidedly less festive level.

Completely eliminating our greatest weakness may prove impossible, given that it likely formed through many years of experience. At a minimum, however, we ought to identify and then stay away from those specific temptations, situations, preconditions, and circumstances that have proved their potential to breach that weakness and thereby cause our downfall. By gaining cognizance of the existence and nature of our Achilles heel, we acquire the opportunity to be alert to whatever warning signals tip off the approach of our special combination of dangerous conditions and therefore exercise extra caution to guard against giving in to our weakness. In *The Picture of Dorian Gray*, Oscar Wilde famously but erroneously declared, "The only way to get rid of a temptation is to yield to it," but actually the best remedy is to understand the temptation and what causes it, strive constantly to remain removed from those causes, stay vigilant for early signs of trouble, and then use all our strength to resist surrender.[4] Doing nothing along these lines makes it far more probable that one day people will gossip about our own stunning failure and shake their heads that we could throw our once-promising careers away on something so blatantly foolish and so entirely obvious (to others) that we should never have gotten caught up in it. Finding and healing our

Achilles heel (or heels) can be one of the greatest favors we ever do for ourselves, our people, and our organization.

Service, Not Self

As young children, we tended to believe that being a leader is an unqualified blessing, amounting to getting our own way all the time and calling all the shots. That might be a fair description of a despotic dictator who rules with an iron fist tightly clenched around a bundle of fear and force. Such tyrants live and die by violence and threats, and their methods have no place in a modern free society—even though some megalomaniacs might imagine themselves as divine-right royalty within their little domains. Paradoxically, in our contemporary, self-centered, Me Century culture, where narcissism and self-esteem are paramount, the best leaders put service to others before service to themselves. To lead people who put themselves first, we would do well to check our own egos at the door and focus on what is best for our people, organization, and culture.

This concept of servant leadership is as old as humanity, but we are fated to relearn it every generation. It feels backwards, as if the leader must put aside the perquisites and privileges of the crown to stay on top—almost abdicating the throne to keep it. But authentic leadership does not involve serving ourselves, and self-aggrandizement remains foreign to the true leader, whose proper aim is to move people to do what is best for the greater good—not what is best for the leader's petty and narrow personal interests. Only by regarding the broader interests of others—employees, colleagues, customers, and society—can leaders prevail in a world where people routinely expect to be first. Of course, over time a leader will strive to impart some measure of other-regarding selflessness to his or her employees as well and move the entire organization into a service mode—but this plan unavoidably begins with the leader's own attitude.[5]

Humility, a modest sense of one's own importance, is basic to reality leadership. For people weaned on a formula of high self-esteem, humility and self-sacrifice would appear oxymoronic—a concept blatantly at odds with itself. But that is precisely why it is so crucial to productive leadership. It is not easy, and it is not obvious—but it is effective. Only by turning outside our constricted, selfish miniworld and looking at what is best for others can we serve them and, ultimately, succeed in our own right. A dictator might demand that his serfs put up a huge statue of him in the city square, but one day that monument to megalomania will be torn down, maybe by those same serfs. The only lasting memorials to leaders are those earned through assiduous devotion to something greater than themselves—and greater than any one person.

That splendid brand of selfless leadership differs greatly from the "best friend" or babysitter leadership you might think appropriate for workers coddled, pampered, and cushioned with an inflated sense of self-esteem since conception. It does no one any favors to dumb down the organization's expected performance level or to numb down our alertness for failure to meet those expectations. Reality leadership demands recognizing the truth about ourselves as well as our coworkers, competitors, customers, and culture—and then insisting on a cooperative and coordinated approach to making that truth work for our organization. No one can do this with sloppy work, lowered standards, tolerance for intolerable attitudes, or excuses for inexcusable behavior. People will eventually respond positively and appropriately to a selfless leader who settles for nothing less than best efforts and high-quality production from everyone—from the leader to the most inexperienced newcomer.

Pampered, grown, and nanny-cosseted self-esteem junkies will probably bristle initially when someone suggests (for maybe the first time in their lives) that their performance is less than above average. However, once it becomes clear that everyone, including the leader, must adhere to a no-excuse, no-kidding production, they too will usually adapt and even take pride in at last meeting and exceeding exacting standards. After all, self-esteem becomes only selfish steam unless real substance lies behind it and we ultimately see undeserved praise as saccharine for the soul. As generations of recruits have learned the hard way from surviving a grueling boot-camp ordeal, they can realize great value by reaching deep within to overcome the steepest challenges of their lives. Furthermore, the genuine sense of pride and camaraderie that comes with such a personal and organizational triumph far outshines any false pride that well-meaning but overly lenient caregivers so easily hand out. Those rewards and accolades we earn are infinitely more satisfying than those given us, precisely because we had to toil, think, struggle, and do more than was comfortable to obtain them. In that sense, the gift of high standards and high expectations for one and all is one of the greatest and truest gifts any reality leader can convey.

Mentoring for Leader Development

One can make a strong argument that leaders are neither born nor passively made; rather, they are developed and develop themselves through education, training, and a special set of experiences. Mentoring offers a good place to begin. It is largely a teaching process, beginning with parental nurturing of children and continuing through the life cycle of organizational and personal interrelationships. A key principle here is that mentoring is both an obligation and a privilege of leadership. It is something we give people. In mentoring, reality leaders provide followers with the guidance they need to make intelligent and informed decisions. Through mentoring, the senior imparts wisdom and experience-derived know-how to the junior. This process includes passing on and discussing principles, traditions, shared values, qualities, and lessons learned. Mentoring provides a framework to bring about a cultural change in the way the organization views the professional development of competent people. In most organizations today, people must take an uphill and bumpy ride on the road to the top—they simply cannot float there, nor will anyone carry them. Mentoring involves guiding and coaching—helping people move in the right direction. Clearly, mentoring is a vital way to help us reach our desired destination.

Perhaps the most powerful method by which we can shape the professional development of our employees, mentoring has become a buzzword, often carelessly shot into the air along with a dust cloud of other jargon from the unofficial, unwritten dictionary of those who consider themselves on the cutting edge of modern leadership and management. Real mentoring, properly understood, is much more than just another clipping from last week's "Dilbert" cartoon. It can and should be adjusted to fit the idiosyncratic needs and situations of both parties to the mentoring partnership, as elastic and malleable as human beings themselves. The antithesis of the old-school, one-size-fits-all, cookie-cutter mentality, mentoring—because of its capacity to conform to individual circumstances—is ideally suited to today's partnering environment. Thus, it is literally a time machine that allows us to have a profound influence many years beyond today's hubbub and humdrum and allows us to make a significant difference in the lives of our people.

A mentor—a trusted advisor, teacher, counselor, friend, and parent, usually older and more senior in the organization than the person being helped—is present when someone needs assistance in an ongoing process, not just a one-shot, square-filling formality. Because of the widely recognized value of mentoring, many organizations have made it routine, turning it into a meaningless exercise in mandatory window dressing—just one more pro forma ritual to perform and check off on some to-do list. With all the blood drained out of it, mentoring becomes just as ineffective as any other quick-fix leadership "secret" copied mindlessly from some leadership-for-losers book. Throughout our society, authentic mentoring can apply to all leaders and supervisors responsible for getting their work done through other people—but it takes much more than a perfunctory patch. As mentors who take the time to do it right, our greatest validation may come one day when we witness our former protégés—the individuals assisted by mentors—in turn undergo metamorphosis and emerge as mentors themselves.

The modeling of proper behavior, an indispensable ingredient of good mentoring, occurs when the leader demonstrates for the protégé exactly what he or she expects. It is an ongoing exercise in "do as I do," follow-the-leader game theory, but we play this never-ending game for keeps. We have seen too many examples of leaders who consider themselves exempt from the rules—even the laws—that apply to everyone. Corruption, scandal, and ruin on both an individual and institutional level metastasize from the leader's attitude of special privilege. The leader who tries to conceal personal dishonesty, immorality, or lawlessness behind a mask of faux integrity can only mentor people into becoming similar frauds because such rottenness will inevitably be exposed, having permeated the organization at every level. The true mentor must prove that "do as I say" and "do as I do" are utterly indistinguishable, without regard for time, place, or circumstance. It may not always be personally convenient or expedient for the mentor-leader to be and do everything he or she asks of the workers, but it is a nonnegotiable prerequisite of genuine leadership excellence.

As mentors, the fact that we can matter, even if for only one protégé, may be one of the most rewarding events a leader experiences. Neither dramatic nor flashy, this outcome may remain invisible to everyone but the protégé, but to that person it has profound significance. This is not the kind of marquee-magic, big-bang leadership legerdemain many people yearn for—just the kind that really does work a quiet, personal form of magic an inch at a time.[6]

Perpetual Learning

Good leaders understand that organizations cannot grow unless people grow, including the leader and everyone else. Professional development or perpetual learning involves becoming capable of doing something we could not do before. It requires growing and developing more capacity and self-confidence in ourselves and in our people. Now more than ever, leaders must ensure that professional development remains a constant activity, as we mentioned in our section about what leaders really do. We do not go to school once in a lifetime and then put education aside forever; we stay in school all of our lives.

Developing people—really developing them, with all the individually tailored effort that entails—is fundamental to how the organization views itself and how it is viewed by leaders, customers, competitors, and colleagues alike. The organization reifies its capabilities through perpetual learning, enhancing every person from the inside out, and working the same internal alchemy on the overarching team structure. Only by holding the "learning constant" foremost in their vision can reality leaders have a chance of keeping their people fully capable of fulfilling an ever-shifting mission under steadily unsteady circumstances. Given the complexity of life in the world today, no one doubts that continuous learning and adaptation are directly related to and absolutely essential for overall, long-term success.[7]

Leadership and Implementing Change

Do not read the following joke if you have already heard it more than forty-three times. How many psychiatrists does it take to change a light bulb? The answer is simple. Only one, but it is very expensive, takes a long time, and the light bulb must want to change. However, unlike changing the legendary light bulb, implementing real change does not necessarily take a long time. It can happen very quickly at some times, while at other times it crawls with imperceptible, glacier-like slowness. This is true of all types of evolution, whether good or bad. A major function of leaders calls for maximizing the former and minimizing the latter. Positive change—the kind that we cause proactively rather than the kind that falls on top of us by default—requires the right strategy. We need a system, including a workable and institutionally internalized process, to bring about the good-news change and identify/dodge the car-crash kind. Without an effective leader engineering useful change, change will inevitably find us even as we sit still, and we will usually not welcome that variety of accidental alteration.[8]

This age of instability can be an uncomfortable time for people who long for things to remain as they are—familiar, well understood, and routine. Since continual change is a given, a leader must resolve to put change to work, squeeze a harness around it, and ride it toward the right horizon. We best predict the future by inventing it, but we cannot do that by mechanically applying any formula from a self-help book, and no do-it-yourself kits exist for this. No matter what neologisms we create to describe our methods and irrespective of how many charts and four-part process lists we concoct to conjure the illusion of quantifiable precision, we still glimpse the future, if at all, through a glass, darkly. But we can look at what we need now and two years from now, and then set purposefully about making it happen. If we devote significant amounts of time on a regular basis to meeting with our people at all levels to brainstorm ideas for dealing with the years to come, we will find ready confirmation of our suspicion that we do not know all the answers and do not have a monopoly on all the good questions. We will also find that action works like a powerful medicine to relieve feelings of fear, helplessness, anger, and uncertainty because we become no longer just passive passengers on a runaway train but engineers with influence over our journey. Instead of changing with the times, we must make a habit of changing just a little ahead of the times and doing what we can to nudge change in the optimal direction; in the process, we will enhance our living with a constructive purpose.[9]

Conclusion

In summary, we reflect on John W. Gardner, who wrote as thoughtfully as anyone on the complexities of leadership. His words almost constitute a leadership creed: "We need to believe in ourselves and our future but not to believe that life is easy. Life is painful and rain falls on the just. Leaders must help us see failure and frustration not as a reason to doubt ourselves but a reason to strengthen resolve. . . . Don't pray for the day when we finally solve our problems. Pray that we have the freedom to continue working on the problems the future will never cease to throw at us."[10]

Perhaps the synthesis and summation of everything we can do to become ethics-based reality leaders call for using our freedom to the fullest and setting our hearts on doing all we can to develop a group of individuals into a cohesive and purposeful problem-crunching team.[11] This will necessarily entail all of the activities we have covered in this article: comprehending the concepts of leadership, conducting genuine mentoring and teaching, healing our Achilles heels, practicing perpetual learning, and inventing our own future at all levels. If we become, at our core, members of that team with no interests out of harmony with what is best for the team and the organization it serves, many of the fancy theoretical notions about leadership will take care of themselves—or we and our teammates will take care of them ourselves. Reality leadership may not fit into any academic textbook's equations or inspire any novelist to rhapsodize us into fictional immortality, but it delivers because it embraces the totality of real things and events that leaders come to grips with on a daily basis.

Disclaimer

The conclusions and opinions expressed in this document are those of the author cultivated through the freedom of expression and the academic environment of Air University. They do not reflect the official position of the US Government, the Department of Defense, the United States Air Force, or the Air University.

Notes

1. Les T. Csorba, *Trust: The One Thing That Makes or Breaks a Leader* (Nashville: Thomas Nelson, Inc., 2004), 23–24.

2. Warren Blank, *The 108 Skills of Natural Born Leaders* (New York: AMACOM, 2001), 13–14.

3. James M. Kouzes and Barry Z. Posner, *The Leadership Challenge: How to Get Extraordinary Things Done in Organizations* (San Francisco: Jossey-Bass, 1987), 15–16.

4. Oscar Wilde, *The Picture of Dorian Gray,* chap. 2, etext no. 174, *Project Gutenberg,* http://www.gutenberg.org/dirs/etext94/dgray10.txt.

5. Ronald A. Heifetz and Marty Linsky, *Leadership on the Line: Staying Alive Through the Dangers of Leading* (Boston: Harvard Business School Press, 2002), 208–209.

6. John C. Kunich and Richard I. Lester, *Survival Kit for Leaders* (Dallas: Skyward Publishing, 2003), 71–73.

7. Paul Hersey, Kenneth H. Blanchard, and Dewey Johnson, *Management of Organizational Behavior: Leading Human Resources,* 8th ed. (Upper Saddle River, NJ: Prentice Hall, 2001), 229.

8. Oren Harari, *The Leadership Secrets of Colin Powell* (New York: McGraw-Hill, 2002), 23.

9. Rick Warren, *The Purpose Driven Life: What on Earth Am I Here For?* (Grand Rapids, MI: Zondervan, 2002), 312–314.

10. John W. Gardner, *On Leadership* (New York: Free Press, 1993), 195, xii.

11. Jeffrey A. Zink, *Hammer-Proof: A Positive Guide to Values-Based Leadership* (Colorado Springs, CO: Peak Press, 1998), 5.

★ ★ ★ 6 ★ ★ ★

Followers as Partners
Ready When the Time Comes

Earl H. Potter III and William E. Rosenbach

THE RECOGNITION THAT THE PERSON on the front line often has the best solution to a difficult problem is at the heart of the systems US forces have put in place to capture the best ideas of every service member. These systems work to uncover new ideas and create an environment that encourages followers to share their best thinking with their leaders. The results save millions for US taxpayers and improve the efficiency and effectiveness of day-to-day operations.

For example, Technical Sergeant James S. Lennartz, a 43rd LSS turbo propulsion craftsman, came up with an idea to fix mount bushings for the oil cooler flap actuator on a C-130 Hercules for 75 cents instead of buying replacements from a depot for $4,808.29. The oil cooler cools the C-130 engine's oil, the flap actuator regulates a flap that brings airflow to the oil cooler, and the mount bushings hold the parts together. "I figured out what size the old bushings were and had the machine shop make up some stock material (for a bushing) to see if it would work, and I sent it off to the engineers, and they approved it," said Lennartz. His idea has been instituted for all C-130 oil cooler flap actuators worldwide.

Telling this story via the Air Force News Service encourages others to try their own ideas and reminds leaders to look for good ideas among their followers. No one would dispute the argument that Lennartz deserved the $10,000 he earned for his innovation, nor would anyone see a threat in encouraging others to offer their ideas. Such problems are objective; there are clear criteria for judging merit and time to evaluate the merit. However, this may not be the case in situations where the risks are higher and the tempo of operations is greater. Yet, the notion that a follower may have the best solution can still be true.

US policy toward Cubans seeking refuge in the United States has changed in the past decade. Where the US Coast Guard had been directed to "rescue" refugees and bring them to port, where they would be processed via US law, the Coast Guard now has orders to stop Cubans attempting to reach the United States before they are "feet dry" and return them to Cuba. Cubans know this and are increasingly resorting to desperate measures to elude interdiction.

On February 4, 2004, eleven Cubans attempted to reach Florida in a 1950s Buick converted into a tail-finned boat. Four women and five children were placed inside the boat/car, the windows were blacked out, and the doors were sealed to keep out the water; the men sat on the roof. The year before, Marciel Basanta Lopez and Luis Grass Rodriguez had tried to reach the United States in a 1951 Chevrolet pickup suspended between pontoons made from empty fifty-five-gallon oil drums. The Coast Guard intercepted Lopez and Rodriguez, sank their "boat," and returned the men to Cuba.

Under normal circumstances, the Coast Guard would fire disabling shots into the engine and board the boat when it stopped. In this situation, however, the vessel was powered by the original V8 engine under the car's hood. The men refused to stop and Coast Guard officials feared the frail vessel would sink if they used aggressive tactics to stop it. Coast Guard Captain Phil Heyl, commanding officer of Coast Guard Group Key West, then in charge of the operation, had his own ideas about how to stop the vessel. But before he gave an order, he asked his team for ideas. There were several suggestions: A chief petty officer suggested that they put sugar in the gas tank. Heyl doubted this suggestion would work but accepted it. The Coast Guard boarded the vessel and placed sugar in the tank. The boat's engine stalled. All personnel aboard were removed safely and returned to Cuba.

Leadership experts have long argued for consultation among leaders and followers when conditions permit. Usually when the problem is complex, expertise is widely distributed among the members of a group and there is time for deliberation. At other times the pace of action is fast and orders are called for. The challenge these days is that the tempo of operations has increased in general. It is too easy to believe that every situation is one in which there is no time for consultation and no place for alternative ideas. Yet the evidence is clear that followers often have information and ideas that are essential to the success of operations. In fact, failure to bring all perspectives to bear on an operation can have disastrous consequences.

On January 28, 1980, the Coast Guard cutter *Blackthorn* sank in Tampa Bay after colliding with an inbound freighter. Twenty-six lives were lost. Investigators determined that each of the six people in the pilothouse that day had information vital to the ship's well-being but did not share that information. An environment that encouraged sharing information did not exist and some personnel "on the bridge" had disengaged from the operation.

Robert Ginnett of the Center for Creative Leadership has studied airline crews to identify the behavior of the most effective pilots in command. Ginnett found that the most effective leaders engaged the entire crew as partners, with the result that each was fully involved in and attentive to the ongoing mission. Moreover, the leader had created an environment in which crew members were enabled to behave as partners, sharing information as they got it, offering alternative perspectives without fear, and actively seeking ways to improve operations at all times.

Partners have the competence and energy to do the job they are assigned but are also attentive to the organization's purpose. Partners understand their leader's goals and use this understanding to focus their own efforts. Such followers seek to master the skills required for their job and maximize their own accomplishments while also seeking to understand their boss's agenda and strategy. Partners understand how to get ideas into play when the tempo of operations is high and when it is time to do what they are told.

If an organization is characterized by strong relationships among leaders and followers, the purpose and direction of the command are transmitted throughout the chain of command. Purpose informs and guides every choice, and contradictions between observed actions and purpose are apparent to all. Questions arise when members can see a deviation from purpose. Seniors welcome questions because they see the question as either an opportunity for improved operations or an opportunity to educate followers to increase their understanding of how the command operates to achieve the mission.

The most effective leaders develop their followers as partners by teaching them how to play this role. But not all organizational members are, or need to be, partners. The role of partner is reserved for mature team members who are high performers with the experience and commitment to understand the big picture. It is a role to which all service members can aspire and does not depend on rank or position. Leaders and followers who behave as partners make the modern military organization work at all times and under all conditions.

Some operations allow for service members who are not yet partners to develop; others require that every member be able to function as a partner. One of these is the six-person intelligence office of the 379th Air Expeditionary Wing at Al Udeid Air Base in Qatar. This operation moves at "breakneck speed with information coming in from a sundry of government agencies via secure computer networks." According to Lieutenant Colonel Ed Polacheck, chief of intelligence for the largest expeditionary wing supporting Operation Enduring Freedom, "Every intel member has to be inquisitive, go beyond the obvious answer, and ask why that piece of information is important to the bigger picture."

If the people you have cannot perform as partners, recruit and hire individuals who share the values of being a partner. At other times, leaders will need to develop partners from those assigned to the unit. In either case, leaders who have to hire or develop partners need a model to guide their efforts. What follows is such a model.

A Model for Evaluating Followers as Partners

Partners and Other Followers

The most effective followers know they cannot be fully effective unless they work in partnership, which requires both a commitment to high performance and a commitment to develop effective relationships with partners (including their boss) whose collaboration is essential to success in their own work. These followers are intent on high performance and recognize that they share responsibility for the quality of the relationship they have with their leaders. These followers are partners, but the two dimensions that define partnership (performance initiative and relationship initiative) also describe three other follower roles familiar to military leaders: the subordinate, the contributor, and the politician. (See Figure 6.1.)

Types of Followers

Subordinate.   The subordinate is the "traditional" follower who does what he or she is told—competent at a satisfactory level but not one to whom the organization looks for leadership or who receives challenging assignments. The subordinate keeps a job and may rise in a seniority-driven organization

FIGURE 6.1   FOLLOWER STYLES

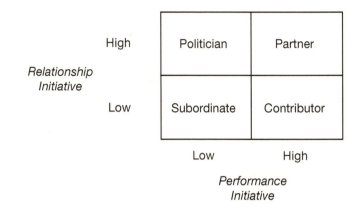

but demonstrates neither a sensitivity to relationships nor a commitment to high performance. The subordinate is the only kind of valued follower in hierarchical organizations that operates only with orders from the top and with obedience from the bottom. In organizational settings where this is desired behavior, "good" followers will exhibit these characteristics even when they are fully capable of, and even desirous of, behaving like individuals described in other quadrants of this analysis. It is also the likely style of a somewhat or completely disaffected follower who is not interested in giving anything extra, or whose job is not one of his or her primary concerns.

Contributor.   This type of follower behaves in an exemplary way—one who works hard and is known for quality work. These people rarely seek to understand the boss's perspective, however, and generally wait for direction before turning to new challenges. They are thorough and creative in obtaining resources, information, and skills that are needed to do the job; however, the interpersonal dynamics of the workplace are not a primary concern and they rarely share their expertise or knowledge. These individuals can develop into full partners by gaining skills and perspectives on the relationship initiative dimension. Alternatively, their valued inclinations can be accommodated and their work value maximized by allowing them to focus where they excel and feel comfortable, removing or minimizing aspects of the job that call for interpersonal relationships with the boss.

Politician.   The politician gives more attention to managing relationships than to maximizing performance. This person possesses valuable interpersonal qualities that are often misdirected or misunderstood. Such followers are un-usually sensitive to interpersonal dynamics and are valuable for their ability to contribute when interpersonal difficulties have arisen or might arise. They can provide valuable assistance to the leader because they are willing and able to give insights into group relationships. However, often these followers neglect the defined aspects of their jobs in favor of the more relationship-oriented or political aspects of their relationship with the boss. This is a particular prob-lem when others rely on them for job performance. Politicians can become full partners by focusing on job performance and learning how to balance these two concerns, or they can be accepted as they are and given responsibil-ities that call primarily for the skills and inclinations they possess.

Partner.   The partner is committed to high performance and effective re-lationships. The energy given to developing relationships gains the kind of understanding that leads to plans and actions that anticipate new directions and contributions that serve unmet needs. Organizations that anticipate and keep pace with change in the global environment are characterized by leaders who encourage partnership and followers who seek to be partners.

Follower Behaviors

These four types of followers can be identified by describing their behavior on the performance initiative dimension and relationship initiative dimension.

Performance Initiative

Performance initiative refers to the follower's active efforts to do a good job. A person who demonstrates a great deal of performance initiative finds ways to improve his or her own performance in the organization, which might in-clude improving skills, sharing resources with team members, and trying new strategies. The people at the high end of this scale understand that their fu-ture depends on the future of the organization and are not content to simply do what they were asked to do yesterday. At the low end of this scale one still finds satisfactory performers, while at the high end one finds experts who lead in their fields and whose contributions strengthen the organization's performance.

To assess this dimension of follower initiative, we need to consider the ex-tent to which the follower thinks of ways to get his or her assigned job done, the extent to which the follower treats himself or herself as a valuable resource, how well the follower works with coworkers, and what view the follower takes toward organizational and environmental change. Followers differ in the extent to which they take positive initiatives in each of the four domains described below:

Doing the Job.   Followers vary in the extent to which they strive to be as good as they can be at what they do. At one end of this continuum are the followers who go through the motions, performing their assigned tasks up to the minimum standards required to keep their jobs, and doing no more. At the other end of this continuum, some followers care deeply about the quality of their performance. They set their own standards, which are higher than the minimum the organization prescribes, and are focused on effective performance rather than on merely meeting defined standards. For these followers, work is an important and integral part of their lives. They take pride in what they do and apply high personal standards for performance from which they can derive personal satisfaction.

Working with Others.   Another important dimension of follower performance is working with others in the organization. At one extreme is the follower who cannot work well with others and is continually involved in arguments and disputes, irritating everyone in the process. These followers actually interfere with others' performance in the organization. In contrast, some followers work alone. They do not have difficulties with others, but they do not really work with them either. Their performance solely depends on what they themselves do (or so they think). But to varying degrees many followers do take advantage of working with others. When followers work effectively with others, they can balance their own personal interests with the interests of others, discovering common purpose and working to achieve common goals. That means emphasizing cooperation over competition, finding success in the success of the whole group instead of in self-achievement only.

Self as a Resource.   Another important aspect of follower performance initiative lies in the extent to which the person treats herself or himself as a valuable but limited resource. Some followers pay little attention to their own well-being, neglecting physical, mental, and emotional health. Although this may yield short-term benefits for the organization if the follower is effective in important ways, in the long run such neglect is likely to lead to burnout or stagnation (depending on the other aspects of follower performance initiative). Followers who will be effective over the long haul recognize that they are their own most valuable resource and take care to maintain their own physical, mental, and emotional health by balancing work and other interests (e.g., family and friends, community activities and relations, physical and nutritional fitness).

Embracing Change.   The other important dimension of follower initiative is the follower's orientation to change. In many cases, a follower's reaction to change is to ignore it or hide from it. Change is threatening and confusing, altering the time-honored and the familiar. Some followers actively resist change, finding ways to prevent things from being done differently. At the positive end of this dimension are the followers who look for new and better ways to do things because they are committed to continuous quality improvement and see change as the vehicle for continuous improvement. These followers see change as an opportunity for improvement for themselves and their organizations. Such followers anticipate or look for change. They can be effective agents for change by explaining to their coworkers the advantages of doing things differently, showing by example that "different" doesn't have to mean "worse."

Relationship initiative refers to the follower's active attempts to improve his or her working relationship with the leader. People who demonstrate a high degree of relationship initiative find ways to help the leader succeed because they know that "you can't succeed if your boss fails."

Relationship Initiative

The other vital but typically neglected dimension of follower initiative is the follower's relationship to the leader. On the relationship initiative dimension, several questions need to be explored. To what extent does the follower understand and identify with the leader's vision for the organization? Does the follower actively try to engender mutual trust with the leader? To what extent is the follower willing to communicate in a courageous fashion with the leader? How actively does the follower work to negotiate differences with the leader? At the low end of this dimension, people take the relationship they are given. At the high end, they work to increase openness and understanding to gain a perspective that can inform their choices as a partner. The following subscales describe relationship initiative:

Identifying with the Leader.   Followers vary considerably in the extent to which they understand and sympathize with the leader's perspective. Many followers simply do not. Viewing the leader as something strange and not quite human, they do not try to think about how things look from the leader's perspective or what the leader's goals or problems might be. In organizations with clear hierarchical structures and relatively strict chains of command, it is probably quite natural to see this element missing in the typical follower's approach to the leader. Followers may even be encouraged to think of their leaders as sufficiently different (i.e., superior) as to defy understanding by mere mortals. In contrast, some followers think more dispassionately about their leaders, understand their aspirations and styles, and develop sufficient respect for the leader that they adopt those aspirations as their own. These followers understand the leader's perspective, do what they can to help the leader succeed, and take pride and satisfaction in the leader's accomplishments.

Building Trust.   Followers can also take the initiative to act in ways that will build their leader's confidence and trust in them. They look for and take advantage of opportunities to demonstrate to the leader that they are reliable, discreet, and loyal. Followers who demonstrate these qualities to their leaders will in turn be asked for their opinions and reactions to new ideas. Followers who do not seek out such opportunities for building trust, who do not understand or see as important this aspect of their relationship with their leaders, will be treated accordingly and will not be in a position to help their leaders as much as they might.

Courageous Communication.   Part of building trust includes being honest, even when that is not the easiest thing to do. This aspect of relationship initiative is important enough to consider in its own right. Some followers fear (often with good reason) being the bearer of bad news and are likely to refrain from speaking unpleasant truths. This can range from the classic notion of the yes-man to simply refraining from speaking one's mind when doing so might be uncomfortable for the speaker and listeners. But followers who take the initiative in their relationships with their leaders are willing to speak the truth to serve the goals of the organization even when others may not enjoy hearing it. A follower who exhibits courageous communication takes risks in order to be honest.

Negotiating Differences.   Another aspect of relationship initiative concerns the follower's approach to differences that arise between leaders and followers. A follower who is oriented toward improving her or his relationship with the leader is in a position to negotiate or mediate these differences. In the case of a difference of opinion between a leader and follower, the follower may engage in open or hidden opposition to the leader's decisions, hiding his or her differences of opinion and quickly agreeing with the leader regardless of true personal opinion. Alternatively, the follower who is concerned about the leader-follower relationship will air these differences to have a real discussion that may persuade either party or lead to a satisfactory compromise.

Developing Partners

Creating the conditions that lead followers to partnership requires first that leaders know what they are looking for in their followers. The model we describe above offers this picture. Creating the right conditions for effective followership next requires a clear understanding of practical steps that invite followers to partnership.

Petty officers, even chief petty officers who are making recommendations on issues outside of their assigned duties, don't make off-the-wall suggestions at critical points in a life-and-death mission unless they have learned that their ideas are valued. Captain Phil Heyl intentionally makes room for partners in his command. When Coast Guard Group Key West reorganized and moved functions among its buildings, Building 48 became the group's new operations center. Heyl decided to paint COAST GUARD in bold letters on the new command center, which had previously been a Navy torpedo facility, and gave the job to a seaman in the deck force. He also gave the seaman license to figure out how to do the job, which would take a week.

As the work unfolded, Heyl could see that the seaman had chosen a different approach than the captain had in mind. He was putting three-foot-tall letters six feet apart so that US COAST GUARD stretched across the entire face of the large building and SEMPER PARATUS (the Coast Guard motto) made a bold statement on the opposite side of the building. Heyl thought about redirecting the young man's efforts, but then thought of the cost to personal initiative of doing so. He decided to let the seaman finish what he had started. In the weeks after the job was done, the command received numerous compliments on the appearance of the new paint job. Heyl decided that the job did look better than what he'd had in mind. More important, one more seaman understood that his ideas were valued, and still more important, Heyl shared his reflections about this event with his crew. The wider result was that the whole team understood how the captain viewed quality, initiative, and teamwork.

When Coast Guard Commandant Admiral Tom Collins visited a few months later, he noted the nonregulation "advertisement" by saying, "Looks like the Coast Guard is in town." Heyl heard both the stated and implied messages and told the commandant how Group Key West had come by its "unauthorized branding." Collins listened to the story and responded, "Well, that's how our system works . . . and why it works."

All military leaders work to move their followers from subordinates to contributors. They drill and rehearse, praise and redirect to develop skill and pride in performance. Leaders who share their own thinking about why they do what they do, and push their followers to think with them about why things work the way they do, push their followers to become partners. Those who encourage feedback on operations and welcome questions from their followers have a greater chance of achieving partnership. Ginnett's work shows that the difference between the best pilots in command and the others is that they directly engage all members of the crew and empower them to be active partners in the mission's success. The best partners learn how to share what they see and think because their leaders teach them when to give their input—and when not to. Leaders who work day-to-day to create partners will find them ready when they need them, and partners who are willing to accept this role will find that their leaders value them. Those with whom we serve and the country we serve deserve no less.

References

Ginnett, R. C. 1990. "Crews as Groups: Their Formation and Their Leadership." In E. L. Wiener, B. B. Kanki, and R. L. Helmreich, eds., *Cockpit Resource Management.* San Diego: Academic.

Heyl, P. J. 2004. Personal communication with the authors concerning the operation of Coast Guard Group Key West, February.

Kelleher, N. H. 2002. "Sergeant's Idea Earns Him $10,000." Air Force News Service, April 4.

McKenna, S. 2002. "Air Force Intelligence Plays a Key Role in OEF." Air Force News Service, April 26.

Pain, J. 2004. "Cubans in Floating Buick to Be Sent Home." *Oregonian,* February 5.

Rosenbach, W. E., T. S. Pittman, and E. H. Potter. 1997. *Performance and Relationship Questionnaire.* Gettysburg, Pa.: Gettysburg College.

Leaders, Managers, and Command Climate

Lieutenant General Walter F. Ulmer Jr.

The Setting

Despite the enormous contemporary stresses on the institution, America's military continues to perform with remarkable competence and commitment, from Afghanistan to Iraq, and simultaneously at multiple danger spots in between. No wonder the American people keep placing America's armed forces at the top of national institutions in poll after poll. Whether this laudatory evaluation will be accurate five years from now is unclear. Budgets that are still marginal at the cutting edge of the forces, awesome advances in technology, structural reconfigurations associated with "right-sizing" and "transformation," a stunning array of missions, and critical scrutiny of roles and doctrines continue to create extraordinary pressures. The past two decades have seen competence and tradition in action—from the spectacular 1991 excursion in the Persian Gulf through the confusion of Mogadishu, the peacekeeping in Bosnia, the spectacular reach into Afghanistan, the tactical resilience that continues in Iraq, and the not insignificant energy devoted to fire and flood relief and to homeland security. However, despite many indicators of robustness and tactical excellence, and the many recent creative initiatives of leaders at all levels, we are far from capitalizing on the human potential in our armed forces. To sustain the reliable and efficient military machine our nation needs, we must attend even more vigorously—and simultaneously with complex, vital operations worldwide—to the revitalization of organizational climates.

No institution is more serious about inculcation of leadership and managerial techniques than our armed forces. The current senior leaders appear particularly sensitive to the role of leadership and the urgent need for change. Still, we have imprecise, unstudied, and randomly supervised concepts for building and sustaining a climate that fosters innovation, aggressiveness, calculated risk-taking, and the special unit tenacity necessary for battlefield superiority. Listening to students at War College seminars or reading the professional journals, one might conclude that different officers had come from different armies. Their stories of motivational techniques, leader priorities, organizational values, training distracters (i.e., any activity required of a commander or the troops that takes away from the critical training mission), and mentoring are extraordinarily diverse. The good stories reveal the enormous power of a proper command climate. The others describe frustration amid mindless bureaucracy—an invitation to avoidable and ultimately debilitating mediocrity in a world environment that allows little room for second best.

The Role of Climate

These described variations in the quality of our organizations do not stem primarily from differences in geography, new equipment, or availability of training devices. Nor do they derive exclusively from differences in leadership style. Rather, they evolve from diverse combinations of leadership and management competencies and the realities of national budgeting and planning that together produce either a supportive or a dysfunctional organizational climate. And what is the essence of a "supportive" climate that promotes esprit and gives birth to "high-performing units"? It may be easier to feel or sense than to describe. Most experienced people can quickly take its measure. There is a pervasive sense of mission. There is agreement on the top priorities. There are clear standards. Competence is prized and appreciated. There is a willingness to share information. There is a sense of fair play. There is joy in teamwork. There are quick, convenient ways to attack problems and fix aberrations in the system. There is a sure sense of rationality and trust. Such climates are the product of strong, insightful leadership embedded in enduring values. Such climates are often seen on television news, as our field operations are now scrutinized in small chunks. Certainly in some organizations these supportive climates are the norm—or nearly so.

However, recent studies and the flow of e-mail from soldiers at the front and coming from or going to the front confirm that within the officer corps remain widely varying opinions about the quality of leadership and favorable command climates. Some sources still contend that the bold, creative officer cannot succeed in today's military, where only spotless and politically correct actions will ensure "survival." Naturally, some complaints may represent merely the cries of unsatisfiable idealists or the whining of those not selected for promotion. My personal experience and recent observations support the disturbing contention that inappropriate constraints on boldness and candor do exist but that remarkably positive command climates that have withstood the stress of combat are also with us. Some young officers disenchanted by their local situation are voting with their feet. However, the fact that excellent units exist alongside those of low or erratic effectiveness confirms that pathways to high performance can be found even in today's hectic, stressful environment.

Trust and Leadership

Leadership is not the exclusive factor determining climate and combat effectiveness. Other nonmaterial factors include the mental and physical abilities of the followers, the managerial skills of the leaders, the level of commitment to institutional values, and the mode of processing information through the organization. One critical component of the morale and cohesiveness mosaic—absence or dilution of which is particularly detrimental to effectiveness over time and under stress—is trust. Trust plays an enormous role in large and small organizations. Trust can generate magic. Nourishing it among active and reserve soldiers coming from a skeptical, periodically traumatized, and often misinformed free society is a continuing challenge. The development of trust represents the consummation of a thousand small acts, while a single isolated event might undermine it. It works or fails upward, downward, and sideways. Our future performance is significantly affected by the trust (or lack of it) our boss places in us. A World War I story has Brigadier General Douglas MacArthur in the trenches with an infantry unit just before dawn. He takes the Distinguished Service Cross ribbon from his own tunic and pins it to the chest of a young major about to lead the battalion in an attack, explaining that he knows the major will perform heroic deeds that day. One general officer serving in a troop command in the 1990s observed the opposite end of the spectrum: "We occasionally practice what we preach, but all in all we're gripped by our collective distrust of our people." My feeling is that the typical commander is somewhat more sensitive to climate and its formation than was the case in the early 1990s. But the distrust that lingers inhibits soldiers from sharing responsibility and taking initiative. Consequently, it is of more than clinical interest in any military unit—especially in a volunteer military.

American bureaucracies have a penchant for solving problems, whether caused by individual ethical flaws or systemic discontinuities, by grafting another set of regulations or another gang of overseers onto the existing superstructure. NASA's quest for guaranteed safety via checklists, the Defense Department's use of oppressive regulations to ensure integrity in the procurement process, the Environmental Protection Agency's flood of minute environmental guidelines, and some bizarre revelations of bureaucratic nonsense during the 9/11 Commission hearings highlight our tendency to rely on detailed proscriptions rather than on ethical common sense. Distrust is the lubricant for oversupervision and centralization. (Trust is both the glue that holds organizations together and the lubricant that allows sustained productivity!)

A few years ago, the US Army implemented a policy whereby a company commander could not be relieved of command without prior approval of a general officer (except in tactical or life-threatening emergencies). This directive sent two messages. The message policy-makers intended to send was that relief was a serious move and that company commanders should be protected from arbitrary and capricious actions by battalion and brigade commanders; the second, unintended message was that the system did not trust the judgment of battalion and brigade commanders. The second message was stronger. The directive was severely misguided, and its author to this day probably remains unaware of the damage.

Some military scholars and defense establishment thinkers recently have developed the concept of a contemporary revolution in military affairs (RMA). The initials RMA are starting to appear here and there in military journals and Department of Defense memoranda. The basic postulate of the RMA is that the microprocessor and other technological innovations will enable a smaller force propelled by creative doctrine to substitute for the larger, slower formations of the Cold War. (Operations in Iraq might have already brought into question the universal application of this conjecture.) In the current discussion of structural and doctrinal change that may fit too comfortably into an era of marginal—if increased—defense spending, there are too few references to the serious challenges to leadership and leader development that will attend any such revolution or transformation. At the top levels of the Department of Defense in particular, fascination with technology, finances, and geopolitics continues to relegate human issues to the back bench, even considering the increased emphasis on pay and housing in the late 1990s to early 2000s. Future force effectiveness will still depend more on sustaining fighting spirit than on utilizing cyberspace.

The tools for building routinely supportive organizational climates are available. Developing and implementing a systematic approach to climate building are the specific avenues to dramatically improved combat readiness. And the prescription is not expensive. The issue is not leadership versus management; it is one of good leadership versus bad leadership, good management versus bad management, and integrating enlightened leadership and sensible management to create the proper climate. It is absurd to imply that skilled managers cannot be skilled leaders. On the contrary, leadership and management must be complementary to create the climates from which high-performing units emerge.

Measuring and Developing Leaders

If we are serious about identifying and developing leaders, we must provide a model for measuring leadership. In this context we define "leadership" as essentially an influence process whereby one gains the trust and respect of subordinates and moves them toward goals without unduly relying on positional authority. (Exercise of positional authority is of course legitimate and necessary, but relying on formal authority alone does not constitute "leadership" as we are using that term.) Given that our standard mode of performance appraisal is exclusively superiors assessing subordinates, it is remarkable that we do as well as we do in selection and development. We would do much better to have subordinates augment the system with periodic input about their superiors. (And experiments of this model are ongoing in more than one service.) When, as occasionally happens, a general makes a spectacle through arrogant or capricious behavior, his or her boss is often surprised and disappointed. The troops might be disappointed as well, but they are never surprised.

An Army War College study in the early 1970s examined leader behavior from three perspectives—self/peer, superior, and subordinate—and eventually incorporated input from more than 30,000 questionnaires. The data confirmed what we intuitively knew: Self-delusion about leadership effectiveness is common. Peers, superiors, and subordinates often see an officer in a way that differs from the officer's self-perception. These data are similar to those collected in the corporate sector fifteen years later by researchers at the Center for Creative Leadership. No matter which definition you use, leadership does not speak of something that happens to, or occurs within, the leader; it speaks of something that happens to, or occurs within, a group of followers. Only followers reliably know how well the leader has led. This is particularly true in evaluating such leader behaviors as candor, commitment, and caring. In any formal organization, but within the long shadow of military tradition in particular, accepting the fact that our subordinates are the best judges of even one facet of our performance is difficult. Such acceptance becomes even more threatening and counterintuitive as we are "successful," hear mostly "good news," and become more chronologically gifted!

Why does any leader ever promote the person everyone else knows is wrong for the job? The answer is rarely cronyism or disregard for leader behaviors. The leader is simply ignorant of the candidate's leadership reputation. Seniors' evaluations of colonels or brigadier generals are especially difficult to make because they are often based on infrequent or intermittent personal contact and tend to be skewed by single, highly visible incidents. Rarely (but more now than in the late 1990s) do we provide useful developmental feedback to colonels, generals, or admirals. The crucial model of successful adult learning with performance feedback as the essential ingredient is slighted in our mainline leadership texts and service school curriculums. (As of 2004, there are efforts to confront these realities in all services. That such issues are being seriously discussed, particularly during stressful times, is encouraging; the history of sustained implementation of leader development at senior levels in either military or commercial organizations is not.)

Because superiors cannot alone measure leadership capability reliably, peer and subordinate input into the evaluation system are essential if the organization wants to identify, reward, and develop leadership. There is simply no alternative, particularly remembering that leadership strengths and weaknesses and ethical imperfections often reveal themselves last to even an experienced boss. (Interestingly, those leaders least in need of behavioral feedback usually seem the ones most interested in receiving it.)

Peer and subordinate ratings raise emotional issues of competitiveness among peers and perceived challenges to authority, often creating theoretical confusion between popularity and competency. Such ratings have been used at our service academies, in other officer training programs, in Ranger school, and in special situations. Input from subordinates and peers can be packaged and administered in relatively unemotional and supportive formats and provided as constructive feedback even within the constraints of a hierarchical organization. However, although it is essential for decision-makers to have access to the viewpoints of subordinates and peers when assessing leader effectiveness, such input could not and should not substitute for the commander's input or decision. There may be justifiable occasions when the boss says, "I know this person to not be a great leader, but I need her or him in that job anyway." (The critical element is that the boss really knows.) A second powerful, underutilized mechanism for providing insight regarding leader strengths and weaknesses is the behavioral assessment. Our senior service colleges have been using a limited battery of psychological tests to provide some awareness of individual personality tendencies. (The ICAF model is probably the most powerful.) A longer, more comprehensive session of assessment earlier in an officer's career is warranted. Assessment—how and why—should be integrated into the normal sequence of promotion, schooling, and assignment and made a formal part of our programs. The results should be used for screening prior to commissioning and for self-development in the middle years, and should be made available to selection boards for key staff and command positions in grades of colonel.

Further, we should give serious consideration to an outrageous concept proposed by Army Colonel Mike Malone. He suggests that an officer apply for the position of brigade commander or equivalent and that the application process include anonymous evaluations of the candidate's leadership from designated peers and subordinates in his prior command assignments. (I suggest that officers should have to apply for attendance at the senior service colleges.)

To further complicate the process of evaluating leadership outcomes, we are not capable of assessing accurately the short-term changes in unit combat effectiveness. Not only are important attributes such as morale, pride, and mental toughness difficult to appraise, but also the more tangible components of readiness, such as matériel status or tactical proficiency, defy precise evaluation. The inherent difficulty of evaluating unit effectiveness is exacerbated by omitting that subject from the military education system.

Climate and Quality

Examinations of climate and culture are anything but new. Systematic but aborted organizational effectiveness initiatives in the military and similar efforts in industry have spotlighted the interaction between environment and productivity. Industrial giants such as Goodyear, Procter & Gamble, General

Electric, and Ford continue to invest big money in reshaping the motivational context of work. "Self-directing" or "self-managing" teams (SMTs) have moved past the conceptual stage, and we know of their strengths and limitations. The role of teams is receiving attention from theorists and practitioners, but already we have found that team presence does not reduce at all the need for leaders. Total quality management (TQM) has entered and departed the managerial lexicon. Both concepts had erratic records of success in the corporate world. None of these old or new managerial twists will fare any better in the governmental sector. Their success at enhancing productivity and reducing personnel turnover will ultimately play out within the context of a supportive organizational climate. When top leaders know how to lead and manage, innovative systems can produce wonders. When leaders lack knowledge of organizational climates and culture, bold new managerial stratagems just don't take. Decentralization, trust, clarity of organizational vision, and empowerment of responsible subordinates appear to be the direct route to unlocking American initiative and producing better tires, paper towels, and switchboards. But it takes leadership of greater energy and confidence to decentralize and empower than to exercise rigid, centralized control. "Freedom to do one's work" (meaning latitude in getting the job done) in the realm of clear goals and priorities is the key stimulant to productivity. Environmental factors in the workplace are even more powerful than personal qualities of the workforce—including exceptional cognitive abilities—in producing innovative solutions. A stifling, overpressured climate with poorly articulated goals and priorities and a dearth of trust is the primary stimulant for ethical misbehavior as employees or soldiers attempt to meet impossible goals with marginal resources. Arthur D. Little Inc. concludes in *Management Perspectives on Innovation* that "creating a favorable climate is the most important single factor in encouraging innovations." And "innovation" translates quickly into the mind-set of intelligent risk-taking and creative problem-solving needed by every fighting element in our armed forces, with or without the RMA. We must get serious about unleashing and focusing our enormous, uniquely American reservoir of human initiative. Too much of it remains pinned beneath the weight of a relentless bureaucracy—but fortunately some of it escapes to produce the daring and creative tactics we have seen in recent battles.

Enhancing Organizational Climate

How can we change the organizational climate? Effective climate-building steps will mean altering the managerial and leadership habits of many of our colonels and generals. Therefore, it must be supported and watched over by the top team. Crucial to leadership at the flag officer level is an understanding of the following: how to communicate a clear vision of an idealized future; how to build supportive, coordinated, internal operating systems; how to modernize methods for evaluating people and units; and how to reinforce traditional values through personal example.

As we move to create an environment that builds and sustains high-performing units, the criticality of competence in management must be recognized. Any diminution of managerial competence and practice is as threatening to organizational effectiveness as is incompetent leadership. Poor managerial practices soak up so much energy that leaders become too tired and frustrated to lead. And the bullets and replacement parts never arrive at the front. Current systems for evaluating unit readiness, for tracking fund expenditure, and for ensuring rationality in local procurement of supplies, for example, create an administrative morass that can cripple any efforts to create a positive climate. (Much frustration in the early days of Operation Iraqi Freedom came from the inability of the bureaucracy to put cash into the hands of officers in the field who had been promised funds in time to pay for the local projects for which they had contracted in good faith.) Again, our service schools have not taught us about the importance of the supportive climate or how to create, sustain, and measure it. Our systems for measuring progress in units—systems that often highlight short-term results, compromise morale, distort priorities, and worship statistics—represent another managerial challenge. They sit alongside the challenges of articulating a vision, decentralizing while maintaining high standards, developing loyal disagreement, generating trust, and scrubbing the nonsense out of the systems.

In relative terms, the US military as an institution is the best on earth. That special aura of selfless commitment and wonderful camaraderie unique to the brotherhood of arms still permeates most of our units. But we must be better if we are to survive perilous times ahead. That can be done only by attracting, developing, and retaining individuals of strong character and quick intellect throughout the forces, and in the first instance by constructing organizational climates that will nurture and excite the enormous human potential at our disposal. Good people are increasingly intolerant of organizational stupidity and vacillating leadership. Poor organizational climates will demotivate the brightest and the best. We need to analyze and learn from specific successes and failures of senior officers as they energize or demoralize their commands. Supportive climates will sustain hope and build the emotional muscle necessary for continued battlefield success. Their creation can be commonplace even in an era of budget austerity and complex wartime challenges. They are in fact the most cost-effective force multiplier imaginable. And the responsibility for moving from routine good intentions to routine best practice clearly falls on those of us who have been, are, or will be the senior leaders of our armed forces.

PART TWO

CHARACTER

The Heart of Leadership

POSITIONS OF LEADERSHIP ARE CRUCIBLES of character. The most difficult tests for military leaders challenge their character as much as their skills. Leaders are challenged and tested many times throughout their careers, and the self-knowledge gained from those tests of character is the heart of leadership. Leading requires a deep understanding of the meaning of personal accountability and responsibility. Character involves motivation, maturity, vision, creativity, ethics, culture, commitment, courage, presence, self-confidence, humility, loyalty to oneself, and self-awareness. Ethics is integrity, morality, and principle. Integrity involves openness, truthfulness, and transparency, all of which lead to trust. Credibility means that the leader is believable, and for the leader to influence followers, he or she must be credible. Courage is the foundation of leadership, which reinforces all other values. The real test of an individual's—or an organization's—ethical fiber, according to psychologist Howard Gardner, is what happens when there are potential pressures. Leaders retain their moral compasses by believing that doing so is essential for the good of the organization or unit and asking themselves tough questions. Having the right answers to those questions is not nearly as important as asking the right questions, which will provide keen insights. When circumstance tempts leaders to betray their moral standards, they practice rigorous self-honesty and are committed to authenticity. Authentic leaders consistently demonstrate a passion for their mission or vision and practice the values that reflect their leadership style and persona. Building character never really ends for military men and women.

In "Leadership Candor" (Chapter 8), Jack Uldrich describes both leadership and followership in the broad context. Insights about General George C. Marshall as a follower and leader highlight the importance of self-knowledge and self-confidence. Vision, integrity, and humility characterized Marshall. He was a politician, but he did not promote himself. Winner of the Nobel Peace Prize, Marshall served as Army chief of staff, secretary of defense, and secretary of state, one of only a few people who were successful leaders in very different contexts or environments.

In "The Potency of Persuasion" (Chapter 9), General Wesley Clark describes power as transactional. More effective than the use of raw power, he argues, is leadership, which is the art of persuasion. According to Clark, one persuades others to follow through education, participation, and the idea of co-option. Before one threatens, he says, seek to build a community of shared interests.

In "When Leadership Collides with Loyalty" (Chapter 10), James M. Kouzes describes the results of a study he conducted with Barry Z. Posner, which indicates that leaders are expected to be forward-looking and inspiring. Leaders and followers each want the other to be capable and effective; they need to be able to trust and depend on one another and set aside their own agendas for that of the organization. Yet being forward-looking and inspiring is often incompatible with being cooperative and dependable, which presents another dilemma. The leader who is both often must choose between leading and following.

In "Leading Warriors in the Long War" (Chapter 11), Sarah Sewall describes the ethical lapses among military members in Iraq and the impact on the mission. There is also a discussion of General David H. Petraeus's response to these professional and legal violations. We elected to include Petraeus's letter to the troops in Iraq as an example of how a leader sets the expectations and tone for ethical leadership. Following the Sewall piece, it allows the reader to have additional context for her paper.

It is not only what you say, but also how you say it that makes a strong leader, according to Brian Friel in "Command Presence" (Chapter 12). To develop the ability to influence people, leaders must start by acting the way they want others to see them, according to Army Lieutenant General Russel Honoré. Here, the key is that followers are influenced more by the example the leader sets than by the words he or she speaks. Setting the example is a key to effective leadership.

In "A Soldier in the Battle to Lead Through Influence" (Chapter 13), Craig Chappelow describes the leadership challenge for credibility by a reserve officer serving as a judge advocate on active duty in Iraq. Interestingly, the key leadership challenge he faced in the civilian world corresponded closely to the one confronting him in Iraq. What this conflict has taught us is that there is a great deal of transferability between civilian careers and the military service of the National Guard and reserve officers. It is yet another lesson we are learning about leadership.

$$\star \; \star \; \star \quad 8 \quad \star \; \star \; \star$$

Leadership Candor

Jack Uldrich

RALPH WALDO EMERSON ONCE SAID, "Great men exist that there may be greater men." Based on what great men have said of George C. Marshall—General of the Army and Secretary of State—there was perhaps no greater leader in the twentieth century. Winston Churchill called him the "organizer of victory." President Eisenhower said of him, "Our people have never been so indebted to any soldier." President Truman referred to him as the "great one of the age."

A review of his extraordinary life reveals why these accolades still ring true:

- As Chief of Staff of the US Army from 1939 to 1945, Marshall transformed the Army from a poorly armed force of 175,000 men into the most powerful military service in history.

- During the war, he was a global strategist, balanced the needs of five theaters of war, and managed the egos of Franklin Roosevelt, Winston Churchill, Douglas MacArthur, and George Patton. He also achieved unity of command among the Allied forces.

- In 1947, as Secretary of State, he introduced the European Recovery Plan—better known as the Marshall Plan—to restore the European continent torn apart by war and nearing financial and political collapse. Many credit him with "winning the peace."

- He served as the president's emissary to China, president of the American Red Cross, and Secretary of Defense. Twice *Time* magazine named George Marshall its Man of the Year.
- In 1953, he became the first soldier to be awarded the Nobel Peace Prize.

Still, the lessons of George Marshall have faded. History's oversight is not so much Marshall's loss as it is ours. For as Colin Powell said, "We have so much to learn from General Marshall from his character, courage, compassion, and commitment to humankind."

Four Leadership Principles

In this short article, I highlight four of Marshall's leadership principles:

1. **Teaching.**   In 1926, after serving in various high-level positions in World War I, Marshall accepted a job at the Army Infantry School because he knew that the next war would be radically different and that America needed to train a new generation of more flexible and innovative leaders. Above all, he urged them to "study the first six months of the next war." It was a lesson that Dwight D. Eisenhower, George Patton and Omar Bradley—along with two hundred other officers who were instructed by Marshall and later became generals in World War II—learned very well.

2. **Candor.**   In November 1938, George Marshall, then deputy Chief of Staff of the Army, attended his first meeting with President Roosevelt. After thirty-five years, he was within reach of his life-long ambition of being appointed Chief of Staff. Called to discuss Roosevelt's plans to build 10,000 war planes to strengthen the Army Air Corps, Marshall was surprised to learn the president only intended to request enough funding from Congress to build the planes—with no money allocated to maintenance or training. Roosevelt asked each advisor for his opinion. Each man offered support for the plan. But Marshall responded, "I am sorry, Mr. President, but I don't agree with you at all." Roosevelt gave Marshall a startled look and adjourned the meeting. The other advisors said his turn in Washington was over.

   Six months later, however, Roosevelt selected Marshall as the next Chief of Staff because he provided honest advice.

3. **Selflessness.**   In late 1943, after Marshall had convinced a stubborn Roosevelt and Churchill of the necessity of an attack on Germany, the vital question of who would lead the invasion arose. By every standard—seniority, knowledge, experience and skill—Marshall had the right to expect he would be chosen. Roosevelt knew that Marshall was the best man for the job. Yet, when the time came to make the decision, Roosevelt balked because he understood how vital Marshall was to the overall war effort.

   Still, Roosevelt decided to offer Marshall the command on the sole condition that he ask for it. Marshall, however, was too duty-bound to ask. He simply said, "I will serve wherever you order me, Mr. President. Feel free to act in the best interest of the country."

   So, the command of the Normandy Invasion—one of Marshall's "deepest hopes" and one of history's surest invitations to glory—went to Dwight D. Eisenhower. Secretary of War Henry Stimson said: "Marshall reached great heights by never thinking of himself."

4. **Vision.**   After leading the US to victory, George Marshall could have retired a satisfied man. He did not retire, however, because he knew that his job was not finished. He recognized that unless the conditions that led to World War II—namely chaos, poverty, and hunger—were alleviated, a lasting peace could never be achieved. Therefore, as Secretary of State, he asked the war-weary American people and a reluctant US Congress to fund the economic recovery of Europe. He did it because it was the right thing to do.

   Perhaps that is Marshall's greatest lesson: Great leaders do not just perform great deeds. They leave their mark on the world by making it a better place. They do this by training the next generation of leaders, setting an example by their actions and by creating the conditions for future prosperity. George C. Marshall still serves as a model for any leader.

ACTION: Practice these four principles.

$$\star\ \star\ \star \quad 9 \quad \star\ \star\ \star$$

The Potency of Persuasion

General Wesley Clark

YOU'RE IN A TOUGH NEGOTIATION. The guy across the table is unconcerned, backed up by his cronies, prepared to wait you out. There is no legal recourse. You need power, real power. Like this: "Mr. President, may I see you outside, alone, for just a moment?" "Certainly," Serb president Slobodan Milosevic replies, with that smug self-assurance characteristic of his dictatorship. "Mr. President," I begin, looking at him eye-to-eye that day in 1998 and speaking in an even voice, "perhaps you don't understand, but the United Nations has directed that you pull out your excess forces from Kosovo now. And if you don't, NATO is going to tell me to bomb you, and I will bomb you good."

That was raw power, the power to destroy, the power to, I hoped, compel—backed by the knowledge that the greatest air force in the world could deliver thousands of tons of bombs and rockets with pinpoint accuracy.

Not many people will ever have that kind of power, or have to use it. Power is essentially about achieving influence over others. Individuals strive for it, as do nations. Power serves to promote interests, compassionate or selfless interests. Employers exert it over employees, charitable donors over beneficiaries, regulators over businesses. For years the US used its nuclear arsenal to deter an attack by the Soviet Union, its system of laws and civil rights to win worldwide admiration, its wealth to support and influence international institutions.

Power is based on certain qualities or capabilities, but power itself is transactional and flows out of relationships, real or perceived. As a career Army officer, a commander in Vietnam, NATO commander during the Kosovo campaign, one-time presidential candidate, and now chairman of an investment bank, I have seen many kinds of power: the power of threats and of praise, of shock and surprise, and of a shared vision. Sometimes threatening works, but it usually brings with it adverse consequences—like resentment and a desire to get even in some way. People don't like to be reminded that they are inferior in power or status. And so, in business, it is important to motivate through the power of shared goals, shared objectives, and shared standards.

Leadership is the art of persuading the other fellow to want to do what you want him to do, General Eisenhower wisely taught us decades ago, and it remains the best recipe I know for developing power. But how do you persuade others to follow? I've found three ways to do so: through education, through participation, and through the idea of co-option. Take training. An ounce of education upfront is worth a pound of threats later on. This is one of the reasons that businesses both big and small spend millions on training and educating their new arrivals and their managers, all the way to the top. Employee education is one of the most cost-effective investments that businesses can make. But it isn't enough: Employees need to become vested in their work through participation. In the budget process, for example, team leaders are often required to present their own projections—in essence forming a contract to do their part to bring in revenues and hold down expenses. Such exercises are critical for empowering employees. Co-option, the third step, is less tangible. It involves building and maintaining the emotional bonds of teamwork, loyalty, and trust. Essentially leaders have to sell themselves and their programs to their teams in order to influence.

As for Milosevic, well, he heard the threat, but he didn't like it. He pulled back his troops, but only temporarily. Soon he resumed the ethnic cleansing, and, following through on our threat, we did bomb Yugoslavia. After seventy-eight days of attacks, coupled with diplomacy, we broke his will and eventually his grip on power. He died in prison in 2006, awaiting conviction as a war criminal. But to this day I often think about how many lives could have been saved if we had successfully persuaded him to share our vision.

Even if the stakes aren't as high, the same lessons should be applied to business—before you're tempted to threaten, seek to build a community of shared interests. Then you won't need to call in the US Air Force.

★ ★ ★ **10** ★ ★ ★

When Leadership
Collides with Loyalty

James M. Kouzes

Despite our cry for more effective leadership, I've become convinced that we are quite satisfied to do without it. We would much rather have loyalty than leadership. Recall the fight between former General Motors board member H. Ross Perot and G.M.'s chairman, Roger B. Smith, that erupted when someone other than the official leader of the corporation began to articulate a strategic vision for the company.

Or take the case of a friend of mine, a former senior vice president of a large packaged goods company. A few years ago he faced a critical leadership challenge. New technology made it possible to introduce a substitute for his company's food product. His market studies clearly indicated that the future of the industry lay in the new substitute product. He was convinced that his company had to revise its long-range plans and develop its own entry into the market or suffer disastrous consequences.

But the board did not share his point of view. It authorized its own independent studies by two prestigious management consulting firms, which to the board's surprise supported the senior vice president's sense of the market. Still unconvinced, the board asked two law firms to determine whether entry into the new market would pose any antitrust issues. Both sets of lawyers agreed there would be no problem.

Despite the overwhelming evidence, the board then sought the opinion of yet a third law firm. This one gave it the answer it was looking for and it abandoned the new product.

The senior vice president would not be false to his beliefs and subsequently left the company. He has since successfully applied his leadership talents to dramatically improve the performance of a business he now owns in another industry. And he was right about the future of his former company. It experienced serious financial losses, went through a dramatic downsizing, and has yet to recover fully from its myopic strategy.

This critical incident illustrates an extraordinarily difficult choice executives must often make: Do I lead or do I follow? While one is frequently a leader and a follower in the same organization, there are times in executive careers when the choice is either or. That is because there are distinct differences in what we expect of followers. These expectations are in dramatic conflict.

During the course of doing research for a book, my co-author, Barry Posner, and I asked top-level managers to complete a checklist of the characteristics they look for and admire most in a leader. According to our study, the majority of senior managers admire leaders who are: honest, competent, forward-looking and inspiring.

In a separate study, we asked a similar group of executives about what qualities they value in a follower. The majority of executives in our study said they admire honesty, competency, dependability and cooperation.

In every survey we conducted in the United States, honesty and competency ranked first and second in our expectations of what we want from our leaders and followers. If we are to follow someone willingly, we first want to know that the person is worthy of our trust. Similarly, when a leader inquires into the status of a project he wants to know that the information is completely accurate.

We also want leaders and followers alike to be capable and effective. When a leader delegates a task he naturally wants assurance that it will be carried out with skill and precision.

But we also expect our leaders to have a sense of direction and a concern for the future of the organization. Leaders must know where they are going. We expect them to be enthusiastic, energetic and positive about the future. It is not enough for a leader to have a dream—he must be able to communicate his vision in ways that uplift and encourage people to go along with it.

Leaders want to know they can count on people to be team players. They want to know they will work together willingly and will be able to compromise and subordinate individual needs to the common purpose.

These qualities are absolutely essential for even the most mundane tasks in organizations. We must be able to rely on each other, to trust each other and to set aside our own agendas for that of the organization. Without dependability and cooperation, nothing would get done, and politics would be rampant.

Yet being forward-looking and inspiring—two essential leadership qualities— is often not harmonious with being cooperative and dependable. This is what happened in the case of the senior vice president of the packaged goods company. His integrity demanded that he stand up for his point of view. The result was that he was perceived not to be a team player.

If an individual's vision of the future is opposed to that of his superiors, he may be perceived as uncooperative and disloyal even if his point of view is correct. Persistently selling a point of view only reinforces this perception and may diminish support within the organization. It may even lead to being branded a renegade and result in being fired, transferred or "voluntarily" dismissed.

As essential as cooperativeness and dependability are, they can be inhibitors of organizational change. If they are too rigidly adhered to, they can result in faithful allegiance to the status quo and unquestioning loyalty to the party line. They also can inhibit the development of the leadership skills we so need in business today.

There is another crucial difference between a pioneering leader and a dependable follower. While success in both is founded on personal credibility, leadership requires the realization of a unique and ideal vision of the future. Following requires cooperative and reliable adherence to that common vision. When an individual's vision is in conflict with the existing strategic vision of an organization, he may have to make a choice: Do I lead or do I follow?

There is no easy path. If organizations inhibit the honest articulation of fresh strategic visions of the future, they will never grow and improve. They will never create a climate that fosters leadership. On the other hand, if individuals cannot learn to subordinate themselves to a shared purpose, then anarchy will rule.

In these times of business transformation, it is wise for executives to encourage and tolerate more internal conflict than we have allowed in the past. If we expect people to show initiative in meeting today's serious business challenges, then we have to relax our expectations of abiding devotion. Instead, we must support the efforts of honest and competent people to find solutions to the problems that are confronting our companies. In short, we must develop the leader in everyone.

11

Leading Warriors
in the Long War

Sarah Sewall

THE ESSENCE OF THE CHALLENGE of modern military leadership is ethical. Counterinsurgency in particular intensifies moral dilemmas about the use of force in military operations, but any sustained combat operation today will reveal battlefield ethics as a central concern. And for the foreseeable future, the US armed forces will confront terrorism and seek to enhance global stability through sustained worldwide military operations conducted under global scrutiny. Thus the various monikers used to describe current and future security challenges—"persistent conflict," "long war," "global war on terror"—suggest that ethical leadership will become more important and complicated in the years ahead.

Battlefield ethics generally relate to discipline in the application of violence in war. Short, intense combat operations avoid reckoning with these issues in real time. In peacetime or during peace operations, military leaders focus on different strata of ethical problems revolving around financial mismanagement, fraternization, or the use of alcohol. Counterinsurgency, although an ancient form of war, is the harbinger of a profound paradigm shift in the American way of war. Not surprisingly, it poses more complex leadership challenges to which the services are still adjusting. Its related moral hazards will eventually demand the attention of not just the military but the broader citizenry as well.

Counterinsurgency (COIN) creates deeper and confounding ethical dilemmas because, unlike in conventional wars, civilian protection lies at the core of the COIN mission.[1] The strategic objective is to protect civilians while destroying insurgents and strengthening the host-nation government. This poses a more radical challenge than is commonly understood.

As a straightforward military task, the protection mission is demanding. It is far more difficult for the counterinsurgent to secure the population than it is for the insurgent to selectively wreak destruction. Moreover, because the civilian is the center of gravity, counterinsurgency demands that US forces assume more risk on behalf of those civilians. And if even a small proportion of COIN forces fail to "get it," their actions can swiftly discredit the larger political objectives of the campaign.

In addition, American COIN forces must fight in a manner consistent with their law, honor, and national values. The insurgent, on the other hand, is free to flout the law of armed conflict and international norms by targeting civilians, shunning uniforms, and hiding amid the population, thus posing constant and enervating ethical conundrums for counterinsurgent forces.

Observers both inside and outside the military have long regarded counterinsurgency as the most internally corrosive form of warfare. The national stakes are high. Algeria in the 1950s is a prime example. The French military's descent into torture and the use of indiscriminate force ultimately weakened the armed forces and rocked the core of French political order. The ethical quandary is particularly intense for any democratic nation that prides itself on its national values and military professionalism.

It is this ethical dilemma that ultimately underlies a lingering complaint about America's defeat in Vietnam. The superficial argument was that political constraints upon the use of force prevented victory. In reality, this was a complaint against the *moral asymmetry* in the application of violence in counterinsurgency—asymmetry because, unlike in conventional war, the other side is almost by definition unburdened by such niceties. In reality, Americans have yet to come to terms with the ethical dilemmas of counterinsurgency. It is no surprise, then, that the toughest military leadership challenges revolve around this issue.

Scoping the Problem

It is essential to recognize that the American military's concerns about battlefield ethics and maintaining moral integrity reflect the fundamental distinction between the US armed forces and the enemy they fight. Still, the military as a whole was slow to recognize and respond to the challenges of COIN.

The common truisms of conventional war apply equally to counterinsurgency: War is hell and people die; individuals will make mistakes in applying force; and bad apples exist within every institution. The ethical performance of US forces in combat cannot easily be measured comparatively because the United States is unparalleled in its combination of precision and discipline in the conduct of war. The challenge is not even one of absolute numbers, because we have such limited ability to define a reasonable level of civilian harm under a given set of circumstances. Instead, the question is whether the US military is doing all it can to achieve its mission of protecting civilians, minimizing the harm that proves so counterproductive in COIN. In sum, are US forces being effective?

One significant objective measure of effectiveness is the number of civilians inadvertently hurt instead of protected in the course of US operations. The record shows that senior leadership attention can have remarkable impact. In 2005, Lieutenant General John R. Vines, leader of Multinational Corps-Iraq, began tracking incidents of civilian harm at checkpoints and during convoy operations. The following year, his successor, Lieutenant General Peter W. Chiarelli, directed subordinate commanders to investigate all "escalation of force" incidents resulting in severe wounding or death of civilians and to report the findings to the Baghdad headquarters.[2]

The information became a routine part of senior leadership briefings, shaping assessment of the COIN effort. The severity of the problem prompted responses, including standardization of checkpoint tactics, techniques, and procedures, and training on those standards. By June 2006, the US military had reduced the number of Iraqi civilians killed at US checkpoints or shot by US convoys to about one a week from about seven a week the previous year.[3] And each soldier and Marine knew, by virtue of the escalation-of-force reporting requirements, that senior leadership in theater cared about the incidents. Real-time civilian casualty data thus provided a useful leadership tool for monitoring and managing ethical behavior—and supporting mission success—in the field.

By 2006, though, a deeper challenge came into clear focus. The commander of Multinational Forces in Iraq, General George W. Casey, had directed that a mental-health survey break new ground by incorporating questions about ground forces' ethical behavior on the battlefield. The fall 2006 survey of some 1,600 soldiers and Marines included questions about troops' attitudes and behavior toward civilians.[4] Though most service members perform with honor under the most trying of circumstances, a noteworthy number evinced disdain for the very civilians whose "hearts and minds" are the contested prize of counterinsurgency.

More than half of US troops surveyed disagreed with the statement that noncombatants should be treated with dignity and respect. Almost 10 percent reported mistreating civilians by kicking them or unnecessarily damaging their possessions. Many claimed they had never been instructed otherwise. According to one-third of the Marines and one-quarter of the soldiers surveyed, their leaders failed to tell them not to mistreat civilians. Is it surprising, then, that fewer than half the troops said they would report a team member's unethical behavior?

The bottom line is that significant numbers of surveyed US troops thought and acted in less visible ways that violated their professional ethics (not to mention the laws of war) and undermined their mission.

Some responsibility for this behavior lies with a post-Vietnam military leadership that ignored counterinsurgency because it wanted never to fight that type of war again. The Army and Marine Corps, for all intents and purposes, relegated COIN to the special-operations community. As a result, regular forces deploying to Iraq had to learn a new trade on the job. Guerrillas, though, were the worst imaginable ethics instructors. It's no wonder that more than a quarter of soldiers and almost a third of Marines faced ethical challenges to which they did not know how to respond. So Army and Marine Corps institutional leadership had failed in a meaningful way, while leaders in the field clearly had also failed to communicate the mission and the moral imperatives that troops desperately needed to fight an unfamiliar type of war.

Organizations rarely want to examine their fundamental weaknesses. Nor is it considered career enhancing to reveal problems eating at the core of great institutions. The US military deserves praise for getting its arms around the dark side of counterinsurgency. Though the follow-on mental health survey in 2007 yielded similar findings about the ethics of forces in Iraq, at least one other recent Army survey suggested progress in attitudes and behavior soldiers reported themselves.[5] The bottom line is that addressing ethics in COIN is an ongoing challenge that has only just begun.

Calibrating Response

There is an enormous difference between troops' purposefully violating the law of war and a close judgment call that results in unintended civilian deaths.

The two circumstances demand different assessment processes (legal investigation versus operational fact-finding) and institutional responses (criminal justice proceedings versus DOTMLPF [Doctrine, Organization, Training, Materiel, Leadership and Education, Personnel, and Facilities] adaptation). But sometimes the two cases begin to blur, and COIN is where that overlap becomes most likely.

The reported massacre of civilians at Haditha, Iraq, in November 2005 caused great concern within the senior Marine Corps leadership. In its aftermath, commanders ordered "refresher training" for Marines in theater.[6] But it seemed a more symbolic than practical response to the incident. More of the same training that already had been provided before the incident offered little reassurance. Nor was it clear that Haditha represented a widespread problem. If it did, however, no quick and simple fixes existed. The case was quickly swallowed up in a shield of legal proceedings, even as the Marine Corps sought to understand the contributing factors.

The hard data about the extent of inadvertent killing of civilians during routine tactical operations, and later the broader survey of troop behavior, illustrated more systemic challenges, raising legal, ethical, and operational issues the Army and Marine Corps began to address more comprehensively.

General David H. Petraeus had recently arrived in theater as the Multinational Forces in Iraq commander when the Pentagon released the results of the battlefield ethics survey. Petraeus had been the central proponent of the new COIN field manual stressing the links between leadership, ethics, and success in counterinsurgency.[7] His prior focus at the Army's Combined Arms Center had been on redirecting service thinking and practice toward the demanding, subtle, and admittedly frustrating practice of counterinsurgency. Petraeus immediately recognized the survey's significance. Its results suggested that many troops in theater were actively undermining the very mission he hoped to reinvigorate with a surge of forces into Baghdad and application of the new COIN manual tenets. The survey also showed that with better leadership, troops were more likely to follow the rules.

Petraeus seized the teaching moment, issuing an open letter to all forces (see Exhibit 11.1). He explained that despite understandable anger at enemy tactics, "adherence to our values distinguishes us from our enemies." Petraeus also knew he would have to rely heavily upon his junior leaders in the field to fill the ethics vacuum. "Leaders, in particular," he wrote, "need to discuss these issues with their troopers—and, as always, they need to set the right example and strive to ensure proper conduct. We should never underestimate the importance of good leadership and the difference it can make."[8] Petraeus

EXHIBIT 11.1

HEADQUARTERS

**MULTI-NATIONAL FORCE - IRAQ
BAGHDAD, IRAQ
APO AE 09342-1400**

10 May 2007

Soldiers, Sailors, Airmen, Marines, and Coast Guardsmen serving in Multi-National Force-Iraq:

Our values and the laws governing warfare teach us to respect human dignity, maintain our integrity, and do what is right. Adherence to our values distinguishes us from our enemy. This fight depends on securing the population, which must understand that we—not our enemies—occupy the moral high ground. This strategy has shown results in recent months. Al Qaeda's indiscriminate attacks, for example, have finally started to turn a substantial proportion of the Iraqi population against it.

In view of this, I was concerned by the results of a recently released survey conducted last fall in Iraq that revealed an apparent unwillingness on the part of some US personnel to report illegal actions taken by fellow members of their units. The study also indicated that a small percentage of those surveyed may have mistreated noncombatants. This survey should spur reflection on our conduct in combat.

I fully appreciate the emotions that one experiences in Iraq. I also know firsthand the bonds between members of the "brotherhood of the close fight." Seeing a fellow trooper killed by a barbaric enemy can spark frustration, anger, and a desire for immediate revenge. As hard as it might be, however, we must not let these emotions lead us—or our comrades in arms—to commit hasty, illegal actions. In the event that we witness or hear of such actions, we must not let our bonds prevent us from speaking up.

Some may argue that we would be more effective if we sanctioned torture or other expedient methods to obtain information from the enemy. They would be wrong. Beyond the basic fact that such actions are illegal, history shows that they also are frequently neither useful nor necessary. Certainly, extreme physical action can make someone "talk"; however, what the individual says may be of questionable value. In fact, our experience in applying the interrogation standards laid out in the Army Field Manual (2-22.3) on *Human Intelligence Collector Operations* that was published last year shows that the techniques in the manual work effectively and humanely in eliciting information from detainees.

We are, indeed, warriors. We train to kill our enemies. We are engaged in combat, we must pursue the enemy relentlessly, and we must be violent at times. What sets us apart from our enemies in this fight, however, is how we behave. In everything we do, we must observe the standards and values that dictate that we treat noncombatants and detainees with dignity and respect. While we are warriors, we are also all human beings. Stress caused by lengthy deployments and combat is not a sign of weakness; it is a sign that we are human. If you feel such stress, do not hesitate to talk to your chain of command, your chaplain, or a medical expert.

We should use the survey results to renew our commitment to the values and standards that make us who we are and to spur re-examination of these issues. Leaders, in particular, need to discuss these issues with their troopers—and, as always, they need to set the right example and strive to ensure proper conduct. We should never underestimate the importance of good leadership and the difference it can make.

Thanks for what you continue to do. It is an honor to serve with each of you.

David H. Petraeus
General, United States Army
Commanding

recognized that his most practical short-term strategy lay in inspiring what he personally hoped to provide in Iraq: a positive command climate of openness and accountability.

The services began responding immediately within familiar parameters, adapting the tools and processes they had long relied upon to prepare leaders and train soldiers and Marines. They set about updating and revising schoolhouse curriculum and battlefield ethics and law-of-war training. There was a great deal of focus on pre-deployment mental-health training and understanding the impact of stress upon decision-making and followership. Yet, as explained by a Marine Corps psychiatrist, "I don't think there's a lot in the study that has prompted us to do something new, because we've been working on many of these things for a long time now and I think the findings have reinforced for us the importance of those things."[9]

Both services rightly view the solution as residing largely in leadership, reinforced by reminders about the laws of armed conflict and expectations of ethical behavior on the battlefield. But familiar labels can be overly reassuring, deceptively suggesting that existing approaches to developing leadership or repeated exposure to existing rules and expectations will suffice. In fact, the moral conundrums in COIN demand significant attention at a deeper level, as the Army and Marine Corps have begun to realize.

The Deeper Leadership Challenge

At its core, the ethical issue revolves around risk. Specifically, how much risk should the service member assume on behalf of the civilian, who is literally the heart of the counterinsurgency mission? This is the nub of the moral dilemma for the American military. It remains unresolved even as the Army and Marine Corps undertake additional battlefield ethics training and education and ask leaders to become more vigilant and responsive to ethical challenges. At the end of the day, the issue may not be resolvable, but it must be more deeply understood.

For decades, conventional US military doctrine and training stressed the primacy of firepower and technology in operations and have increasingly emphasized the importance of force-protection measures. Force protection has also been a priority at the lower end of the spectrum of operations, such as during stability operations in the Balkans. The broader risk aversion of American society generally has helped create a political-military culture that, in *relative* terms, has been shielded from risk.

Add to this the earlier discussion about traditional military understandings of mission, and you can see the makings of a perfect storm confronting counterinsurgency's demands for assuming risk on behalf of the civilian and larger intangible, political objectives. Simply put, COIN's absolute levels of risk and mission objectives are a dramatic departure from the post-Vietnam experience of the US military.

The operational design of COIN poses additional barriers to assuming greater risk in practice. Successful conduct operations require empowering lower-level commanders with maximum flexibility to adapt to local conditions and opportunities. Decentralized operations require decentralized responsibilities. Yet, in unappreciated ways, this devolved authority increases tension for the small-unit leader. Tradeoffs between achieving the mission and protecting the men, real enough for the battalion commander, are both starker and more intimate for the lieutenant or captain. This can create additional psychological barriers to reducing the emphasis on force protection in the name of reallocating risk to accomplish the mission.

Thus junior officer leadership is truly central in COIN—it is where the struggle for ethical conduct will be won or lost. Senior leaders, as Petraeus and Chiarelli have demonstrated, can make a significant difference. And in many ways the inverse is even easier to see. Consider the command climate that tolerated ethical collapse in Haditha. But the decision to plant a weapon on a dead civilian or repeatedly fire without positive identification or, perhaps most important, to fail to report those ethical lapses will in many cases hinge upon the character of junior leaders.

Furthermore, it is not just the officers, but often the noncommissioned officers, who will have the greatest influence in the field. They face a subtly different set of pressures in the men-versus-mission tradeoff. Their career revolves around their unit, and their futures are linked to the men with whom they fight. Officers are expected to move up and on, while the noncommissioned officers (NCOs) are expected to retain the focus on the troops. Ultimately charged with discipline and training, NCOs effectively uphold the "pointy end" of the ethics spear. Thus, it is critical that they accept COIN principles—particularly the tenet that greater short-term risk yields both enhanced force protection and mission accomplishment in the longer term. Otherwise, asking ever more of their men seems not just counterintuitive but also sacrilegious, contrary to their core professional responsibility.

The problem is of course amplified by the apparent absence of immediate and concrete advantage in assuming greater risk. Simply put, COIN success is elusive and difficult to measure. Instead of a radical and lasting tactical military or political victory, success often lies in simply mitigating counterproductive effects (avoiding the foul). Yet justifying decisions is easier when, at the end of the day, the hill is clearly taken, despite the losses that may have been incurred. When greater risk simply avoids harming overall operational objectives—without providing measurable progress—risk assumption may prove harder to sustain. Again, this is likely to be particularly acute in decentralized operations where the bigger picture is harder for a unit commander to assemble. Calculated in a strictly military context, the cost/benefit analysis of force protection can produce an equilibrium that does not meet the larger political campaign goals most effectively.

For all of these reasons, it may be necessary for the Army and Marine Corps as institutions to appear to overstate the risk-assumption requirement to inducing the requisite changes in troops' understanding and actions. But can either the services as institutions or the junior leaders in the field actually do that? COIN confronts an institutional history, practice, and set of assumptions that run in the other direction. There are always risks that such an overemphasis will be perceived as straying from prudent force protection. These are essential political concerns, not military concerns. American standing rules of engagement reiterate the right to self-defense, and any risk reorientation for COIN would reiterate the centrality of self-defense even as the escalation of force is to be more tightly controlled. But what would it mean for civilian protection to truly be a core objective of counterinsurgency? If the civilian is the mission, where does self-defense fit in if it comes at the civilian's expense?

Mission first: This is the core of what it means to serve in the armed forces, the implicit self-sacrifice that comes with accomplishing the mission. The US military has, through its study of history and its own operational experience, evolved an understanding of what constitutes a mission. It is not always destroying the tank or taking the hill. The military teaches the value of a diversion in which there will be no tangible immediate military gain but rather an indirect contribution toward mission success. The military accepts the need to protect diplomats or congresspeople working in the theater, even if their direct contributions to the fight are unclear. The military understood the need to eliminate Iraqi Scud missiles during Operation Desert Storm, not because Scud attacks were militarily significant but because of their political significance for a major US ally and, therefore, indirectly, the unity of the assembled fighting coalition. These are all commonly accepted military missions that require an assumption of risk.

Yet the civilian in counterinsurgency still faces an uphill battle—not conceptually, but in the concrete, tactical calculation of risk assumption. Sustained change in the conduct of counterinsurgency requires expanded appreciation of the relationship of risk assumption to mission success and a COIN exit strategy. This is the logical conclusion of emergent efforts to define and implement escalation-of-force measures. To avoid creating more new enemies than a given operation eliminates; to demonstrate the professionalism, moral distinction, and commitment of US forces; and to enable non-American and nonmilitary actors to assume ultimate responsibility for the COIN effort, military forces must tolerate higher levels of risk in conducting COIN operations.

What messages do services send with regard to these issues? The Army and Marine Corps have updated battlefield vignettes to provide updated teaching materials for their schoolhouses. These counterinsurgency case studies more accurately reflect the tensions described above, and the schoolhouse discussion questions surely raise the right issues. Yet without an institutional nod to a different answer, the traditional default answers are likely to emerge. The discussion will hint at the need for an alternative approach but will settle with the standard way of looking at tradeoffs between men and mission. The civilian protection mission will not be internalized without real pushing and reinforcement from the top. Inevitably, that means staking a view regarding the correct response. Thus far, the services have largely stepped back from this brink.

The longstanding and understandable reluctance to second-guess decisions in the field makes sense when the paradigms are understood, but may not suffice when a deeper conceptual shift is required. The US Army and Marine Corps counterinsurgency doctrine suggests as much in a narrower context: "The use of discriminating proportionate force as a mindset goes beyond the adherence to the rules of engagement."[10] In other words, the right answer may differ from the minimum required by the rules or by common practice.

Unlike laws or rules of engagement, ethics reflect a deeper cultural and institutional ethos. They provide an internal compass to help troops "know what to do" in challenging circumstances. Counterinsurgency ethics are particularly perplexing and complex. In COIN, the primacy of civilian protection appears at odds with military service values that stress loyalty to fellow Marines and soldiers. Thus, the toughest dilemmas are rarely legal or rule-based issues per se. They are more often struggles between competing personal values and service values, between force protection and mission accomplishment.

The COIN field manual notes that morality and honor are closely linked. A promising route to reconciling the apparent dilemmas consistent with service traditions is to emphasize battlefield ethics not as a strictly legal or ethical matter, but as a matter of service values. During an early tour of duty in Iraq, an exemplary Marine Corps leader found himself doing just that as he sought tools to help his men internalize the COIN mission and its often discordant implications.

Intuitively, Lieutenant Colonel Todd Desgrosseilliers turned to Marine Corps values to transmit principles of behavior he wanted his young men to follow in the field. Honor, courage, and commitment were expanded upon in what he dubbed his "virtue ethics" pocket cards. He essentially recast the unfamiliar new demands in the terminology and code of service identity. Combined with strong personal leadership, Desgrosseilliers's approach helped fill the vacuum of counterinsurgency training and education in which US forces operated at that time.

It will take time for each service to articulate, inculcate, and tend an ethic of counterinsurgency consistent with its culture. This process must be seen as genuine evolution of those values, not a short-term expedient or an instrumental manipulation.

It requires another complementary evolution, too, which is the expansion of what honor in battle means and how it is rewarded. The modern Marine Corps or Army warrior ethos must adapt to modern warfare. This requires recognition of heroism as a matter of restraint, of the action *not* taken, of the risks assumed on behalf not just of the fellow serviceman but the local civilian. It is the next step in proving institutional commitment to support the actions the military demands in the field. And these are issues of institutional responsibility—a leadership challenge of a different order.

A truly comprehensive approach to COIN leadership must cast a wider net around leadership, focusing on junior officers and noncommissioned officers. It must continue improving tools for assessing and responding to identified problems, such as surveys and casualty data. It demands a deeper and more prominent effort to address the conflicts among values and the tensions between force protection and the mission. And it requires institutional support at the highest levels for redefining leadership. Underlying these leadership challenges is the need for a deeper understanding of the ethical challenges COIN presents.

Notes

1. For a more comprehensive discussion, see Sarah Sewall, "Introduction: A Radical Field Manual," *US Army and Marine Corps Counterinsurgency Field Manual FM3-24* (Chicago, IL: University of Chicago Press, 2007).

2. Greg Jaffe, "US Curbs Iraqi Civilians' Deaths in Checkpoint, Convoy Incidents," *Wall Street Journal*, June 6, 2006.

3. Ibid.

4. Office of the Surgeon, Multinational Force-Iraq and Office of the Surgeon General, US Army Medical Command, Mental Health Advisory Team (MHAT-III), Operation Iraqi Freedom 04–06, May 29, 2006. Available at www.armymedicine.army.mil/news/mhat/mhat_iii/MHATIII _Report_29May2006-Redacted.pdf. Last viewed July 8, 2008.

5. Office of the Surgeon, Multinational Force-Iraq, and Office of the Surgeon General, US Army Medical Command, Mental Health Advisory Team (MHAT-IV), Operation Iraqi Freedom 05–07, November 17, 2006. Available at www.armymedicine.army.mil/news/mhat/mhat_iv/ MHAT_IV_Report_17NOV06.pdf. Last viewed July 8, 2008.

6. Hamza Hendawi, "US Troops in Iraq to Get Ethics Training," Associated Press, June 2, 2006.

7. David Petraeus and James Amos, *US Army and Marine Corps Counterinsurgency Field Manual FM3-24* (Chicago, IL: University of Chicago Press, 2007).

8. Ibid.

9. Assistant Secretary of Defense for Health Affairs S. Ward Casscells, DoD News Briefing, May 4, 2007. Available at www.defenselink.mil/transcripts/transcript.aspx?transcriptid=3958. Last viewed July 8, 2008.

10. Petraeus and Amos, *US Army and Marine Corps Counterinsurgency Field Manual*, section 7–37.

12

★ ★ ★   **12**   ★ ★ ★

Command Presence

Brian Friel

IT'S NOT ONLY WHAT YOU say, but how you say it that makes a strong leader.

Watching the retrospective coverage of the government's response to Hurricane Katrina that marked the one-year anniversary of the 2005 disaster, it was striking to observe the number of leaders who cried publicly.

Louisiana Governor Kathleen Blanco did. So did New Orleans Mayor Ray Nagin. And New Orleans Police Chief Edwin Compass. Jefferson Parish President Aaron Broussard cried as well. Mississippi Governor Haley Barbour said President Bush cried when they met up shortly after the storm.

The tears reflected the overwhelming nature of the disaster—and the difficulty leaders had trying to respond to it. Some also showed their anger and frustration by shouting, pouting or cursing.

It was on that wave of emotion that Army Lieutenent General Russel Honoré, commander of the military Joint Task Force Katrina, came into New Orleans to assume control of the rescue-and-recovery operations.

He did not cry, at least publicly. Upon his arrival in New Orleans, Nagin described the soldier as "one John Wayne dude." Shortly after Honoré got to town, he was famously seen on camera yelling at military and law enforcement personnel to stop pointing their weapons because he didn't want New Orleanians to feel like they were being policed rather than helped. "Hey!

Weapons down!" Honoré shouted as he walked through an intersection. "Weapons down! Weapons down, damn it! Put your weapons down!"

"Command presence," in military and law enforcement circles, describes the physical way in which leaders lead: their body movements, tone of voice, the way they stand, how they make eye contact. At a pivotal moment during the Katrina recovery efforts, Honoré's command presence helped restore a sense of control in New Orleans. The way he walked, the way he carried himself, the way he projected his voice, even the fact that he frequently smoked cigars—all those elements of his command presence conveyed a leadership message. All that would have been meaningless if he had failed to deliver a strong military response. But it was strong, so his command presence was an appropriate communicator of the actions he was taking.

In the military, command presence is part of the training. As a simple example, military officers are taught how to use their voices to give commands, learning which volume, pitch and tone to use for various purposes. In the civilian world, however, such physical training often is overlooked. Civilian managers have to teach themselves such skills or seek out such training.

In a world where management often is done via computer, managers can't forget that their physical presence matters. Every leader isn't a "John Wayne dude," but everyone communicates not only with words but also with the way they deliver those words. In a 2002 article in *Military Review,* Honoré pointed out that interpersonal skills are a key component of command. "Leadership begins with influencing people," he wrote. And to develop the ability to influence people, leaders must start by acting the way they want others to see them.

$\star\;\star\;\star$ **13** $\star\;\star\;\star$

A Soldier in the Battle to Lead Through Influence

Craig Chappelow

Send lawyers, guns, and money . . .
—*Warren Zevon*

BILL DYER IS HITTING MIDSTRIDE in his successful legal career. You might think that Dyer, an attorney with Finnegan, Henderson, Farabow, Garrett & Dunner, one of the largest and most prestigious intellectual property firms in the United States, would be firmly focused on his specialty—patent and trademark litigation. But nowadays when Dyer gets ready to go to work each morning, he doesn't pack case files into his briefcase. He doesn't have to contend with the Atlanta rush-hour traffic or crowded commuter trains. Dyer has swapped the traditional tools of his trade for desert camouflage fatigues, body armor, a Kevlar helmet, and a Beretta 9 mm pistol. He is a major in the US Army Reserve, one of the thousands of men and women called from civilian life to fill a military role in Operation Iraqi Freedom. Dyer looks young for his age—forty-one—and his erect posture and close-cropped hair betray his military background, which includes college at Virginia Military Institute (where he earned a B.S. degree in electrical engineering) and a stint as an Air Force officer.

The United States has depended on citizen-soldiers such as Dyer since 1908, when Congress authorized the Army to establish a reserve corps of medical officers. Since then the armed forces' reserves have been key players in every military conflict in which the United States has been involved. Army reservists now fulfill critical functions not only in medicine but also in such other areas as engineering, policing, maintenance, linguistics, and—yes—law.

135

Until recently my mental image of a battle-ready modern Army did not include lawyers. (After all, wouldn't their shiny wingtips reveal the troops' position on nighttime missions?) But it turns out that there is plenty of legal work to go around. Dyer has been called on to handle criminal matters such as assaults and drug use, to brief soldiers on legal issues such as the laws of war and the rules of engagement, and to manage the grim task of helping soldiers prepare their wills.

A Different World

In Iraq, Dyer is the judge advocate (military jargon for lawyer) for a fifteen-person engineering design unit. As Dyer explains, his team of reservists provides expertise that isn't available from active-duty combat engineering units, which are geared toward tasks such as breaching obstacles and blowing up bridges. Dyer's engineering unit is the type that is needed most in Iraq right now, consisting of managers of large-scale construction projects, architects, and power-distribution experts.

Dyer's technical background in electrical engineering has been a tremendous advantage in his current assignment. He finds himself switching back and forth between his legal and engineering duties. When he first arrived in Iraq he was one of the few Americans on hand with any knowledge of the gas turbines Iraq uses to generate power, and he was able to help Iraqi engineers get generators back on the power grid. As a judge advocate he has been dealing largely with the legal aspects of construction, service, and procurement contracts and issues such as destroyed Iraqi civilian property.

I have been interviewing Dyer via e-mail and, because of his strong attention to detail and ability to tell a good story, have gotten a vivid image of what life is like for a successful lawyer thrust into a war environment. His missives reveal that in most ways his day-to-day existence in Iraq is diametrical to his life in suburban Atlanta. Instead of coming home to the leafy neighborhood where he, his wife, Jill, and two young daughters keep a tidy house at the top of a steep driveway, Dyer bunks along the Tigris River in a building in Baghdad that formerly housed bureaucrats of Saddam Hussein's Baath Party. The sound of gunfire across the river is common, especially at night. Dyer says that although he is able to deal with the brutal heat, it is the smell that he has not adjusted to. He describes it as resulting from his own closely quartered troops, raw sewage being dumped into the Tigris, and the black smoke and noxious fumes from old vehicles and diesel-powered generators.

Common Ground

Despite the night-and-day contrast between Dyer's life back in the States and in Iraq, there is one aspect he has found to be tremendously similar—his leadership duties. He says the main leadership challenge he faces in his military role is the same one he faces in working with clients at the law firm.

"Without question, the toughest leadership challenge is leading without being *in charge,* per se," he wrote in one e-mail. "I'm not in command here, and I'm not *leading* anyone in the sense that a combat commander tells a hundred of his men to take a hill. I'm part of a staff, but not all opinions that come from staff members—even if they hold equal positions in the pecking order—are given equal weight."

Dyer says there's a striking parallel with his experiences at the law firm: "In many cases clients are looking to their counsel for that leadership. Not necessarily someone to just tell them what to do but someone with experience, wisdom, and selfless motives who can help guide them on a course of action that is right for their company—without simply telling them what they have to do."

John Kotter, a professor of leadership at Harvard Business School and author of a number of best-selling books on leadership, has written extensively on the subject of leadership through influence. He suggests that leaders who are effective at using influence rather than a command-and-control approach do three things well: They use information to appeal to others' reason and convince them that a certain action is consistent with their goals; they sense how others will react to various words, events, settings, and stories and use these symbols to appeal to their feelings; and they use role modeling to demonstrate the kinds of behaviors and actions they desire from others.

I am sure Dyer did not have Kotter's leadership model on his mind during a recent incident in Iraq, but his actions followed that theory as he and three other soldiers were returning from Baghdad International Airport to their residence. They were on edge because there had been several recent attacks on American troops along the route they were taking, which is known as Ambush Alley. About two miles past the last checkpoint (the last secure place for about a ten-mile stretch), their Humvee died. It seems that their gas gauge had gotten stuck on half full.

> We had no radio or extra fuel. One of our guys had a badly sprained ankle, and the other two were in the throes of Saddam's revenge . . . one had a fever and both had bad stomach cramping. It was midday, about 115 degrees, and we

had no idea when a friendly vehicle might come by. I was the ranking guy in the group, so I set up the other three guys in a defensive perimeter around the vehicle and took off running back to the last checkpoint, with the weapon drawn and all of my gear on (flak vest, Kevlar helmet, etc.). As I came into view of the Abrams tank at the checkpoint, I saw activity there. The machine gunner turned his barrel toward me, and somebody scrambled to the top of the tank—I hoped somebody with good vision. They recognized me as American, and the young lieutenant who was on the top of the tank jumped down and met me. I explained the situation, he radioed for help, and we had fuel in a few minutes. Later that afternoon there was another attack about a half a mile from where we broke down.

The physical and mental stress resulting from these events is further evidence of the contrast between Dyer's life in Iraq and in the civilian world, where he confesses that the most grueling routines he faces are an occasional lunchtime workout and "hand-cranking the windows on my old Saab."

Sound Choices

Dyer has developed a strategy of selective guidance, honing it first at the law firm and more recently during his work sorting out problems in Iraq:

In my position [in Iraq], I couldn't just stand up and declare that I had the answer and that other ideas were bad—at least not without suffering a complete loss of credibility. Instead I gradually laid a foundation of leadership over time. Offering knowledge when I had it, silence when I didn't, and a commitment to whatever course of action was best for my "client"—either the Iraqi people or my unit. Over time I have found that my opinions and input have carried more weight than they probably should have, given my place in the hierarchy here.

Dyer notes that the key leadership challenge he faces in the civilian world corresponds closely to the one confronting him in Iraq:

As someone to whom clients have come for advice and counsel, I have an obligation to influence their decision-making process in the direction of sound legal and business choices. Companies that retain top firms expect this kind of leadership from their counsel, but the reality is that being able to deliver on this leadership challenge while not crossing the boundaries of who is in charge is a huge test of one's abilities and resources that many lawyers haven't figured out. It took me a long time, and I'm still working on it. From my experience, many counselors have trouble finding the middle ground between telling their clients what to do and simply providing directionless, legalistic answers to questions. Leading your client is a much more satisfying arrangement for both attorney and client, but it requires a balance that can be difficult to strike.

Making the Most

I get the impression that Dyer may be understating his ability to strike that balance and his impact as a leader on his clients in civilian life and his military colleagues in Iraq. I spoke with Roger Taylor, managing partner of Finnegan, Henderson's Atlanta office, and his remarks seem to confirm my suspicion. "Bill is respected and well liked within our firm," Taylor said.

> Intellectual property work is complex and time pressured. We depend on Bill to direct and review the work of the younger attorneys. He also serves as a chief interface with clients, and we can't send just *anyone* to work directly with them. His style and expertise establish credibility with the clients.

Dyer remains philosophical about his approach to leadership, and one of his e-mail comments contains some telling insights for others who work in an environment where the leadership paradigm seems to be shifting. "It would have been much easier for me to lead if I had been General Tommy Franks, but I'm not," he wrote.

> I've had to make the most of my position, experience, et cetera, to influence people and events around me. Not everyone can be a CEO or a commanding general. It's a real test of leadership, I think, to lead when you aren't in charge. And I'm learning as I go.

PART THREE

GENERAL OFFICERS

Leadership Challenges and Opportunities

Movies and literature are replete with images of courageous, brash, and smart generals, such as MacArthur, Patton, and Schwartzkopf, who rally the spirits of their troops to accomplish the impossible and defeat our enemies. These images typify Americans' notion of military leadership and underpin consistent post-Vietnam public opinion polls that show military leaders holding some of the most respected professional occupations in the country. Given positive perceptions about senior military leaders, it is not surprising that the public often calls upon them to pursue leadership positions in the political arena. George Washington was the first, and Dwight David Eisenhower will not be the last former general to hold the highest office in the land.

But what makes those legendary generals tick? Scholars and practitioners alike have analyzed the keys to succeeding as a senior military officer. Some of the conclusions reached by thinkers centuries ago remain salient today. Most agree, for example, that senior military leaders must possess extraordinary intellect and some form of courage. Yet changes in both the nature of warfare and the military's relations with a democratic society have almost certainly added complexity to the already significant expectations of general officers. Generals now must not only devise military tactics and strategy but also advise senior civilian decision-makers and Congress on the prospects and feasibility of their policy objectives in such places as Iraq and Afghanistan.

The previous section of this book illuminated some of the general characteristics and traits effective military leaders possess. In this section, we take a deeper look at the senior-most military leaders and the contemporary challenges they face. As the senior leaders in their respective services, generals and admirals should—at least in theory—embody the best of military leadership. Part III examines leadership by senior military officers from the ground up. It begins with writings by military officers who offer their perspective on the key tenets of senior military leadership. The challenges facing generals today is assessed in this part and concludes with a piece that reflects on the type of general the military of the future will require.

In his classic text "Generalship: The Diseases and Their Cure" (Chapter 14), Major General J. F. C. Fuller articulates his personal perspective on the problems associated with generals' leadership and then suggests remedies for those problems. The chapter includes an excerpt of one section from his book that highlights the three factors Fuller believes represent the "essentials in generalship." Fuller, who wrote the book in 1936, reflects on lessons he learned about leadership during service in the First World War. The danger of war weighs heavily on his analysis of the essence of leadership. He asserts, for example, that "heroism is the soul of leadership" and "courage is the pivotal moral virtue in the system of war." But courage alone does not make a general: Fuller believes that effective generals must also have "creative intelligence." The mental capacity to "do something that the enemy does not expect" and the intellect to think creatively allow the best generals to succeed in the art of war. Finally, Fuller recommends that successful generals must remain physically fit for command because a leader's mind must remain clear.

General Montgomery C. Meigs, commander of Stabilization Forces in Bosnia from 1998 to 1999, provides a more contemporary reflection of the essential characteristics of generalship in "Generalship: Qualities, Instincts, and Character" (Chapter 15). Like Fuller, however, Meigs bases many of his observations on historic analysis of past leaders such as Ulysses Grant, Matthew Ridgway, and Dwight Eisenhower. Four characteristics compose Meigs's model of generalship: force of intellect, energy, selflessness, and humanity. Meigs believes that successful generals have a strong *force of intellect,* from which the elements of decision and execution derive. Smart generals must also have the *energy* to both engage problems at their source and bolster troops' efforts through an engaged presence. But Meigs distinguishes from Fuller's belief in the importance of courage; he believes that courage is based in an underlying *selflessness* that also allows leaders to forge consensus amid conflicting guidance from subordinates. In conclusion, Meigs highlights the importance of humanity in developing the "loyalty of subordinate to leader that underlies the spirit of great units."

But must an outstanding senior military leader in the twenty-first century be a man? In "Breaking Through 'Brass' Ceilings: Female Military Leaders" (Chapter 16), Major Paula D. Broadwell examines the concern that women's path to the highest ranks in the armed forces may include institutional, societal, or cultural barriers. The piece explores the leadership competencies of female general officers who have overcome the "brass ceiling" and now serve at the highest ranks in the Army. Broadwell proposes that the Department of Defense can—and should—do more to enable future female leaders.

During a time of war, the responsibilities of senior military leaders grow in magnitude and complexity. So how have America's generals performed in the run-up to and execution of the war in Iraq? According to Lieutenant Colonel Paul Yingling, there has been "A Failure in Generalship" (Chapter 17). Upon its original publication in 2007, Yingling's piece set off an intense and controversial discussion about the competence and judgment of American generals. Yingling argues that the military's senior leaders "repeated the mistakes of Vietnam" in Iraq in at least three ways. First, Yingling believes that military leaders failed to anticipate future military operations and warfare after the Cold War. The US military was not equipped, manned, or trained for low-intensity conflicts. Second, the generals miscalculated the means and methods necessary to secure post-Saddam Iraq and failed to adapt to the demands of counterinsurgency warfare. Finally, Yingling asserts that the senior-most military leaders did not accurately reflect the security situation in Iraq to the public or to policy-makers.

Junior and midlevel officers in the military are not typically rewarded for challenging the decisions senior military leaders make. The military's success depends on organizational clarity and discipline. But how have senior military leaders in the Army responded to criticism from lower-ranking officers, such as Paul Yingling? In his piece, "Challenging the Generals" (Chapter 18), Fred Kaplan explores the Army's reaction to critiques of its senior leaders. Kaplan notes that many Army generals openly and candidly discussed criticisms of their leadership with junior officers. Yet, it is unclear how the reverberations from high-profile criticism of senior Army leaders will affect the model of future leaders. Some Army generals want to promote officers whose careers mirror their own, while others are more open to intellectual leaders cast in the mold of General David Petraeus. The challenge is clear: The Army needs to develop future generals who possess the tactical knowledge, analytical prowess, and "moral courage" to advise policy-makers.

Senior military leaders must balance the dual roles of advising civilian decision-makers on the military implications of their policies and representing the interests of their subordinates. The war in Iraq has heightened the inherent tension between senior military leaders and national security policy-makers that has existed since the Vietnam War. In "Bush and the Generals" (Chapter 19), Michael C. Desch explains that this tension did not start with President George W. Bush; however, civilian policy-makers' low regard for military expertise and their micromanagement of tactics and operations made it worse. President Bill Clinton's tense relationship with the military hampered his ability to carry out several of his key policy initiatives. But Desch asserts that former Secretary of Defense Donald Rumsfeld's deeply entrenched distrust of the military and willingness to immerse himself in operational and tactical issues exacerbated friction with the military. The proper balance in the relationship between generals and policy-makers should provide civilian leaders with authority over political decisions and the military with latitude in making the operational decisions to complete the mission.

14

Generalship

The Diseases and Their Cure

Major General J. F. C. Fuller

"THE MORAL IS TO THE physical as three to one," is a catchphrase which parrot-wise has been repeated a million times, and yet few soldiers pay any attention to what morality in war really means. Above all things it means heroism, for heroism is the soul of leadership, whether a man is leading himself by placing his convictions before his interests, or whether he is risking his life to save the lives of his comrades, or to help win the cause his country is fighting for. Both forms are essential in generalship, for until a man learns how to command himself it is unlikely that his command over others will prove a profitable business.

War is, or anyhow should be, an heroic undertaking; for without heroism it can be no more than an animal conflict, which in place of raising man through an ideal debases him through brutality.

Many years ago now this was pointed out by John Ruskin in his lecture on war, which he gave at the Royal Military Academy, Woolwich, in 1865,[1] the year the Civil War in America ended. I intend to quote freely from this lecture, probably the most noted ever delivered at the Royal Academy, and certainly one which we should study today. I intend to do so because Ruskin gets down to the heart of this subject, showing that if war is bereft of the personal factor in command, it cannot but degenerate into a soulless conflict in which the worst and not the best in man will emerge.

An artist and a lover of peace, he said to his youthful audience:

You may imagine that your work is wholly foreign to, and separate from mine. So far from that, all the pure and noble arts of peace are founded on war; no great art ever yet rose on earth, but among a nation of soldiers. There is no art among a shepherd people, if it remains at peace. There is no art among an agricultural people, if it remains at peace. Commerce is barely consistent with fine art; but cannot produce it. Manufacture not only is unable to produce it, but invariably destroys whatever seeds of it exist. There is no great art possible to a nation but that which is based on battle.

To Ruskin war "is the foundation of all the arts" because "it is the foundation of all the high virtues and faculties of men"; then he says:

It is very strange to me to discover this; and very dreadful—but I saw it to be quite an undeniable fact. The common notion that peace and the virtues of civil life flourished together, I found to be wholly untenable. Peace and the *vices* of civil life only flourish together. We talk of peace and learning, and of peace and plenty, and of peace and civilization; but I found that those were not the words which the Muse of History coupled together; that, on her lips, the words were—peace, and sensuality—peace, and selfishness—peace, and death. I found, in brief, that all great nations learned the truth of word, and strength of thought, in war; that they were nourished in war, and wasted by peace; taught by war, and deceived by peace; trained by war, and betrayed by peace; in a word, that they were born in war, and expired in peace.

But what type of war does Ruskin refer to? Not "the rage of a barbarian wolf-flock," not wars begotten by bankers, squabbling merchants or jealous politicians, but wars of self-defense. "To such war as this," he says, "all men are born; in such war as this any man may happily die; and out of such war as this have arisen throughout the extent of past ages, all the highest sanctities and virtues of humanity." Then turning towards his audience he said:

If you, the gentlemen of this or any other kingdom, choose to make your pastime of contest, do so, and welcome; but set not up ... unhappy peasant pieces upon the chequer of forest and field. If the wager is to be of death, lay it on your own heads, not theirs. A goodly struggle in the Olympic dust, though it be the dust of the grave, the gods will look upon, and be with you in; but they will not be with you, if you sit on the sides of the amphitheatre, whose steps are the mountains of earth, whose arena its valleys, to urge your peasant millions into gladiatorial war.

And further on:

First, the great justification of this game is that it truly, when well played, determines *who is the best man*—who is the highest bred, the most self-denying, the most fearless, the coolest of nerve, and the swiftest of eye and hand. You can not test their qualities wholly, unless there is a clear possibility of the struggle's ending in death. It is only in the fronting of that condition that the full trial of the man, soul and body, comes out. You may go to your game of wickets, or of hurdles, or of cards, and any knavery that is in you may stay unchallenged all the while. But if the play may be ended at any moment by a lance thrust, a man will probably make up his accounts a little before he enters it. What ever is rotten and evil in him will weaken his hand more in holding a sword hilt than in balancing a billiard cue; and on the whole, the habit of living lightly hearted, in daily presence of death, always has had, and must have power both in the making and testing of honest men.

These two quotations contain within them the essence of true generalship. The true general is not a mere prompter in the wings of the stage of war but a participant in its mighty drama, the value of whose art cannot be tested "unless there is a clear possibility of the struggle's ending in death." If he will not, or if the system of command prohibits him from experiencing this danger, though he may feel for his men, his men cannot possibly feel for him as they would were he sharing danger with them. Morally the battle will be thrown out of tune, because Death is the band master of War, and unless all, general to drummer boy, follow the beat of his baton, harmony must eventually give way to discord. On the modern battlefield Death beats one tune to the soldier, and frequently the modern general, out of sight of his baton, beats another. No single one of the great warriors of past ages has dared to be so presumptuous.

Courage is the pivotal moral virtue in the system of war expounded by Clausewitz. He writes: "Primarily the element in which the operations of war are carried on is danger; but which of all the moral qualities is the first in danger? *Courage.*"[2] And again: "War is the province of danger, and therefore courage above all things is the first quality of a warrior."[3] And yet again: "As danger is the general element in which everything moves in war, it is also chiefly by courage, the feeling of one's own power, that the judgment is differently influenced. It is to a certain extent the crystalline lens through which all appearances pass before reaching the understanding."[4]

Should the general consistently live outside the realm of danger, then, though he may show high moral courage in making decisions, by his never being called upon to breathe the atmosphere of danger his men are breathing, this lens will become blurred, and he will seldom experience the moral influences his men are experiencing. But it is the influence of his courage upon the hearts of his men in which the main deficit will exist. It is his personality which will suffer—his prestige.

"The personality of the general is indispensable," said Napoleon; "he is the head, he is the all, of an army. The Gauls were not conquered by the Roman legions, but by Caesar. It was not before the Carthaginian soldiers that Rome was made to tremble, but before Hannibal. It was not the Macedonian phalanx which penetrated to India, but Alexander. It was not the French Army which reached the Weser and the Inn, it was Turenne. Prussia was not defended for seven years against the three most formidable European Posers by the Prussian soldiers, but by Frederick the Great."[5] In a similar strain Robert Jackson writes: "Of the conquerors and eminent military characters who have at different times astonished the world, Alexander the Great and Charles the Twelfth of Sweden are two of the most singular; the latter of whom was the most heroic and most extraordinary man of who history has left any record. An army which had Alexander or Charles in its eye was different from itself in its simple nature, it imbibed a share of their spirit, became insensible of danger, and heroic in the extreme."[6]

So we see that without the personal contact of the commander with his men, whether of a subordinate general or of the general-in-chief, such enthusiasm cannot be roused and such heroism cannot be created, for as Thomas Carlyle says: Heroism is "the divine relation . . . which in all times unites a Great Man to other men."

There are yet other factors besides those which appertain to the heart. Marshal Saxe realizes this when he says: Though "the first quality a general should possess is courage, without which all others are of little value; the second is brains, and the third good health."[7] "He must be as active in mind as in body,"[8] says the Prince de Ligne. Mind and body, let us see what the great soldiers have said about these.

Baron von der Goltz writes: "One of the most important talents of a general we would call that of a 'creative mind'; because to term it 'inventive faculty' appears to us too shallow." Originality, not conventionality, is one of the main pillars of generalship. To do something that the enemy does not expect, is not prepared for, something which will surprise him and disarm him morally. To be always thinking ahead and to be always peeping round corners. To spy out the soul of one's adversary, and to act in a manner which will astonish and bewilder him, this is generalship. To render the enemy's general ridiculous in the eyes of his men, this is the foundation of success. And what is the dry rot of generalship? The Archduke Albert puts his finger on it when he says:

> They thus acquire an unmerited reputation, and render the service a burden, but they above all do mischief in preventing development of individuality, and in retarding the advancement of independent and capable spirits.
>
> When war arises the small minds, worn out by attention to trifles, are incapable of effort, and fail miserably. So goes the world.[9]

Frederick the Great, as may be expected, is more sarcastic. Before a gathering of generals he said:

> The great mistake in inspections is that you officers amuse yourselves with God knows what buffooneries and never dream in the least of serious service. This is a source of stupidity which would become most dangerous in case of a serious conflict. Take shoemakers and tailors and make generals of them and they will not commit worse follies![10]

What does this meticulous-mindedness lead to? Marshal Saxe gives us the answer, saying:

> Many Generals in the day of battle busy themselves in regulating the marching of their troops, in hurrying aides-de-camp to and fro, in galloping about incessantly. They wish to do everything, and as a result do nothing.
>
> If he wishes to be a sergeant-major and be everywhere, he acts like the fly in the fable who thought that it was he who made the coach move.
>
> How does this happen? It is because few men understand war in its larger aspects. Their past life has been occupied in drilling troops, and they are apt to believe that this alone constitutes the art of war.[11]

Finally we come to the third factor, physical fitness, a factor which can more easily be cultivated and controlled, for whilst, should he lace them, it is impossible to endow a general with courage and intelligence, it is possible to pick fit men and young men who are likely to remain fit for command. Baron von der Goltz says:

> Good health and a robust constitution are invaluable to a general. . . . In a sick body, the mind cannot possibly remain permanently fresh and clear. It is

stunted by the selfish body from the great things to which it should be entirely devoted.[12]

These, then, are the three pillars of generalship—courage, creative intelligence and physical fitness; the attributes of youth rather than of middle age.

Notes

1. *The Crown of Wild Olives*, John Ruskin, 1900 edition.

2. *On War*, Karl von Clausewitz, English edition, vol. 1, p. 20 (1908).

3. Ibid., vol. 1, p. 47.

4. Ibid., vol. 1, p. 101.

5. *Memoirs écrits a Sainte-Helene*, Montholon, vol. 2, p. 90 (1847).

6. *A Systematic View of the Formation, Discipline and Economy of Armies*, Robert Jackson, pp. 218–219 (1804). Jackson (1750–1827), military surgeon and medical writer, was concerned mainly with the study of fevers. Driven from the Army, Jackson "pursued private practice in Stockton and published works discussing principles for Army discipline and for organizing medical departments. His book on Army discipline, *A Systematic View of the Formation, Discipline and Economy of Armies*, was the fruit of this period. It was the only work republished after his death."

7. *Mes Reveries*, Marshal Saxe (1757).

8. *Oeuvres Militaires*, Prince de Ligne (1806).

9. *Les Methodes de la Guerre*, Pierron (1889–1895).

10. Quoted from *Battle Studies*, Ardant de pieq, American edition, p. 10 (1921).

11. *Mes Reveries*, Marshal Saxe (1757).

12. *The Nation in Arms*, Colmar von der Goltz, English edition, p. 75 (1906).

15

Generalship

Qualities, Instincts, and Character

General Montgomery C. Meigs

Great military ideas are actually extremely simple. . . . Greatness lies in the freedom
of the intellect and spirit at moments of pressure and crisis,
and in the willingness to take risks.
—*Hans Delbruck,* History and the Art of War, 1900[1]

Battle is the ultimate to which the whole life's labor of an officer should be directed. He
may live to the age of retirement without seeing battle; still he must always be getting
ready for it exactly as if he knew the hour of the day it is to break upon him. And then,
whenever it comes later or early, he must be willing to fight—he must fight.
—*Major General C. F. Smith*[2]

Successful senior leadership in any institution, including the
military, depends on attributes that differ markedly from the skills needed in
middle management. "Generalship" is perhaps the most important thing
about military leaders, the aspect of our leadership which should make us
uniquely valuable to our institution and to the nation. Duty as a general is different from what goes before. Flag officers are more visible; subordinates can
defer and waffle because of one's rank and not necessarily stand on the quality of one's ideas. The elements of decisions made at the senior level are more
abstract. One often receives conflicting guidance. One usually has less personal control over events. And in spite of all that, senior leaders are more fully

---

This article was developed from a presentation given by the author to the Brigadier General
Training Course at Fort Leavenworth in late November 2000.

accountable and more personally so for results than they were in their duties as more junior officers.

There seems to be no real conclusive body of thought on what makes a good general. So as a start point, study of the leadership attributes of generals, past and present, should be useful. Historians and commentators alike usually cite character as the essential ingredient of enlightened senior leadership, especially of military leaders. When one attempts to break character down into its essence, one finds it defined as a set of qualities, "the complex of accustomed mental and moral characteristics and habitual ethical traits marking a person." But what is the essence of the person that compels him or her to exhibit those traits? And how do aspiring military leaders develop that kind of character?

From reading history, from walking many battlefields with scholars to re-create the dilemmas of command of those bloody grounds, and from watching a number of flag officers good and bad, some common characteristics emerge that define successful generalship. One of the most important things a soldier does is to prepare himself for the time when the nation calls, when he is thrown into a situation in which his decisions and his ability to drive execution affect national interests. Soldiers as a group are interested in advancing their own professional development. If one agrees that self-development is one of the essential aspects of the personal growth of military leaders, we must get the characteristics of generalship right. These characteristics are the windows to the warrior's soul, the traits one must develop in oneself in order to know, to be, and to do as a general. When the crucial test comes for a senior military leader, whether in peacetime or in war, it is too late then for preparation. Flag officers face decisions that risk careers, if not lives, and national treasure along with national interests. A better understanding of the link between what historians term as character and instincts honed over years of service should highlight the qualities that will help senior leaders to prevail in "the hour of the day," to paraphrase C. F. Smith's words, "that the fight breaks upon you."

The list of essential characteristics of generalship starts with force of intellect, from which derive the elements of decision and execution—competence, intuition, and will. In addition to force of intellect, good generals have energy. They get around. They influence the battle with their presence. The best ones have that uncanny knack of being at the critical point at just the right time. Selflessness also lies at the core of what is essential in a general, for both moral and physical courage derive from self-abnegation. Finally, no general is worth his salt unless he has the basic humanity that gives him a feel for the troops that engenders the bond between leader and led which is so fundamental to the personal sacrifices that bring victory. These four characteristics—intellect, energy, selflessness, and humanity—are worth our study. What are some examples of how these characteristics have counted in our past?

Intellect

General Ulysses S. Grant comes immediately to mind as an example of the force of intellect. Grant was no scholar. He graduated at the halfway mark in his West Point class. His distinguishing characteristic as a cadet, and later as a young officer, was a startling aptitude for horsemanship. After promising regimental service in the Mexican War followed by the boredom of the frontier army and resulting depression, Grant left the Army as a captain, went home to Illinois, and tried his hand in the civilian economy. He failed in business and farming—several times. It took the subsequent challenges of the Civil War to uncover the character that made him a great captain. Two examples of Grant's generalship stand out, one at Shiloh, one before Vicksburg.

By the Battle of Shiloh, Grant had moved from regimental command to command of an army. His experiences in the Mexican War and the fighting at Belmont and Forts Henry and Donelson had given him the basic tactical competence and confidence that served as the foundation of his operational decisions.

At Shiloh, Grant arrived on the battlefield with the situation in doubt. Albert Sidney Johnson had attacked and driven into the unsuspecting and unprepared camps of the Union divisions, who fell back attempting to regroup. Many Union soldiers had abandoned their regiments and cowered under the cover of the bluff above the river's edge upon which the Union right was hinged. Grant arrived well into a fight going badly, and late in the day. He had a sprained ankle and was helped onto his horse and propped there by a crutch lashed to his saddle. He rode from division commander to division commander, giving orders to restore the line, reissue ammunition, defend in place. Halfway up the line of divisions, Grant stopped and from the saddle wrote to Buell, who controlled reinforcements on their way downriver:

> The attack on my forces has been very spirited since early this morning. The appearance of fresh troops in the field now would have a powerful effect both by inspiring our men and disheartening the enemy. If you can get upon the

field, leaving all your baggage on the east bank of the river, it will be a move to our advantage and possibly save the day to us. The rebel force is estimated at over 100,000 men. My headquarters will be in the log building on top of the hill, where you will be furnished a staff officer to guide you to your place on the field.[3]

In the midst of the fight, Grant had the mental discipline to give Buell a clear commander's intent that laid out exactly what he needed to do to intervene successfully in the battle: "spirited attack . . . 100,000 men . . . appearance of fresh troops . . . powerful effect . . . get on the field without tarrying with the baggage . . . save the day to us . . . my headquarters is on the hill above the Landing—go there for final orders." Written in haste under the greatest stress, this fragmentary order shows mental clarity and discipline.

Throughout the day, Grant rode through his command rallying the force in spite of the lateness of reinforcements. As matters reached the culminating point, Grant supervised the placement of artillery batteries hub-to-hub to defend the point where his left flank hooked into the high ground above the landing. The Confederate attack began to weaken. That night, after Grant's divisions had stabilized the situation and the Confederate momentum had stalled, Sherman met Grant under a tree near the Union headquarters. Grant was not able to sleep. The cabin in which he had placed his headquarters became a hospital. Unable to stand the gore and agony of the ongoing surgery, he left the cabin. It was raining. Grant was wet and tired, in pain from his ankle; he had been shot at all day; a cigar was clamped between his teeth. Running on pure nervous energy, he was caught in the temporary lethargy that comes after great effort: Sherman: "We've had the Devil's own day, haven't we?" Grant: "Yes. . . . Yes, lick 'em tomorrow though." He later issues the order to "advance and recapture our original camps."[4]

Later in the Western campaign, Grant was stymied before Vicksburg. He had attacked the city six times. He had failed at places like Chickasaw Bluff, Yazoo Pass, Lake Providence. The Ole Miss had risen unexpectedly and spoiled his attempt to build a canal west of the city to provide a route for his flotilla to pass south out of the range of the batteries at Vicksburg. In addition, McClernand, a subordinate and a political general, was lobbying with friends in Washington to secure Grant's removal. His efforts caused Lincoln to remark that he remained Grant's only supporter. Grant had a mess on his hands.

He responded by closeting himself in the former ladies' cabin of the steamer *Magnolia* while he pored over maps pondering the situation. Refusing the company of his more amiable subordinates, he studied the alternatives. The plan that resulted was to have the navy run the batteries at Vicksburg and the army simultaneously march to the west and south to a point south of the city where Admiral Porter's ships could ferry them across the river, allowing Grant to cut his opponent's lines of communication and take Vicksburg from the rear. Grant was willing to take the risk of putting his army across the river separated from its own lines of communication and between the two opposing forces of Pemberton, the defender of Vicksburg, and J. E. Johnston, the district commander. He did this based on a detailed study of the realities of the situation, the risks, and a sense of the abilities of his opponents.

This type of behavior is not unique to nineteenth-century generals. Omar Bradley, a general noted more for his human qualities and toughness than for his operational brilliance, showed a similar trait. In July 1944 his army was held up between the beaches and the *bocage* (wooded area) in Normandy. The British VIII Corps was slow to arrive. Bradley's divisions had consolidated but were caught up in the interlacing hedgerows held by veteran German units. There was great pressure to break out of the beachhead, but the US divisions experienced extreme difficulty against the German defenses. Imagine the consternation of Bradley's staff when he called for a big blacked-out tent, and then for duckboards for flooring, and then for a big table. Remember, Bradley had a reputation as the "soldier's soldier." Why in a time of trial would he be building himself a tent palace?

Bradley's next demand would cut through the confusion. He asked for a large map oriented in the way the terrain lay. Then he summoned all his subordinate commanders to study the map, assess the possibilities, and develop a new concept of operations. The result was the plan for the breakout, Operation Cobra. While divisions and brigades developed entirely new tactics for breaking through the serial ambushes the German veterans conducted in the system of hedgerows in Normandy, Bradley and his corps commanders derived the concept of a breakout that combined the maneuver of corps enabled by carpet bombing. Again faced with adversity and possible reverse, like Grant, Bradley went back to basics, put his mind to work, and overmatched physical reality through the use of intellect and will.

Again and again, we have seen American generals do this: Washington at Trenton, MacArthur at Inchon, Ridgway in Eighth Army, Abrams in reorienting US military strategy in Vietnam. Under the greatest pressures, successful flag officers have shown the ability to think their way through problems to derive innovative solutions. They calculated and accepted the risks inherent in those solutions and through force of personality disciplined their organizations to execute their intent. Remember, the great military ideas are really very simple. However, this ability does not require only intellect and will, it also takes a fair amount of energy and drive.

Energy

Influencing the battle with one's presence remains a crucial aspect of generalship to this day. Being at the place where things are about to happen takes stamina and great effort. I've walked the Gettysburg battlefield a number of times. More than any other part of the battle, the events of the afternoon of the second day stand out.

On the first day, the Army of the Potomac fought a delaying battle and managed to hold on to the key terrain, the ridge above the town. The second day consisted of a seesaw battle in which Lee sought a flank or a breakthrough. On the afternoon of the second day, through the incompetence of Sickles, who moved his corps forward into the Peach Orchard opening a gap in the Union line, the Confederates gained an unrecognized advantage. But George Gordon Meade was a very good tactical commander. Remember, it was his corps that made the greatest advance at bloody Fredericksburg. Meade knew how to fight a corps. Meade rode the line during the battle and visited Sickles. He recognized the mistake immediately, reprimanded Sickles, and, realizing there was no time to move the troops back, gave orders to hold and rode back to get reinforcements to close the gap. Regiments and brigades literally ran to arrive just in time. Barksdale's Mississippeans could not break through. Longstreet's brigades were stopped, but barely. The battle flowed to the right up onto Little Round Top. Again commander presence won the day, this time by Gouverneur Warren, who put a brigade onto the dominant hill just in time.

If you dissect the events of the second day at Gettysburg, you find similar patterns all over the Army of the Potomac. Hancock, Meade, Schofield, Warren—all were more aggressive and active than their Confederate counterparts. They controlled the tactical tempo of the battlefield. Precisely because of their energy and being at the right place at the right time and the quality of their tactical decisions, they fought a better battle than their gray-clad opponents. Their actions established the conditions for the fateful events of the third day.

We can find similar examples in European military history. Take, for instance, the Duke of Marlborough. At Ramillies, at a critical point in the battle he led a cavalry charge into the French Maison du Roi, the equivalent of the household cavalry, which was involved in a seesaw battle for control of the center of the line. In the words of one of his generals, "Milord Marlborough was rid over, but got other squadrons which he led up. Major Bingfield holding his stirrup to give him another horse was shot with a cannonball which went through Marlborough's legs; in truth there was no scarcity of 'em."[5]

Two months later at Oudenarde, Marlborough was once again mixed in the melee: "Marlborough, himself in the height of action only a few hundred yards behind the swaying, quivering infantry fighting line, [deprived] himself first of Lottum and then of Lumley [subordinate English units Marlborough sent from his point on the battlefield to other parts of the field to reinforce allies] for the sake of the general battle. It is these traits of serene comprehensive judgment, serene in disappointment or stress, unbiased by the local event in which he was himself involved, this fixing with untiring eye and absolute selflessness the problem as a whole. . . ."[6]

In these battles, as at Blenheim, Marlborough was in the thick of the fight while his French opponents hung back, out of touch with events at the point of the spear. Marlborough fought his battles from the saddle at whatever place on the field became the critical point from which to seize the initiative.

In today's campaigns we do not have the ability to see the battle from one or two vantage points. Campaigns cover huge expanses of territory. But we do have good examples of energy and standing up before the troops in our history of the past century. Before he made the decision to launch the D-Day invasion, Eisenhower made sure he understood the temper of his units. In his diary in May 1944 he wrote,

> Recent inspections of troops have shown them to be tough, well trained, and in good fettle. I have visited approximately 20 airfields, some 20 divisions, and four units of the American Navy. I believe that all these units are ready to operate effectively. . . . This coming week is crowded with more inspections.[7]

Ike was influencing the morale of the troops to the extent he could and assessing whether the troops were ready.

Matthew Ridgway played a similar role when he assumed command in Korea. Eighth Army reeled from the Chinese army's attack south. Again like Grant, Meade, and Marlborough, Ridgway was a tactically competent officer, as illuminated by his record in World War II. Within forty-eight hours of taking command, Ridgway moved his headquarters north, closer to the fighting, and visited every corps and division commander. Through personal presence, he demanded proper tactics be used. He walked the ground with commanders, schooling them on how to fight, instilling confidence, looking for leaders who were no longer capable of offensive action. He improved logistical procedures, ensuring hot food for the troops. He demanded standards be maintained, and through personal knowledge based on visits to units he removed weak, exhausted leaders. In the words of one of his subordinates:

> He breathed humanity into that operation. He got their spirits up, he saw the soldiers were warm, properly fed, properly led. Sure, a few people had to go. They were good people, most of them, but they were tired, they had been in that war too long, they were worn out. . . . He kept the spirit of the offensive, spirit of the bayonet, call it what you will.[8]

But the critical aspect of Ridgway's generalship lay in the standards enforced by his own presence all over the Army. In his words, "*A basic element in troop leadership is the responsibility of the commander to be where the crisis of action is going to happen.*"[9] That kind of command presence day after day takes tremendous stamina and energy. And more than in times past, it is the only way a modern commander can impose his will on events across a large organization.

This practice is not unique to wartime or to the military. After retirement, Lucius Clay assumed duties as CEO of Continental Can Corporation. During his early months in the firm, he visited every factory in the company, ensuring he understood the realities of the shop floor and the people at the cutting edge of operations. In today's management literature one reads about "management by walking around." Gaining a fingertip feel for what is going on in the core of a business or on the battlefield comes only through being at the point of the spear enough times to develop an accurate, relevant, situational awareness. That kind of presence takes a tremendous investment of time, energy, and sweat. It also requires that one get out from under the pressure of the calendar and focus on the human element of the organization.

Selflessness

Force of intellect, and energy expressed in the ability to be at the place where the critical events are going to take place, underlie the decision and execution needed to bring campaigns to a successful conclusion. But there is another trait crucial to good generalship: selflessness. Marlborough certainly was not worrying about his own skin when he placed himself in danger at Ramillies and Oudenarde, nor was Meade while sitting astride his horse at the Peach Orchard. Both were focused mentally and physically on controlling events. Selflessness underlies physical courage, but equally important, it is the basis for the moral courage so critical on the political-military stage where the events of the day play out. Good generals are not worried about themselves when they make the tough decisions.

Think of Eisenhower on 5 June 1944. He had irrevocably unleashed the D-Day assault in what would be—along with the Battle of Britain, Midway, Stalingrad, and the events in the Battle of the Atlantic in spring 1943—one of the significant turning points of the war. But that night, the outcome was not certain. The weather looked promising for only a short time. No one knew how deeply the hook of Allied strategic deception had sunk into the German High Command's strategic appreciations. No one could have known how much Hitler's personal interference would hamstring the Wehrmacht's ability to counterattack the landings. Knowing the outcome was in doubt and that in case of failure an accounting would be made, Ike wrote this short message to have on hand in case of a reverse:

> Our landings in the Cherbourg-Havre area have failed to gain a satisfactory foothold and I have withdrawn the troops. My decision to attack at this time and place was based upon the best information available. The troops, the Army and the Navy did all that bravery and devotion to duty could do. If any blame or fault attaches to the attempt it is mine alone.—July 5[10]

Ike was not worrying about himself. He was preparing for the eventuality that, if defeat came, he would have to leave command taking responsibility for it.

Ike's diary is very useful for understanding the powerful, self-effacing nature of his generalship. In February 1944 Ike was newly assigned as Supreme Allied Commander. He mused about the events of 1942 in northern Africa and the assessment the British press made of his contribution to the campaign—mere "friendliness in welding an Allied team," not boldness or initiative. Ike wrote privately to himself:

> The truth is that the bold British commanders in the Med were [Admiral Cunningham] and Tedder. (Not the English ground commanders.) I had

peremptorily to order the holding of the forward air fields in the bitter days of January 1943. I had to order the integration of an American corps and its use on the battlelines. I had to order the attack on Pantelleria. And finally the British ground commanders (but not Sir Andrew and Tedder) wanted to put all our ground forces into the toe of Italy. They didn't like Salerno—but after days of work I got them to accept. On the other hand, no British commander ever held back when once an operation was ordered. We had a happy family— and to all the C-in-C's must go the great share of the operational credit. But it wearies me to be thought of as timid, when I've had to do things that were so risky as to be almost crazy.—Oh hum—.[11]

Ike's reaction, "Oh hum," gives an understanding of his unique contribution as Supreme Allied Commander. He could forge consensus and order reluctant generals with large followings in their own country to take risky action precisely because his absence of self-interest was a given. Ike could manage the precarious balance between American and British strategic points of view and the personalities that represented them, and he could bring together dissenting American and British generals simply because he advocated on the merits and without animus or personal bent what was right operationally and what would work, and he had the patience to see the issue through.

This dynamic works so often in our affairs. Read General Bruce Palmer Jr.'s *The 25-Year War.* He gives one a strong sense of Creighton Abrams's leadership. Abrams and Ambassador Ellsworth Bunker routinely received conflicting guidance in parallel from the White House and the Secretary of Defense. The White House came to accept the military assessments of General Al Haig, then Henry Kissinger's deputy on the National Security Council staff and at the time a very junior general officer, over those of Abrams and Bunker. In the extremely challenging operational and diplomatic situation in Vietnam, these complications created tremendous difficulty. Palmer describes Abrams's frustration with "the inevitable urgent and sometimes contradictory messages that daily arrived from Washington." Years later, Palmer urged General Abrams to consider writing his memoirs, "however brief":

His reply was vehement, "Never." And when I asked why, he gave two reasons— because memoirs become larded with the "vertical pronoun" and because he would never reveal certain aspects of his service in Vietnam.[12]

Abrams' response reveals a total absence of self-interest. In the toughest times the best decisions are made by men and women who focus on the realities, the opportunities, and the risks inherent in a given situation, with no thought to themselves. One will never shoulder the tremendous risks involved in the critical operational and strategic decisions if he is worried about how he will look if things go poorly.

Finally, generals often must execute a course of action with which they do not completely agree. One may know a better way. One may have even offered that alternative to the boss, and may have even argued for it strongly. Or, as with General Abrams, one may find oneself constrained by guidance from political leadership that mitigates military effectiveness and increases risk. In these moments it is always a good thing to attempt to put yourself in the boss's shoes. What are the constraints with which he must deal? Is there something he has factored into the decision that you have missed or underrated? Is there a way to meet his intent with an innovative course of action not yet proposed but within your own latitude for initiative? It also never hurts to accept that none of us is right all the time.

In the final analysis, if an order is illegal or negligent or totally inimical to success, one may have to object even to the point of requesting relief. But remember you owe to your commander the same faith given to you by your soldiers simply because you are their commander. Even when faced with a less than optimum decision, and perhaps especially when your commander does not have the human touch to engender confidence, once any discussion is over and the decision is made we each must execute loyally and with enthusiasm. Sherman's relationship with Grant comes to mind, most specifically the letter he wrote to Grant after Vicksburg.

When Grant was deciding to move south around Vicksburg, Sherman wrote to him arguing for another course of action, begging for a council of war but pledging, "Whatever plan of action [you] may adopt will receive from me the same zealous cooperation and energetic support as though conceived by myself."[13] When the order was given, Sherman did execute with total loyalty to his commander. After the operation, he admitted his concern that Grant's plan was too risky and gave him full credit for the result: "Until this moment, I never thought your expedition a success. I never could see the end clearly, until now. But this is a campaign, this is a success, if we never take the town."[14] You don't have to always agree completely with the boss to support him.

Even in peacetime, when in the eye of a storm of national events in which decisions about policy and resourcing are being made—let alone in wartime when decisions affecting the fate of the nation are at hand—the pressures are tremendous. Only those who have trained themselves to remove any self-interest from the equation will be able to successfully face the dilemmas, abstractions, and uncertainty, and handle the stress, to apply their intellect to frame the best possible decision or to render the best advice. Only those who can put away their own self-interest to face with equanimity the risk to reputation in peacetime and the physical risk in combat will be able to do what is right.

Humanity

Because generalship concerns leading people in the most demanding circumstances, it involves motivation and consensus and the ability to elicit personal sacrifice. In short, it requires a basic humanity from which stems the loyalty of subordinate to leader that underlies the spirit of great units. Combat and peacekeeping operations always involve risk of failure. Despite the best plans and the best training, the outcome is always subject to random factors and to error and is in doubt. The difference between winning and not winning lies often in the faith of the unit in their leader and in their ability together to persevere through that last final push that breaks the enemy's will. To engender that faith, generals must have a human touch and a feel for the troops.

I remember in my early days as a company-grade officer a division commander whom everyone disliked and feared. Those were the dog days of the Army in the post-Vietnam mid-seventies. The Army was more than hollow; parts of it were very rotten. We had a great deal of rebuilding to do. Many in company command in our division were combat veterans in our second or third company command. When our commanding general would visit, we never knew how things would turn out. To his credit, that officer had well-stated priorities and clear standards. But his untrusting and adversarial approach to officers, NCOs, and soldiers alike and his emotional outbursts in front of the troops did nothing to create the energy and confidence units needed. He would arrive, check those things he had mandated, and if any small thing was out of order, launch into a tantrum that sometimes involved throwing things around the motor pool or yelling at soldiers and sergeants. None of us thought that officer could lead us in combat.

I also remember the day our corps commander visited our outfit. He had great military bearing and exuded quiet confidence. He stressed standards but spoke to us in a way that recognized our standing as soldiers. I'll never forget my motor sergeant coming up to me when the corps commander departed. Looking at the party leaving the area, he said quietly though tellingly, "Now there's a general." I think he was advising me that if you ever get to be a general, which in those days was certainly doubtful, that's the way we want you to be. Later, in another job, I escorted the same general to a dining-in. He carried his own bags. I liked that. It taught me that as a general, one should occasionally think about how others see you as opposed to how you feel about yourself.

A general respected by his soldiers for being at the right place at the right time also exerts tremendous power on the battlefield and in peacetime. At the Battle of the Wilderness on the second day, Confederate General Longstreet's corps was about to be penetrated. Wilcox's line went to pieces. The way to the rear of the Army of Northern Virginia was open. General Lee at the critical point ordered the wagon trains to be withdrawn and then he moved forward into the smoke of battle. A trickle of new troops began to arrive and hastily formed to counterattack. Lee spurred himself past the line of gun pits with the troops, the leading units of Hood's Texans. "Go back General Lee, go back," they shouted. "We won't go on unless you go back."[15] It is not completely clear what happened, whether Lee's aide brought him out of danger or whether some of the Texans grabbed his horse's reins and held him in place. What is clear is that the image of "ole Marse Robert" in danger at the key point in the battle had a galvanizing effect on Hood's men, who attacked and repelled the Union advance and stabilized the situation.

Not only does this kind of emotion matter in combat. It matters in peacetime as well. In one of the most poignant moments of our republic's history, George Washington's standing with the officers of the Continental Army secured for us Americans what is unique about our revolution, the willing submission of the military arm of the revolution to political will. Recall March of 1783. The American War of Revolution was over. The officers of the Continental Army made up perhaps the most cohesive and most national of institutions. The new states were now independent. There existed no system for taxation, no federal government to speak of. There was great concern that the revolutionary experiment was doomed even as it was being born. There was no historical example of a successful democracy that our founding fathers could follow. Nationalists argued for a military coup. Many of a more republican mind argued for restraint.

Washington was caught in the middle of this debate and pressured from both sides. He decided not to intervene. The Army's officers became restive, seditious, and called a secret meeting. Washington at first refused to attend, but then did so unannounced, surprising those in the hall. He addressed the officers, endorsing moderation. But the officers remained angry, unsettled, and ill-disposed toward his message. Remember, these were men who had served with Washington, many since Brooklyn and the reverses that led to Trenton. They had weathered Valley Forge and a number of defeats and near-victories that finally had culminated at Yorktown. They had risked the hangman's noose. They had followed Washington through seven years of tough soldiering during which the outcome remained always in doubt.

Finally, Washington remembered a letter he was carrying from a representative in the Congress and decided to read it to the audience to buttress his argument. He pulled out the letter and stared at it for a moment, seemingly uncomprehendingly. Then he took from his pocket a pair of eyeglasses most of the officers had never seen him use. He said simply, "Gentlemen, you will permit me to put on my spectacles, for I have not only grown gray but almost blind in the service of my country."[16] This simple human gesture carried the day and shifted the mood of the officers present. The Continental Army disbanded and went home, no longer a threat to the evolution of a republican government it had fought so hard to foster. There is no question that Washington's Newburgh Address and his stand against any usurpation of the government by the officers of the Continental Army was a crucial moment in our history, as well as a founding precept of our citizen Army. It was Washington's human touch and the hard-won emotional loyalty of his officers that made his intervention effective.

The Complete Package

In all of these examples the four qualities seem to overlap. Under the tremendous pressures of national decision, selflessness helps to ensure that a powerful force of intellect focuses solely on the causal aspects of the decision at hand and the risks that must be borne to achieve success. Ferreting out the best course of action, assessing and minimizing the risk and then accepting it require intellect and an absence of self-interest. Forcing execution to a successful conclusion by being with the troops when they need us most demands tremendous energy and drive. In addition, creating consensus among men and women of great emotion, talent, and ego requires that one's own ego be under control. Creating consensus also requires the intellectual and emotional stamina to keep advancing convincing arguments in ways that do not offend and that always offer an aspect of logic unanticipated by the dissenter. Stamina and energy make possible the ability to see the battle by being where, in the words of Ridgway, things are going to happen, not just where they are happening or, worse yet, where they just happened. Force of intellect, energy, selflessness, and a human touch—how does one develop those traits?

These traits are innate in all of us to some degree. Perhaps the path to generalship begins with an understanding of what it takes to be a successful commander. Perhaps the understanding that one will probably be thrown into difficult decisions while a flag officer serves as a motivator. Perhaps it helps to understand that generals, like athletes, are made not born, despite the fact that some are born with a natural ability that gives them more promise than the rest of us. But all of us need development to progress to the level of competence and character our potential allows. Knowing what is required and, in the aftermath of our own decisions and actions, introspectively demanding of ourselves why we did not do better can help us to develop our own measures of character and to hone our instincts. Those instincts are the crucial balancing link between behavior and that inner-self that drives behavior. I am always struck when someone I have known for years in the service, when faced with a confusing, tough decision, goes to his gut, to his instincts, and comes down on balance oriented toward the right course. One cannot change one's inner motivations, but one can surely discipline and refine one's instincts and the way one approaches objective reality and leads others in achieving results.

That idea leads to the premise that it is incumbent on each of us to develop these characteristics in ourselves. By personal study of history and the art and science of leadership, one understands what worked and what did not. In a letter to his son on the eve of D-Day, George S. Patton wrote: "To be a successful soldier you must know history. Read it objectively. . . . What you must know is how man reacts. Weapons change, but the men who use them change not at all."[17]

General J. Lawton Collins served as head of the machine-gun committee at Ft. Benning when George Marshall was Commandant of the Infantry School. Daily, he would supervise set-up of the training, ensure all was going well, and then retire to the bleachers to read and study professional matters. Don't for a minute think, however, that Collins was a dilettante. The officers of the machine-gun committee, as a professional standard, were required to be able to operate the machine-guns taught in their courses at least as well as the NCO instructors. In Collins's words, "As an instructor there, I always prided myself that I could mount a machine-gun just as fast as Sergeant Wolf could, which was something, I can assure you. . . . We wanted to know as much about it as Wolf did, and McNerny and McGony, and if we could do that, then we knew our business."[18] Impressed with Collins, Marshall noted his reading habit and invited him to weekly gatherings at his quarters for "conversation, reading, and recitation." Marshall's group trained many of the generals who fought World War II. Throughout the history of our profession, intense professional study has been one of the essential tools soldiers have used to advance their military art, and their generalship. As with Collins and his sergeants, moreover, intellectual development has walked hand-in-hand with technical mastery.

Seeking the tough jobs provides another means of self-development. As a general, it is understood that when offered an assignment by the Chief of Staff, the officer without question enthusiastically and willingly accepts it. But there are times when one is given the opportunity to express a preference before the offer is made officially. Some choices are more comfortable than others. In my opinion, the officer who accepts the challenge of the difficult, independent assignment is far ahead of the one who leans toward assignments where he or she is usually a subordinate. One learns more from the greater challenge of the independent role and takes on the case-hardening it provides. When the opportunity presents itself, seek independent command or directive authority. When the more risky job is offered, grab it. And along the way, don't be afraid to ask your own commander as well as your peers how you could do the job better.

Finally, one last piece of advice. Assuming one can enhance one's force of intellect, sustain the elemental energy needed to compel execution, maintain control of one's ego, and develop a human touch, there are two more things to remember. Officers are selected for duties as a general officer because they have already exhibited these four characteristics to some degree. Don't forget what brought you to the dance—don't change the way you play the game, just resolve to get better. And last, as you perform your duties at the hectic pace at which we work in the military, remember, the fun is in the getting there, not in the arriving.

Notes

The author wishes to acknowledge the help of Lieutenant Colonel George Hull, Dr. Richard Swain, and Major General William Stofft (USA Ret.)

1. Justin Wintle, *The Dictionary of War Quotations* (New York: The Free Press, 1989), p. 98.

2. Bruce Catton, *This Hallowed Ground: The Story of the Union Side of the Civil War* (New York: Doubleday, 1956), p. 72. General Smith made these remarks to then-Colonel Lew Wallace, who in finding he was about to be promoted to brigadier general came to Smith to ask his advice on whether to accept the commission.

3. John Keegan, *The Mask of Command* (New York: Viking Penguin, 1987), p. 226.

4. Brooks D. Simpson, *Ulysses S. Grant: Triumph Over Adversity, 1822–1865* (Boston: Houghton Mifflin, 2000), p. 134.

5. Winston S. Churchill, *Marlborough: His Life and Times* (New York: Scribner and Sons, 1968), p. 520.

6. Ibid., p. 615.

7. Robert H. Ferrell, ed., *The Eisenhower Diaries* (New York: W. W. Norton, 1981), p. 117.

8. Matthew B. Ridgway and Walter F. Winton Jr., "Troop Leadership at the Operational Level: The Eighth Army in Korea," *Military Review* 70 (April 1990), p. 68.

9. Ibid., p. 60 (emphasis added).

10. Steven Ambrose, *The Supreme Commander: The War Years of General Dwight D. Eisenhower* (New York: Doubleday, 1968), p. 418.

11. Ferrell, p. 111.

12. Bruce Palmer Jr., *The 25-Year War: America's Military Role in Vietnam* (New York: Simon and Schuster, 1984), p. 133.

13. Simpson, p. 183.

14. Ibid., p. 202.

15. Douglas Southall Freeman, *Lee at the Wilderness* (New York: Scribner and Sons, 1961), pp. 375–376.

16. Dave R. Palmer, *1794: America, Its Army, and the Birth of a Nation* (Novato, Calif.: Presidio Press, 1994), p. 19.

17. Edgar F. Puryear Jr., *American Generalship: Character Is Everything: The Art of Command* (Novato, Calif.: Presidio Press, 2000), pp. 158–159.

18. J. Lawton Collins, *Lightning Joe: An Autobiography* (Baton Rouge, La.: LSU Press, 1979), p. 51.

Breaking Through "Brass" Ceilings

Female Military Leaders

Major Paula D. Broadwell

There is much work to be done in breaking the glass ceiling. However, each era has it a little bit better than the last and [we] never forget it is our responsibility to continue to improve the situation for the women that come behind us.[1]

—*Female general officer, May 2008*

MULTIPLE STUDIES ON WOMEN IN the military have illuminated concern about the progression of women officers into senior leadership positions. Many of the studies question whether women face either real or perceived institutional, societal, and cultural barriers to their ability to reach the highest levels of military leadership.[2] Female leaders in the military have come a long way, but there is much room for improvement. Women fully contribute to the military workforce, yet female officers do not ascend to the same proportion of senior leadership positions as men. What contributes to the low numbers? Is the "brass ceiling" a reality or a misperception?

This article explores the leadership competencies of female general officers, primarily in the Army, who have pushed through the "brass ceiling" to overcome institutional or sociocultural barriers and serve at the highest ranks in the military. The survey composed and conducted for this article provides unique perspectives on military leadership from active and reserve Army, Navy, and Air Force female colonels and generals, including highlights of impediments (e.g., self-inflicted restrictions, lack of command assignments, domestic responsibilities) and enabling factors (e.g., reputation, mentoring, mission versus career attitude) that have hindered or helped in their progression. After examining the self-described leadership attributes these successful women embrace, I offer some "pearls of wisdom" that provide learning points for future generations of leaders.

Why is this important for military leadership? According to many sources—such as multiple articles by world-renowned Harvard Business School professor and sociologist Rosabeth Moss Kanter, and Darlene Iskra's research on elite military women—the "perception of opportunity for an individual in an organization can affect how an individual performs or behaves."[3] Theories in management, leadership, and even gender-related pedagogy hold that those maintaining low expectations for promotion to high levels will fail to aspire to elite positions and to work in a manner that would enable them to achieve such a goal. One active-duty general officer in this study felt that "unless a 4-star leader takes the initiative to not only promote males, women will be limited at the top of our senior leadership . . . and when they are limited, what is the motivation for them to stay?"[4]

Though this assessment is somewhat bleak, most survey respondents were positive about the number and quality of women in the leadership pipeline and that, given time, numbers would improve. Most felt that, as in the private sector, women and men aspiring to high levels of leadership would have to make choices and sacrifices to do so. Influencing societal norms about women's role in work and family would have more impact on influencing retention than institutional changes. As one woman stated, "perhaps some redefinition of gender preconceptions is in order. After all, what could be more feminine than to want to protect and defend what one cares about?"[5]

The Score Card

On June 11, 1970, Colonel Anna Mae Hays, chief of the Army Nurse Corps, became the first woman in the history of the US Army to attain general officer rank of brigadier general. In 1997, Claudia Kennedy became the first US Army and third US military woman to reach lieutenant general. Only two women have reached three stars in the Army, and four women in all services combined (within just over the past decade). In June 2008, President George W. Bush nominated Lieutenant General Ann E. Dunwoody to serve as head of the Army's supply arm. This marks the first time a female officer has been nominated for promotion to four stars—a landmark move because by law women are excluded from combat jobs, the typical path to four-star rank in the military.

Is there room for more trailblazers in the defense sector? No woman has served as a chief of staff of the Army, Navy, or Air Force. No woman has served as secretary of defense or secretary of veterans affairs.

When I was born in 1972, women composed 1.8 percent of the military. That figure has increased significantly over the past thirty-five years, but the proportional number of women in senior leadership positions has not. Women compose 14 percent of our overall armed services, but only 5 percent of active Army GOs are women. There are 901 general officers in the active duty armed services out of a total officer corps of 220,641 (excluding the Coast Guard, which is part of the Department of Homeland Security).[6] In addition, women compose 9 percent of the reserve GO corps.

The Department of Defense has traditionally excluded women from serving at the highest ranks of the armed services because of a lack of combat command experience, joint service, or special assignments. Promisingly, the promotion of Lieutenant General Dunwoody to four stars may be a harbinger of a shift in DoD policy. Under current DoD policy, women do not have the opportunity to serve in the combat arms branches: They cannot lead rifle platoons or command infantry brigades. Yet at the level of crafting strategy and managing organizations—especially one immersed in nation-building, peacekeeping, or support and stabilization operations—senior military women have the same functional and leadership skills as male cohorts.

All cadets and all officer basic training courses subscribe to the same leadership development coursework—they are gender neutral, as is the Army Strategic Leadership Development Course for GOs. And with women serving de facto in combat environments in Bosnia, Kosovo, Afghanistan, and Iraq, the gender gap in field experience closes even more. To date, more than one hundred women have died in Operation Enduring Freedom in Afghanistan and Operation Iraqi Freedom, and thousands have been in direct contact with the enemy. One female GO even stated that "when [citizens] read in the paper that women are not in combat roles, it decimates morale and dilutes the truth."[7]

General officers, regardless of the number of stars on their shoulders, are by definition "generalist" leaders. Why then shouldn't senior women ostensibly be qualified for a Training and Doctrine Command or even chief of staff of one of our services?

When asked how the service secretaries or the next US president could retain or place more women in higher levels in the military, a majority of survey respondents advocated two things. First, the military should reform the exclusion of women from combat leadership roles. Second, the military should assess the value of the combat arms one-billet system for jobs key to advancing to the level of general officer. Other notable responses for improving career advancement included: improved care for female veterans; recognizing staff time as equal to command; gender parity in awarding opportunities for advanced schooling; and resourcing and extensively using collaborative tools to reduce the amount of TDY (temporary duty) for travel (applicable to males and females to reduce constraints imposed by domestic responsibilities).

On a positive note, 100 percent of respondents were confident that DoD is heading in the right direction and is possibly ahead of other government agencies and the private sector.

Trailblazers: Where Did They Start?

With these statistics in mind, it is worth considering where the current female "stars" in the Army were commissioned and how that impacts women's career progression. For women to achieve the highest ranks of military leadership that our system will allow, the armed services must first recruit, train, and commission women.

West Point has sought to develop female leaders over three decades. Of the seventeen active-duty Army female general officers, two are graduates of West Point. Women were first admitted to the two-hundred-year-old academy in 1976. The first class of women included 129 entrants, although only 60 graduated. There are currently over 3,000 female graduates, and approximately 80 percent of those who enroll now graduate.[8] According to US Military Academy public affairs, the entering USMA class of 2011 has a record number of female cadets, at 17 percent of the aspiring 1,314 future Army officers.

West Point's male-centric traditions also are beginning to evolve. In the spring of 2008, for example, the West Point superintendent promoted the idea of replacing the lyrics of several of the Corps' most beloved songs from "men" and "sons" to more gender-neutral lyrics. Superintendent Lieutenant General Franklin "Buster" Hagenbeck testified to a congressional oversight committee that "the changes aren't being pushed by female cadets, but that this is a commonsense move considering the role women play in today's military."[9]

Army Reserve Officers' Training Corps, including women who train at the Citadel, Virginia Military Institute, or Norwich, traditionally commissions some 60 percent to 70 percent of the second lieutenants who join the active Army, the Army National Guard, and the US Army Reserve. More than 40 percent of all current active-duty Army general officers were commissioned through the ROTC. In parallel, eight of the seventeen current Army female flag officers (47 percent) received an ROTC commission. Overall, women traditionally constitute some 20 percent of the corps of cadets and more than 15 percent of those commissioned.[10] The first group of women from ROTC were commissioned in the 1975–1976 school year.

The majority of the generation of women who are now eligible (based on time in service) for GO rank (cohorts of women from the 1940s through the early 1970s) were commissioned via direct appointment (DA) or through the various branches of Women Officer Training schools. Seven (41 percent) of today's seventeen female GOs were DAs to the military. Officers with "professional" or technical backgrounds, including the Nurse Corps, Medical Corps, Medical Service Corps, Dental Corps, or Judge Advocate General's Corps, typically receive DA commissions, although today's female GOs with DA commissions also belong to the military intelligence and maintenance corps.

Impediments Female Army Leaders Face

Regardless of commissioning source, female officers express varied opinions on existing professional obstacles. One female GO claimed there are no "structural barriers" preventing women from the military's top ranks and stated, "We all have challenges—mental, physical, interpersonal—and we all handle them in our own way."[11] Echoing this sentiment, many women believed that "more women would progress into leadership roles if they just stuck around." However, the majority of other female GOs strongly agreed that impediments exist—some personal and some institutional.

These real and perceived barriers invariably include today's cultural and societal norms for women. Barriers exist, but as one female general officer optimistically stated, "Every soldier that ever served was challenged or tested. We need to look at challenges as opportunities to prove ourselves and to gain momentum. If we live up to a challenge, great! If you don't, then prove yourself by putting in the effort to correct individual deficiencies . . . devote personal time to retrain and demonstrate proficiency." Many of the challenges to which she alluded are gender neutral as well, but others apply specifically to women in the field.

Personal Barriers

Low confidence or domestic responsibilities are ascribed reasons for the lack of senior women across many sectors. Often attributed to an "ambition gap," these numbers—across many sectors—do not reach parity with those of men, and it is disheartening that there is no discernable change in these numbers. Surveying thousands of business leaders, educators, and political activists, one private-sector study claimed "clear and compelling evidence that women, even in the highest tiers of professional accomplishment, are substantially less likely than men to demonstrate ambition to seek elected office."[12] A majority of women participating in this study indicated that women faced such barriers as self-inflicted restrictions, domestic responsibilities, and lack of assignments of increasing responsibility. Others cited layered discrimination (e.g., a difficulty perceiving whether one faced inequity because of gender, color, reserve versus active status, academy-graduate, or otherwise) or personal decision to focus on family or a spouse's career.

Incidentally, in one study of over 240 active and reserve female general officers in all services, 23 percent of the active officers never married, and 6 percent of the reserve component had never married. Of those who responded to the survey about their spouses' professional affiliation, 82 percent were or had been married to men who had been in the military, indicating the value of a military spouse or simply spousal validation and support. Of 98 respondents, Iskra found that fewer than a third had children. Most studies show that single life, not having children, or having a spouse whose career was either military or subordinate to the female officer is more conducive to enabling flag officership.[13]

In the survey conducted for this piece, a significant number of women (a majority of whom were married with children) indicated that the military had done a lot to support family welfare, especially compared to the private sector. Notably, most respondents did not feel the military should or could be responsible for affecting work-life balance. Individuals and families must make choices, participants stated, and find ways to outsource the domestic responsibilities that encumber working parents. Most of the survey participants felt that, regardless of public or private sector, women must invariably continue to face this choice to achieve high ranks. The highest-ranking female officer ever in the Department of Defense admitted she was "not sure if [she] could have pursued military career with children too."[14]

According to the 2007 Army Demographics report, military women are less likely to marry than their male peers: 48 percent of men versus 29 percent of women married while on active duty.[15] Senior women reported that either their spouses became jealous of their success, and thus unsupportive, or as they rose in rank, their selection of mates decreased because of the "intimidation factor."[16] All of the married women in this survey indicated the value of finding a supportive spouse and managing expectations for domestic responsibilities. Few respondents indicated that having a family had been detrimental to their careers, as long as they were meeting their obligations. However, one Naval officer juxtaposed her commander's perception of fairness: "When I was a lieutenant, one commander told me that he had given the #1 ranking to my male counterpart because he had a family to support and I had a husband who could support us. He meant it sincerely. I have gone to sea every time I should have. I do know some women who have not so they probably were impacted. I do think that the types of commands that I was assigned had far more impact than my family on not being able to get promoted." Another respondent cautioned, "Don't use the excuse of family/children to justify nonperformance. That is the number one thing that frustrates supervisors and will negatively impact your career."[17] Most women eschewed the perception that "only single women make it to the top" while admitting that managing it all is extremely challenging, but it is a choice many working women across myriad sectors must make.

Several senior women indicated that leaving active duty—but staying active in the reserves—was a method for survival. Most of these women supported new legislation that might create this reserve opportunity as a "holding environment" to support retention. Almost all respondents mentioned the critical point of mentoring intervention at the mid-career (O3 and O4s) mark—recognizing that this is a time when many women are starting families while also serving in command or important staff jobs that if "skipped" could negatively affect their career path.

Notably, military women are not alone in their challenge to balance work with a personal life. In a 2008 study on women in politics, the female survey participants were significantly less likely than the men to be married or have children. Of those who were married, 60 percent of the women, compared with 4 percent of the men, said they were responsible for the majority of child care, reflecting a "nondiscriminatory" age-old dilemma for working mothers.[18]

In another corporate survey examining barriers to women progressing into leadership roles, domestic responsibilities were overwhelmingly the number-one cause for workforce departure.[19]

Formal and Informal Institutional Barriers

In the survey conducted for this piece, women cited formal institutional challenges less frequently than societal barriers. The most prevalent issue the women explicitly highlighted was an anachronistic promotion system based primarily on command time in combat-oriented positions. Several participants strongly argued for the need to abdicate the combat exclusion policy for women to further promotion opportunities to positions such as chief of staff of the Army or commander of US Army Forces Command or Training and Doctrine Command. Women advocated for creating additional channels (through combat service support or combat service branches) for women to achieve higher ranks. Some suggested giving additional credit for senior staff time, which is often equally as demanding as command, depending on the assignment. No participant advocated for quotas, and all agreed that more important than gender parity was filling the top ranks with selfless soldiers who put mission ahead of career.

Two studies indicate that military women also face informal institutional barriers. These include "lack of peer support and mentoring, and their token status results in unique pressures including high degrees of visibility, isolation, gender-stereotyping, sexual harassment, and blocked mobility."[20] Other studies indicate that women who find themselves outnumbered in the workplace frequently have to struggle to join the informal network connections that lead to upper-management positions.

Most of the women in this survey painted an optimistic landscape overall. Though there may exist "old boys'" or West Point networks, no one advocated for a "women's network." Many instead expressed a strong desire for more integration and inclusive networking among all senior GO leaders. There was nearly unanimous agreement that working hard, placing mission over career, and staying the course would pay off in the military.

Personal Leadership Attributes Women Embrace

Real or perceived impediments to promotion to the highest levels may exist. So what personal attributes and factors allow female GOs—like their male cohorts—to succeed in overcoming these challenges?

In this survey, no single attribute stood out as a driving force, although self-discipline and willpower, willingness (eagerness) to accept responsibility, stamina, judgment in action, initiative, values, people skills or the ability to build teams and consensus, and the ability to multitask all ranked highly. Individual participants elaborated by citing their high energy, technical and tactical proficiency, pursuit of jobs that met one's skill set rather than "check the block" positions, never resting on one's laurels, and a deliberate effort to focus on team versus self-interests. One respondent stated that "collegial dialogue and 360 leadership are very important to me . . . and they make the difference between good and great organizations."[21]

For the question of what factor had influenced the participant's success the most, the most prevalent answer was "dedication to serving, not just personal achievement." Many women also responded that support and mentoring received from men was important. Mentorship, a welcome experience for almost all, remained an important enabling factor throughout individual careers but was critical in junior years. Interestingly, no respondents indicated ever having a female mentor; most elaborated that gender should not matter in mentorship. For many, the most important factor is a role model who sets an example for a principled value system, strength of character, contributions to our force, and passion for leadership. Many of the female leaders also emphasized the importance of personal determination, pursuit of hard assignments, strong communication skills, self-discipline, faith, and dedication to meeting mission requirements.

Conclusion

According to a Naval Postgraduate School thesis, "The survival of women in long-standing work cultures that are dominated by male ideology depends on their willingness to confront barriers."[22] The female GOs in this study invariably confronted many of these barriers, blazing a trail for others to emulate. Fortunately, subjective barriers, such as "believing one has the ability" to achieve high ranks, are easier to change than objective institutional challenges. With this landscape in mind, there is a shared hope that as more women rise in rank, others will follow. It is in the interest of national security that we attract and enable the top talent to these high positions to ensure the quality of our force.

With other "Generation X-ers" and "Millennials" in the pipeline who "want it all," the military may be forced to create additional mechanisms to retain these women in the future. If these generations have lingering perceptions about limited possibilities for advancement, the military will have to work diligently not to discourage highly motivated females from joining, and to decrease the turnover of women who could potentially remain career military professional.[23] With today's high operations tempo, midcareer officers are leaving the military to carve out family time during their childbearing years and are not returning to service. The current trend among women is to leave the Army and pursue civilian careers that both allow flexibility and recognize the challenge of two-career families with children. They may still go on to do great things in the public or private sector, but this trend leaves a void of important leadership in the military.

While not advocating that women make better warriors or would run a more effective US military, one might argue that at least at the highest ranks, the United States must pay more attention to society's penchant for "brass ceilings" that prevent female warriors from being "all they can be." With more female role models, more mentors who can empathize with the challenges of "doing it all," and more positions open to women, perhaps more of the nation's best and brightest women would choose the military as long-term career.

Promisingly, the National Defense Authorization Act for Fiscal Year 2009 may authorize novel pilot programs that help address some of the explicit barriers to career progression that women state. This act allows service members (male and female) to leave active service for up to three years and return at the same grade and years of service.[24] For midcareer women (or men) struggling to balance work and family with multiple deployments, even the option of a six- to twelve-month time-out could create incentives to stay the military course. Perhaps service members could continue to serve in a reserve or national service to maintain exposure and contact.

In conclusion, in this survey, respondents offered a few of the following "pearls of wisdom" for mentoring junior and midlevel officers:

Be yourself.

Stay on the moral high ground; do the right thing for the right reason.

Do the best you can in every job.

Don't "think and do" with the mind-set of attaining rank—this comes naturally if you do what is ethically, legally, and morally right . . . doing what is right for the soldiers and being yourself will get you where you ought to be.

Have fun in your job, enjoy your work, and the rest will follow.

For those struggling to balance work and life, realizing that you can't "do it all, all at the same time" is important, but this compromise is a challenge to both men and women. Outsource domestic functions to free up time to spend with your family.

Surround yourself with people who are strong in areas where you are weak, and take care of the folks working for you.

Recognize achievement and reward frequently. Always keep personnel actions professional and your mission focused, and explain your actions for expectation management.

Seek tough operation and command assignment. Find a mentor to guide you. Stay positive and enjoy the journey!

Notes

1. Interview with GOR4, May 20, 2008.

2. These include Defense Advisory Committee on Women in the Service, Office of Management and Budget, Air Force Manpower and Innovation Agency, USMC Manpower and Reserve Affairs, and others. For research on the Marine Corps and Air Force, see A. F. Evertson and A. M. Nesbitt, "The Glass-Ceiling Effect and Its Impact on Mid-Level Female Military Officer Career Progression in the United States Marine Corps and Air Force" (master's thesis, Naval Postgraduate School, March 2004), available at www.academywomen.org/resource/research.

3. R. M. Kanter, *Men and Women of the Corporation* (New York: Russell Sage Foundation, 1977). See also D. M. Iskra, "Breaking Through the 'Brass' Ceiling: Elite Military Women's Strategies for Success" (PhD diss., University of Maryland, College Park, November 2007).

4. Survey question 18, respondent 4 (GOA8).

5. Survey question 16, respondent 13 (GOA10).

6. Department of Defense Active Duty Military Personnel by Rank/Grade, as of March 31, 2008.

7. Survey question 25, respondent 3.

8. Department of Defense Active Duty Military Personnel by Rank/Grade, as of March 31, 2008.

9. Lieutenant General Franklin "Buster" Hagenbeck, "USMA Chief Wants Gender-Neutral West Point Songs," *The Advocate,* May 29, 2008, available at www.advocate.com/news_detail _ektid54496.asp.

10. See www.princetonreview.com/cte/articles/military/rotchist.asp.

11. Interview with GR10, May 28, 2008.

12. Richard Fox and Jennifer Lawless, "Why Are Women Still Not Running for Public Office?" Brookings Institution, May 30, 2008, available at www.brookings.edu/papers/2008/05 _women_lawless_fox.aspx.

13. Iskra, "Breaking Through the 'Brass' Ceiling," p. 159.

14. Survey question 10, respondent 12 (GOA1).

15. Defense Manpower Data Center, HQ Department of the Army, Deputy Chief of Staff of Personnel Human Resources Policy Department, May 2008.

16. Iskra, "Breaking Through the 'Brass' Ceiling," p. 151.

17. Survey question 11, respondent 12.

18. Fox and Lawless, www.brookings.edu/papers/2008/05_women_lawless_fox.aspx.

19. S. Manning, program director, women's programs, National School of Government. United Kingdom. The National School of Government conducted a short survey on the theme of women and leadership during its 2006 conference to mark International Women's Day. Available at www.nationalschool.gov.uk/downloads/WomenAndLeadershipSurvey3.pdf.

20. S. A. Davies-Netzley, "Women Above the Glass Ceiling: Perceptions on Corporate Mobility and Strategies for Success," *Gender and Society* 12, no. 3 (June 1998): 339–355.

21. Survey question 1, respondent 4.

22. Evertson and Nesbitt, "The Glass-Ceiling Effect," p. 14.

23. B. R. Ragins, B. Townsend, and M. Mattis, "Gender Gap in the Executive Suite: CEOs and Female Executives Report on Breaking the Glass Ceiling," *Academy of Management Executive* 12, no. 1 (February 1998): 28–42.

24. Completion of Markup for the National Defense Authorization Bill for Fiscal Year 2009; Press Release and Summary: US Senate Committee on Armed Services, Washington, D.C., May 1, 2008.

17

A Failure in Generalship

Lieutenant Colonel Paul Yingling

For the second time in a generation, the United States faces the prospect of defeat at the hands of an insurgency. In April 1975, the US fled the Republic of Vietnam, abandoning our allies to their fate at the hands of North Vietnamese communists. In 2007, Iraq's grave and deteriorating condition offers diminishing hope for an American victory and portends risk of an even wider and more destructive regional war.

These debacles are not attributable to individual failures, but rather to a crisis in an entire institution: America's general officer corps. America's generals have failed to prepare our armed forces for war and advise civilian authorities on the application of force to achieve the aims of policy. The argument that follows consists of three elements. First, generals have a responsibility to society to provide policymakers with a correct estimate of strategic probabilities. Second, America's generals in Vietnam and Iraq failed to perform this responsibility. Third, remedying the crisis in American generalship requires the intervention of Congress.

The Responsibilities of Generalship

Armies do not fight wars; nations fight wars. War is not a military activity conducted by soldiers, but rather a social activity that involves entire nations. Prussian military theorist Carl von Clausewitz noted that passion, probability and policy each play their role in war. Any understanding of war that ignores one of these elements is fundamentally flawed.

The passion of the people is necessary to endure the sacrifices inherent in war. Regardless of the system of government, the people supply the blood and treasure required to prosecute war. The statesman must stir these passions to a level commensurate with the popular sacrifices required. When the ends of policy are small, the statesman can prosecute a conflict without asking the public for great sacrifice. Global conflicts such as World War II require the full mobilization of entire societies to provide the men and matériel necessary for the successful prosecution of war. The greatest error the statesman can make is to commit his nation to a great conflict without mobilizing popular passions to a level commensurate with the stakes of the conflict.

Popular passions are necessary for the successful prosecution of war, but cannot be sufficient. To prevail, generals must provide policymakers and the public with a correct estimation of strategic probabilities. The general is responsible for estimating the likelihood of success in applying force to achieve the aims of policy. The general describes both the means necessary for the successful prosecution of war and the ways in which the nation will employ those means. If the policymaker desires ends for which the means he provides are insufficient, the general is responsible for advising the statesman of this incongruence. The statesman must then scale back the ends of policy or mobilize popular passions to provide greater means. If the general remains silent while the statesman commits a nation to war with insufficient means, he shares culpability for the results.

However much it is influenced by passion and probability, war is ultimately an instrument of policy and its conduct is the responsibility of policymakers. War is a social activity undertaken on behalf of the nation; Augustine counsels us that the only purpose of war is to achieve a better peace. The choice of making war to achieve a better peace is inherently a value judgment in which the statesman must decide those interests and beliefs worth killing and dying for. The military man is no better qualified than the common citizen to make such judgments. He must therefore confine his input to his area of expertise—the estimation of strategic probabilities.

The correct estimation of strategic possibilities can be further subdivided into the preparation for war and the conduct of war. Preparation for war consists in the raising, arming, equipping and training of forces. The conduct of war consists of both planning for the use of those forces and directing those forces in operations.

To prepare forces for war, the general must visualize the conditions of future combat. To raise military forces properly, the general must visualize the quality and quantity of forces needed in the next war. To arm and equip military forces properly, the general must visualize the matériel requirements of future engagements. To train military forces properly, the general must visualize the human demands on future battlefields and replicate those conditions in peacetime exercises. Of course, not even the most skilled general can visualize precisely how future wars will be fought. According to British military historian and soldier Sir Michael Howard, "In structuring and preparing an army for war, you can be clear that you will not get it precisely right, but the important thing is not to be too far wrong, so that you can put it right quickly."

The most tragic error a general can make is to assume without much reflection that wars of the future will look much like wars of the past. Following World War I, French generals committed this error, assuming that the next war would involve static battles dominated by firepower and fixed fortifications. Throughout the interwar years, French generals raised, equipped, armed and trained the French military to fight the last war. In stark contrast, German generals spent the interwar years attempting to break the stalemate created by firepower and fortifications. They developed a new form of war—the blitzkrieg—that integrated mobility, firepower and decentralized tactics. The German Army did not get this new form of warfare precisely right. After the 1939 conquest of Poland, the German Army undertook a critical self-examination of its operations. However, German generals did not get it too far wrong either, and in less than a year had adapted their tactics for the invasion of France.

After visualizing the conditions of future combat, the general is responsible for explaining to civilian policymakers the demands of future combat and the risks entailed in failing to meet those demands. Civilian policymakers have neither the expertise nor the inclination to think deeply about strategic probabilities in the distant future. Policymakers, especially elected representatives, face powerful incentives to focus on near-term challenges that are of immediate concern to the public. Generating military capability is the labor of decades. If the general waits until the public and its elected representatives are immediately concerned with national security threats before finding his voice, he has waited too long. The general who speaks too loudly of preparing for war while the nation is at peace places at risk his position and status. However, the general who speaks too softly places at risk the security of his country.

Failing to visualize future battlefields represents a lapse in professional competence, but seeing those fields clearly and saying nothing is an even more serious lapse in professional character. Moral courage is often inversely proportional to popularity and this observation is nowhere more true than in the profession of arms. The history of military innovation is littered with the truncated careers of reformers who saw gathering threats clearly and advocated change boldly. A military professional must possess both the physical courage to face the hazards of battle and the moral courage to withstand the barbs of public scorn. On and off the battlefield, courage is the first characteristic of generalship.

Failures of Generalship in Vietnam

America's defeat in Vietnam is the most egregious failure in the history of American arms. America's general officer corps refused to prepare the Army to fight unconventional wars, despite ample indications that such preparations were in order. Having failed to prepare for such wars, America's generals sent our forces into battle without a coherent plan for victory. Unprepared for war and lacking a coherent strategy, America lost the war and the lives of more than 58,000 service members.

Following World War II, there were ample indicators that America's enemies would turn to insurgency to negate our advantages in firepower and mobility. The French experiences in Indochina and Algeria offered object lessons to Western armies facing unconventional foes. These lessons were not lost on the more astute members of America's political class. In 1961, President Kennedy warned of "another type of war, new in its intensity, ancient in its origin—war by guerrillas, subversives, insurgents, assassins, war by ambush instead of by combat, by infiltration instead of aggression, seeking victory by evading and exhausting the enemy instead of engaging him." In response to these threats, Kennedy undertook a comprehensive program to prepare America's armed forces for counterinsurgency.

Despite the experience of their allies and the urging of their president, America's generals failed to prepare their forces for counterinsurgency. Army Chief of Staff General George Decker assured his young president, "Any good soldier can handle guerrillas." Despite Kennedy's guidance to the contrary, the Army viewed the conflict in Vietnam in conventional terms. As late as 1964, General Earle Wheeler, chairman of the Joint Chiefs of Staff, stated flatly that "the essence of the problem in Vietnam is military." While the Army made minor organizational adjustments at the urging of the president, the generals clung to what Andrew Krepinevich has called "the Army concept," a vision of warfare focused on the destruction of the enemy's forces.

Having failed to visualize accurately the conditions of combat in Vietnam, America's generals prosecuted the war in conventional terms. The US military embarked on a graduated attrition strategy intended to compel North Vietnam to accept a negotiated peace. The US undertook modest efforts at innovation in Vietnam. Civil Operations and Revolutionary Development Support (CORDS), spearheaded by the State Department's "Blowtorch" Bob Kromer, was a serious effort to address the political and economic causes of the insurgency. The Marine Corps' Combined Action Program (CAP) was an innovative approach to population security. However, these efforts are best described as too little, too late. Innovations such as CORDS and CAP never received the resources necessary to make a large-scale difference. The US military grudgingly accepted these innovations late in the war, after the American public's commitment to the conflict began to wane.

America's generals not only failed to develop a strategy for victory in Vietnam, but also remained largely silent while the strategy developed by civilian politicians led to defeat. As H. R. McMaster noted in *Dereliction of Duty*, the Joint Chiefs of Staff were divided by service parochialism and failed to develop a unified and coherent recommendation to the president for prosecuting the war to a successful conclusion. Army Chief of Staff Harold K. Johnson estimated in 1965 that victory would require as many as 700,000 troops for up to five years. Commandant of the Marine Corps Wallace Greene made a similar estimate on troop levels. As President Johnson incrementally escalated the war, neither man made his views known to the president or Congress. President Johnson made a concerted effort to conceal the costs and consequences of Vietnam from the public, but such duplicity required the passive consent of America's generals.

Having participated in the deception of the American people during the war, the Army chose after the war to deceive itself. In *Learning to Eat Soup with a Knife*, John Nagl argued that instead of learning from defeat, the Army after Vietnam focused its energies on the kind of wars it knew how to win— high-technology conventional wars. An essential contribution to this strategy of denial was the publication of *On Strategy: A Critical Analysis of the Vietnam War*, by Colonel Harry Summers. Summers, a faculty member of the US Army War College, argued that the Army had erred by not focusing enough on conventional warfare in Vietnam, a lesson the Army was happy to hear. Despite having been recently defeated by an insurgency, the Army slashed training and resources devoted to counterinsurgency.

By the early 1990s, the Army's focus on conventional war-fighting appeared to have been vindicated. During the 1980s, the US military benefited from the largest peacetime military buildup in the nation's history. High-technology equipment dramatically increased the mobility and lethality of our ground forces. The Army's National Training Center honed the Army's conventional war-fighting skills to a razor's edge. The fall of the Berlin Wall in 1989 signaled the demise of the Soviet Union and the futility of direct confrontation with the US. Despite the fact the US supported insurgencies in Afghanistan, Nicaragua and Angola to hasten the Soviet Union's demise, the US military gave little thought to counterinsurgency throughout the 1990s. America's generals assumed without much reflection that the wars of the future would look much like the wars of the past—state-on-state conflicts against conventional forces. America's swift defeat of the Iraqi Army, the world's fourth-largest, in 1991 seemed to confirm the wisdom of the US military's post-Vietnam reforms. But the military learned the wrong lessons from Operation Desert Storm. It continued to prepare for the last war, while its future enemies prepared for a new kind of war.

Failures of Generalship in Iraq

America's generals have repeated the mistakes of Vietnam in Iraq. First, throughout the 1990s our generals failed to envision the conditions of future combat and prepare their forces accordingly. Second, America's generals failed to estimate correctly both the means and the ways necessary to achieve the aims of policy prior to beginning the war in Iraq. Finally, America's generals did not provide Congress and the public with an accurate assessment of the conflict in Iraq.

Despite paying lip service to "transformation" throughout the 1990s, America's armed forces failed to change in significant ways after the end of the 1991 Persian Gulf War. In *The Sling and the Stone*, T. X. Hammes argues that the Defense Department's transformation strategy focuses almost exclusively on high-technology conventional wars. The doctrine, organizations, equipment and training of the US military confirm this observation. The armed forces fought the global war on terrorism for the first five years with a counterinsurgency doctrine last revised in the Reagan administration. Despite engaging in numerous stability operations throughout the 1990s, the armed forces did little to bolster their capabilities for civic reconstruction and security force development. Procurement priorities during the 1990s followed the Cold War model, with significant funding devoted to new fighter aircraft and artillery systems. The most commonly used tactical scenarios in both schools and training centers replicated high-intensity interstate conflict. At the dawn of the twenty-first century, the US is fighting brutal, adaptive insurgencies in Afghanistan and Iraq, while our armed forces have spent the preceding decade having done little to prepare for such conflicts.

Having spent a decade preparing to fight the wrong war, America's generals then miscalculated both the means and ways necessary to succeed in Iraq. The most fundamental military miscalculation in Iraq has been the failure to commit sufficient forces to provide security to Iraq's population. US Central Command (CENTCOM) estimated in its 1998 war plan that 380,000 troops would be necessary for an invasion of Iraq. Using operations in Bosnia and Kosovo as a model for predicting troop requirements, one Army study estimated a need for 470,000 troops. Alone among America's generals, Army Chief of Staff General Eric Shinseki publicly stated that "several hundred thousand soldiers" would be necessary to stabilize post-Saddam Iraq. Prior to the war, President Bush promised to give field commanders everything necessary for victory. Privately, many senior general officers both active and retired expressed serious misgivings about the insufficiency of forces for Iraq. These leaders would later express their concerns in tell-all books such as *Fiasco* and *Cobra II*. However, when the US went to war in Iraq with less than half the strength required to win, these leaders did not make their objections public.

Given the lack of troop strength, not even the most brilliant general could have devised the ways necessary to stabilize post-Saddam Iraq. However, inept planning for postwar Iraq took the crisis caused by a lack of troops and quickly transformed it into a debacle. In 1997, the US Central Command exercise "Desert Crossing" demonstrated that many postwar stabilization tasks would fall to the military. The other branches of the US government lacked sufficient capability to do such work on the scale required in Iraq. Despite these results, CENTCOM accepted the assumption that the State Department would administer postwar Iraq. The military never explained to the president the magnitude of the challenges inherent in stabilizing postwar Iraq.

After failing to visualize the conditions of combat in Iraq, America's generals failed to adapt to the demands of counterinsurgency. Counterinsurgency theory prescribes providing continuous security to the population. However, for most of the war American forces in Iraq have been concentrated on large forward-operating bases, isolated from the Iraqi people and focused on capturing or killing insurgents. Counterinsurgency theory requires strengthening the capability of host-nation institutions to provide security and other essential services to the population. America's generals treated efforts to create transition teams to develop local security forces and provincial reconstruction teams to improve essential services as afterthoughts, never providing the quantity or quality of personnel necessary for success.

After going into Iraq with too few troops and no coherent plan for postwar stabilization, America's general officer corps did not accurately portray the intensity of the insurgency to the American public. The Iraq Study Group concluded that "there is significant underreporting of the violence in Iraq." The ISG noted that "on one day in July 2006 there were 93 attacks or significant acts of violence reported. Yet a careful review of the reports for that single day brought to light 1,100 acts of violence. Good policy is difficult to make when information is systematically collected in a way that minimizes its discrepancy with policy goals." Population security is the most important measure of effectiveness in counterinsurgency. For more than three years, America's generals continued to insist that the US was making progress in Iraq. However, for Iraqi civilians, each year from 2003 onward was more deadly than the one preceding it. For reasons that are not yet clear, America's general officer corps underestimated the strength of the enemy, overestimated the capabilities of Iraq's government and security forces and failed to provide Congress with an accurate assessment of security conditions in Iraq. Moreover, America's generals have not explained clearly the larger strategic risks of committing so large a portion of the nation's deployable land power to a single theater of operations.

The intellectual and moral failures common to America's general officer corps in Vietnam and Iraq constitute a crisis in American generalship. Any explanation that fixes culpability on individuals is insufficient. No one leader, civilian or military, caused failure in Vietnam or Iraq. Different military and civilian leaders in the two conflicts produced similar results. In both conflicts, the general officer corps designed to advise policymakers, prepare forces and conduct operations failed to perform its intended functions. To understand how the US could face defeat at the hands of a weaker insurgent enemy for the second time in a generation, we must look at the structural influences that produce our general officer corps.

The Generals We Need

The most insightful examination of failed generalship comes from J. F. C. Fuller's "Generalship: Its Diseases and Their Cure." Fuller was a British major general who saw action in the first attempts at armored warfare in World War I. He found three common characteristics in great generals—courage, creative intelligence and physical fitness.

The need for intelligent, creative and courageous general officers is self-evident. An understanding of the larger aspects of war is essential to great generalship. However, a survey of Army three- and four-star generals shows that only 25 percent hold advanced degrees from civilian institutions in the social sciences or humanities. Counterinsurgency theory holds that proficiency in foreign languages is essential to success, yet only one in four of the Army's senior generals speaks another language. While the physical courage of America's generals is not in doubt, there is less certainty regarding their moral courage. In almost surreal language, professional military men blame their recent lack of candor on the intimidating management style of their civilian masters. Now that the public is immediately concerned with the crisis in Iraq, some of our generals are finding their voices. They may have waited too long.

Neither the executive branch nor the services themselves are likely to remedy the shortcomings in America's general officer corps. Indeed, the tendency of the executive branch to seek out mild-mannered team players to serve as senior generals is part of the problem. The services themselves are equally to blame. The system that produces our generals does little to reward creativity and moral courage. Officers rise to flag rank by following remarkably similar career patterns. Senior generals, both active and retired, are the most important figures in determining an officer's potential for flag rank. The views of subordinates and peers play no role in an officer's advancement; to move up he must only please his superiors. In a system in which senior officers select for promotion those like themselves, there are powerful incentives for conformity. It is unreasonable to expect that an officer who spends twenty-five years conforming to institutional expectations will emerge as an innovator in his late forties.

If America desires creative intelligence and moral courage in its general officer corps, it must create a system that rewards these qualities. Congress can create such incentives by exercising its proper oversight function in three areas. First, Congress must change the system for selecting general officers. Second, oversight committees must apply increased scrutiny over generating the necessary means and pursuing appropriate ways for applying America's military power. Third, the Senate must hold accountable through its confirmation powers those officers who fail to achieve the aims of policy at an acceptable cost in blood and treasure.

To improve the creative intelligence of our generals, Congress must change the officer promotion system in ways that reward adaptation and intellectual achievement. Congress should require the armed services to implement 360-degree evaluations for field-grade and flag officers. Junior officers and non-commissioned officers are often the first to adapt because they bear the brunt of failed tactics most directly. They are also less wed to organizational norms and less influenced by organizational taboos. Junior leaders have valuable insights regarding the effectiveness of their leaders, but the current promotion system excludes these judgments. Incorporating subordinate and peer reviews into promotion decisions for senior leaders would produce officers more willing to adapt to changing circumstances and less likely to conform to outmoded practices.

Congress should also modify the officer promotion system in ways that reward intellectual achievement. The Senate should examine the education and professional writing of nominees for three- and four-star billets as part of the confirmation process. The Senate would never confirm to the Supreme Court a nominee who had neither been to law school nor written legal opinions. However, it routinely confirms four-star generals who possess neither graduate education in the social sciences or humanities nor the capability to speak a foreign language. Senior general officers must have a vision of what future conflicts will look like and what capabilities the US requires to prevail in those conflicts. They must possess the capability to understand and interact with foreign cultures. A solid record of intellectual achievement and fluency in foreign languages are effective indicators of an officer's potential for senior leadership.

To reward moral courage in our general officers, Congress must ask hard questions about the means and ways for war as part of its oversight responsibility. Some of the answers will be shocking, which is perhaps why Congress has not asked and the generals have not told. Congress must ask for a candid assessment of the money and manpower required over the next generation to prevail in the Long War. The money required to prevail may place fiscal constraints on popular domestic priorities. The quantity and quality of manpower required may call into question the viability of the all-volunteer military. Congress must reexamine the allocation of existing resources and demand that procurement priorities reflect the most likely threats we will face. Congress must be equally rigorous in ensuring that the ways of war contribute to conflict termination consistent with the aims of national policy. If our operations produce more enemies than they defeat, no amount of force is sufficient to prevail. Current oversight efforts have proved inadequate, allowing the executive branch, the services and lobbyists to present information that is sometimes incomplete, inaccurate or self-serving. Exercising adequate oversight will require members of Congress to develop the expertise necessary to ask the right questions and display the courage to follow the truth wherever it leads them.

Finally, Congress must enhance accountability by exercising its little-used authority to confirm the retired rank of general officers. By law, Congress must confirm an officer who retires at three- or four-star rank. In the past this requirement has been pro forma in all but a few cases. A general who presides over a massive human rights scandal or a substantial deterioration in security ought to be retired at a lower rank than one who serves with distinction. A general who fails to provide Congress with an accurate and candid assessment of strategic probabilities ought to suffer the same penalty. As matters stand now, a private who loses a rifle suffers far greater consequences than a general who loses a war. By exercising its powers to confirm the retired ranks of general officers, Congress can restore accountability among senior military leaders.

Mortal Danger

This article began with Frederick the Great's admonition to his officers to focus their energies on the larger aspects of war. The Prussian monarch's innovations had made his army the terror of Europe, but he knew that his adversaries were learning and adapting. Frederick feared that his generals would master his system of war without thinking deeply about the ever-changing nature of war, and in doing so would place Prussia's security at risk. These fears would prove prophetic. At the Battle of Valmy in 1792, Frederick's successors were checked by France's ragtag citizen army. In the fourteen years that followed, Prussia's generals assumed without much reflection that the wars of the future would look much like those of the past. In 1806, the Prussian Army marched lockstep into defeat and disaster at the hands of Napoleon at Jena. Frederick's prophecy had come to pass; Prussia became a French vassal.

Iraq is America's Valmy. America's generals have been checked by a form of war that they did not prepare for and do not understand. They spent the years following the 1991 Gulf War mastering a system of war without thinking deeply about the ever changing nature of war. They marched into Iraq having assumed without much reflection that the wars of the future would look much like the wars of the past. Those few who saw clearly our vulnerability to insurgent tactics said and did little to prepare for these dangers. As at Valmy, this one debacle, however humiliating, will not in itself signal national disaster. The hour is late, but not too late to prepare for the challenges of the Long War. We still have time to select as our generals those who possess the intelligence to visualize future conflicts and the moral courage to advise civilian policymakers on the preparations needed for our security. The power and the responsibility to identify such generals lie with the US Congress. If Congress does not act, our Jena awaits us.

18

Challenging the Generals

Fred Kaplan

ON AUGUST 1, 2007, GENERAL RICHARD Cody, the United States Army's vice chief of staff, flew to the sprawling base at Fort Knox, Kentucky, to talk with the officers enrolled in the Captains Career Course. These are the Army's elite junior officers. Of the 127 captains taking the five-week course, 119 had served one or two tours of duty in Iraq or Afghanistan, mainly as lieutenants. Nearly all would soon be going back as company commanders. A captain named Matt Wignall, who recently spent sixteen months in Iraq with a Stryker brigade combat team, asked Cody, the Army's second-highest-ranking general, what he thought of a recent article by Lieutenant Colonel Paul Yingling titled "A Failure in Generalship." The article, a scathing indictment that circulated far and wide, including in Iraq, accused the Army's generals of lacking "professional character," "creative intelligence" and "moral courage."

Yingling's article—published in the May [2007] issue of *Armed Forces Journal*—noted that a key role of generals is to advise policy makers and the public on the means necessary to win wars. "If the general remains silent while the statesman commits a nation to war with insufficient means," he wrote, "he shares culpability for the results." Today's generals "failed to envision the conditions of future combat and prepare their forces accordingly," and they failed to advise policy makers on how much force would be necessary to win and stabilize Iraq. These failures, he insisted, stemmed not just from the civilian leaders but also from a military culture that "does little to reward creativity and moral courage." He concluded, "As matters stand now, a private who loses a rifle suffers far greater consequences than a general who loses a war."

General Cody looked around the auditorium, packed with men and women in uniform—most of them in their mid-twenties, three decades his junior but far more war-hardened than he or his peers were at the same age—and turned Captain Wignall's question around. "You all have just come from combat, you're young captains," he said, addressing the entire room. "What's your opinion of the general officers corps?"

Over the next ninety minutes, five captains stood up, recited their names and their units and raised several of Yingling's criticisms. One asked why the top generals failed to give political leaders full and frank advice on how many troops would be needed in Iraq. One asked whether any generals "should be held accountable" for the war's failures. One asked if the Army should change the way it selected generals. Another said that general officers were so far removed from the fighting, they wound up "sheltered from the truth" and "don't know what's going on."

Challenges like this are rare in the military, which depends on obedience and hierarchy. Yet the scene at Fort Knox reflected a brewing conflict between the Army's junior and senior officer corps—lieutenants and captains on one hand, generals on the other, with majors and colonels ("field-grade officers") straddling the divide and sometimes taking sides. The cause of this tension is the war in Iraq, but the consequences are broader. They revolve around the obligations of an officer, the nature of future warfare and the future of the Army itself. And these tensions are rising at a time when the war has stretched the Army's resources to the limit, when junior officers are quitting at alarming rates and when political leaders are divided or uncertain about America's—and its military's—role in the world.

Colonel Yingling's article gave these tensions voice; it spelled out the issues and the stakes; and it located their roots in the Army's own institutional culture, specifically in the growing disconnect between this culture—which is embodied by the generals—and the complex realities that junior officers, those fighting the war, are confronting daily on the ground. The article was all the more potent because it was written by an active-duty officer still on the rise. It was a career risk, just as, on a smaller scale, standing up and asking the Army vice chief of staff about the article was a risk.

In response to the captains' questions, General Cody acknowledged, as senior officers often do now, that the Iraq War was "mismanaged" in its first phases. The original plan, he said, did not anticipate the disbanding of the Iraqi Army, the disruption of oil production or the rise of an insurgency. Still, he rejected the broader critique. "I think we've got great general officers that are meeting tough demands," he insisted. He railed instead at politicians for cutting back the military in the 1990s. "Those are the people who ought to be held accountable," he said.

Before and just after America's entry into World War II, General George Marshall, the Army's chief of staff, purged thirty-one of his forty-two division and corps commanders, all of them generals, and 162 colonels on the grounds that they were unsuited for battle. Over the course of the war, he rid the Army of 500 colonels. He reached deep into the lower ranks to find talented men to replace them. For example, General James Gavin, the highly decorated commander of the 82nd Airborne Division, was a mere major in December 1941 when the Japanese bombed Pearl Harbor. Today, President Bush maintains that the nation is in a war against terrorism—what Pentagon officials call "the long war"—in which civilization itself is at stake. Yet six years into this war, the armed forces—not just the Army, but also the Air Force, Navy and Marines—have changed almost nothing about the way their promotional systems and their entire bureaucracies operate.

On the lower end of the scale, things have changed—but for the worse. West Point cadets are obligated to stay in the Army for five years after graduating. In a typical year, about a quarter to a third of them decide not to sign on for another term. In 2003, when the class of 1998 faced that decision, only 18 percent quit the force: Memories of 9/11 were still vivid; the war in Afghanistan seemed a success; and war in Iraq was under way. Duty called, and it seemed a good time to be an Army officer. But last year, when the 905 officers from the class of 2001 had to make their choice to stay or leave, 44 percent quit the Army. It was the service's highest loss rate in three decades.

Colonel Don Snider, a longtime professor at West Point, sees a "trust gap" between junior and senior officers. There has always been a gap, to some degree. What's different now is that many of the juniors have more combat experience than the seniors. They have come to trust their own instincts more than they trust orders. They look at the hand they've been dealt by their superiors' decisions, and they feel let down.

The gap is widening further, Snider told me, because of this war's operating tempo, the "unrelenting pace" at which soldiers are rotated into Iraq for longer tours—and a greater number of tours—than they signed up for. Many soldiers, even those who support the war, are wearying of the endless cycle.

The cycle is a result of two decisions. The first occurred at the start of the war, when the senior officers assented to the decision by Donald Rumsfeld, then the secretary of defense, to send in far fewer troops than they had recommended. The second took place two years later, well into the insurgency phase of the war, when top officers declared they didn't need more troops, though most of them knew that in fact they did. "Many junior officers," Snider said, "see this op tempo as stemming from the failure of senior officers to speak out."

Paul Yingling did not set out to cause a stir. He grew up in a working-class part of Pittsburgh. His father owned a bar; no one in his family went to college. He joined the Army in 1984, at age seventeen, because he was a troubled kid—poor grades and too much drinking and brawling—who wanted to turn his life around, and he did. He went to Duquesne University, a small Catholic school, on an ROTC scholarship; went on active duty; rose through the ranks; and, by the time of the 1991 Persian Gulf war, was a lieutenant commanding an artillery battery, directing cannon fire against Saddam Hussein's army.

"When I was in the Gulf War, I remember thinking, 'This is easier than it was at training exercises,'" he told me earlier this month. He was sent to Bosnia in December 1995 as part of the first peacekeeping operation after the signing of the Dayton accords, which ended the war in Bosnia. "This was nothing like training," he recalled. Like most of his fellow soldiers, he was trained almost entirely for conventional combat operations: straightforward clashes, brigades against brigades. (Even now, about 70 percent of the training at the Captains Career Course is for conventional warfare.) In Bosnia, there was no clear enemy, no front line and no set definition of victory. "I kept wondering why things weren't as well rehearsed as they'd been in the Gulf War," he said.

Upon returning, he spent the next six years pondering that question. He studied international relations at the University of Chicago's graduate school and wrote a master's thesis about the circumstances under which outside powers can successfully intervene in civil wars. (One conclusion: There aren't many.) He then taught at West Point, where he also read deeply in Western political theory. Yingling was deployed to Iraq in July 2003 as an executive officer collecting loose munitions and training Iraq's civil-defense corps. "The corps deserted or joined the insurgency on first contact," he recalled. "It was a disaster."

In the late fall of 2003, his first tour of duty over, Yingling was sent to Fort Sill, Oklahoma, the Army's main base for artillery soldiers, and wrote long memos to the local generals, suggesting new approaches to the war in Iraq. One suggestion was that since artillery rockets were then playing little role, artillery soldiers should become more skilled in training Iraqi soldiers; that, he thought, would be vital to Iraq's future stability. No one responded to his memos, he says. He volunteered for another tour of combat and became deputy commander of the Third Armored Cavalry Regiment, which was fighting jihadist insurgents in the northern Iraqi town of Tal Afar.

The commander of the third regiment, Colonel H. R. McMaster, was a historian as well as a decorated soldier. He figured that Iraq could not build its own institutions, political or military, until its people felt safe. So he devised his own plan, in which he and his troops cleared the town of insurgents—and at the same time formed alliances and built trust with local sheiks and tribal leaders. The campaign worked for a while, but only because McMaster flooded the city with soldiers—about 1,000 of them per square kilometer. Earlier, as Yingling drove around to other towns and villages, he saw that most Iraqis were submitting to whatever gang or militia offered them protection, because United States and coalition forces weren't anywhere around. And that was because the coalition had entered the war without enough troops. Yingling was seeing the consequences of this decision up close in the terrible insecurity of most Iraqis' lives.

In February 2006, Yingling returned to Fort Sill. That April, six retired Army and Marine generals publicly criticized Rumsfeld, who was still the secretary of defense, for sending too few troops to Iraq. Many junior and field-grade officers reacted with puzzlement or disgust. Their common question: Where were these generals when they still wore the uniform? Why didn't they speak up when their words might have counted? One general who had spoken up, Eric Shinseki, then the Army chief of staff, was publicly upbraided and ostracized by Rumsfeld; other active-duty generals got the message and stayed mum.

That December, Yingling attended a Purple Heart ceremony for soldiers wounded in Iraq. "I was watching these soldiers wheeling into this room, or in some cases having to be wheeled in by their wives or mothers," he recalled. "And I said to myself: 'These soldiers were doing their jobs. The senior officers were not doing theirs. We're not giving our soldiers the tools and training to succeed.' I had to go public."

Soon after Yingling's article appeared, Major General Jeff Hammond, commander of the Fourth Infantry Division at Fort Hood, Texas, reportedly called a meeting of the roughly two hundred captains on his base, all of whom had served in Iraq, for the purpose of putting this brazen lieutenant colonel in his place. According to the *Wall Street Journal*, he told his captains that Army generals are "dedicated, selfless servants." Yingling had no business judging generals because he has "never worn the shoes of a general." By implication, Hammond was warning his captains that they had no business judging generals, either. Yingling was stationed at Fort Hood at the time, preparing to take command of an artillery battalion. From the steps of his building, he could see the steps of General Hammond's building. He said he sent the general a copy of his article before publication as a courtesy, and he never heard back; nor was he notified of the general's meeting with his captains.

The "trust gap" between junior and senior officers is hardly universal. Many junior officers at Fort Knox and elsewhere have no complaints about the generals—or regard the matter as way above their pay grade. As Captain Ryan Kranc, who has served two tours in Iraq, one as a commander, explained to me, "I'm more interested in whether my guys can secure a convoy." He dismissed complaints about troop shortages. "When you're in a system, you're never going to get everything you ask for," he said, "but I still have to accomplish a mission. That's my job. If they give me a toothpick, dental floss and a good hunting knife, I will accomplish the mission."

An hour after General Cody's talk at Fort Knox, several captains met to discuss the issue over beers. Captain Garrett Cathcart, who has served in Iraq as a platoon leader, said: "The culture of the Army is to accomplish the mission, no matter what. That's a good thing." Matt Wignall, who was the first captain to ask General Cody about the Yingling article, agreed that a mission-oriented culture was "a good thing, but it can be dangerous." He added: "It is so rare to hear someone in the Army say, 'No, I can't do that.' But sometimes it takes courage to say, 'I don't have the capability.'" Before the Iraq War, when Rumsfeld overrode the initial plans of the senior officers, "somebody should have put his foot down," Wignall said.

Lieutenant Colonel Allen Gill, who just retired as director of the ROTC program at Georgetown University, has heard versions of this discussion among his cadets for years. He raises a different concern about the Army's "can do" culture. "You're not brought up in the Army to tell people how you can't get things done, and that's fine, that's necessary," he said. "But when you get promoted to a higher level of strategic leadership, you have to have a different outlook. You're supposed to make clear, cold calculations of risk—of the probabilities of victory and defeat."

The problem, he said, is that it's hard for officers—hard for people in any profession—to switch their basic approach to life so abruptly. As Yingling put it in his article, "It is unreasonable to expect that an officer who spends twenty-five years conforming to institutional expectations will emerge as an innovator in his late forties."

Yingling's commander at Tal Afar, H. R. McMaster, documented a similar crisis in the case of the Vietnam War. Twenty years after the war, McMaster wrote a doctoral dissertation that he turned into a book called *Dereliction of Duty*. It concluded that the Joint Chiefs of Staff in the 1960s betrayed their professional obligations by failing to provide unvarnished military advice to President Lyndon B. Johnson and Secretary of Defense Robert McNamara as they plunged into the Southeast Asian quagmire. When McMaster's book was published in 1997, General Hugh Shelton, then chairman of the Joint Chiefs, ordered all commanders to read it—and to express disagreements to their superiors, even at personal risk. Since then, *Dereliction of Duty* has been recommended reading for Army officers.

Yet before the start of the Iraq War and during the early stages of the fighting, the Joint Chiefs once again fell silent. Justin Rosenbaum, the captain at Fort Knox who asked General Cody whether any generals would be held accountable for the failures in Iraq, said he was disturbed by this parallel between the two wars. "We've read the McMaster book," he said. "It's startling that we're repeating the same mistakes."

McMaster's own fate has reinforced these apprehensions. President Bush has singled out McMaster's campaign at Tal Afar as a model of successful strategy. General David Petraeus, now commander of United States forces in Iraq, frequently consults with McMaster in planning his broader counterinsurgency campaign. Yet the Army's promotion board—the panel of generals that selects which few dozen colonels advance to the rank of brigadier general—has passed over McMaster two years in a row.

McMaster's nonpromotion has not been widely reported, yet every officer I spoke with knew about it and had pondered its implications. One colonel, who asked not to be identified because he didn't want to risk his own ambitions, said: "Everyone studies the brigadier-general promotion list like tarot cards—who makes it, who doesn't. It communicates what qualities are valued and not valued." A retired Army two-star general, who requested anonymity because he didn't want to anger his friends on the promotion boards, agreed. "When you turn down a guy like McMaster," he told me, "that sends a potent message to everybody down the chain. I don't know, maybe there were good reasons not to promote him. But the message everybody gets is: 'We're not interested in rewarding people like him. We're not interested in rewarding agents of change.'"

Members of the board, he said, want to promote officers whose careers look like their own. Today's generals rose through the officer corps of the peacetime Army. Many of them fought in the last years of Vietnam, and some fought in the Gulf War. But to the extent they have combat experience, it has been mainly tactical, not strategic. They know how to secure an objective on a battlefield, how to coordinate firepower and maneuver. But they don't necessarily know how to deal with an enemy that's flexible, with a scenario that has not been rehearsed.

"Those rewarded are the can-do, go-to people," the retired two-star general told me. "Their skill is making the trains run on time. So why are we surprised that, when the enemy becomes adaptive, we get caught off guard? If you raise a group of plumbers, you shouldn't be upset if they can't do theoretical physics."

There are, of course, exceptions, most notably General Petraeus. He wrote an article for a recent issue of the *American Interest*, a Washington-based public-policy journal, urging officers to attend civilian graduate schools and get out of their "intellectual comfort zones"—useful for dealing with today's adaptive enemies.

Yet many Army officers I spoke with say Petraeus's view is rare among senior officers. Two colonels told me that when they were captains, their commanders strongly discouraged them from attending not just graduate school but even the Army's Command and General Staff College, warning that it would be a diversion from their career paths. "I got the impression that I'd be better off counting bedsheets in the Baghdad Embassy than studying at Harvard," one colonel said.

Harvard's merits aside, some junior officers agree that the promotion system discourages breadth. Captain Kip Kowalski, an infantry officer in the Captains Career Course at Fort Knox, is a proud soldier in the can-do tradition. He is impatient with critiques of superiors; he prefers to stay focused on his job. "But I am worried," he said, "that generals these days are forced to be narrow." Kowalski would like to spend a few years in a different branch of the Army—say, as a foreign area officer [FAO]—and then come back to combat operations. He says he thinks the switch would broaden his skills, give him new perspectives and make him a better officer. But the rules don't allow switching back and forth among specialties. "I have to decide right now whether I want to do ops or something else," he said. "If I go FAO, I can never come back."

In October 2006, seven months before his essay on the failure of generalship appeared, Yingling and Lieutenant Colonel John Nagl, another innovative officer, wrote an article for *Armed Forces Journal* called "New Rules for

New Enemies," in which they wrote: "The best way to change the organizational culture of the Army is to change the pathways for professional advancement within the officer corps. The Army will become more adaptive only when being adaptive offers the surest path to promotion."

In late June 2007, Yingling took command of an artillery battalion. This means he will most likely be promoted to full colonel. This assignment, however, was in the works nearly a year ago, long before he wrote his critique of the generals. His move and probable promotion say nothing about whether he'll be promoted further—or whether, as some of his admirers fear, his career will now grind to a halt.

Nagl—the author of an acclaimed book about counterinsurgency *(Learning to Eat Soup with a Knife)*, a former operations officer in Iraq and the subject of a *New York Times Magazine* article a few years ago—has since taken command of a unit at Fort Riley, Kansas, that trains United States soldiers to be advisers to Iraqi security forces. Pentagon officials have said that these advisers are crucial to America's future military policy. Yet Nagl has written that soldiers have been posted to this unit "on an ad hoc basis" and that few of the officers selected to train them have ever been advisers themselves.

Lieutenant Colonel Isaiah Wilson, a professor at West Point and former planning officer in Iraq with the 101st Airborne Division, said the fate of Nagl's unit—the degree to which it attracted capable, ambitious soldiers—depended on the answer to one question: "Will serving as an adviser be seen as equal to serving as a combat officer in the eyes of the promotion boards? The jury is still out."

"Guys like Yingling, Nagl and McMaster are the canaries in the coal mine of Army reform," the retired two-star general I spoke with told me. "Will they get promoted to general? If they do, that's a sign that real change is happening. If they don't, that's a sign that the traditional culture still rules."

Failure sometimes compels an institution to change its ways. The last time the Army undertook an overhaul was in the wake of the Vietnam War. At the center of those reforms was an officer named Huba Wass de Czege. Wass de Czege (pronounced VOSH de tsay-guh) graduated from West Point and served two tours of duty in Vietnam, the second as a company commander in the Central Highlands. He devised innovative tactics, leading four-man teams—at the time they were considered unconventionally small—on ambush raids at night. His immediate superiors weren't keen on his approach or attitude, despite his successes. But after the war ended and a few creative officers took over key posts, they recruited Wass de Czege to join them.

In 1982, he was ordered to rewrite the Army's field manual on combat operations. At his own initiative, he read the classics of military strategy—Clausewitz's *On War,* Sun Tzu's *Art of War,* B. H. Liddell Hart's *Strategy*—none of which had been on his reading list at West Point. And he incorporated many of their lessons along with his own experiences from Vietnam. Where the old edition assumed static clashes of firepower and attrition, Wass de Czege's revision emphasized speed, maneuver and taking the offensive. He was asked to create a one-year graduate program for the most promising young officers. Called the School of Advanced Military Studies, or SAMS, it brought strategic thinking back into the Army—at least for a while.

Now a retired one-star general, though an active Army consultant, Wass de Czege has publicly praised Yingling's article. (Yingling was a graduate of SAMS in 2002, well after its founder moved on.) In an essay for the July 2007 issue of *Army* magazine, Wass de Czege wrote that today's junior officers "feel they have much relevant experience [that] those senior to them lack," yet the senior officers "have not listened to them." These junior officers, he added, remind him of his own generation of captains, who held the same view during and just after Vietnam.

"The crux of the problem in our Army," Wass de Czege wrote, "is that officers are not systematically taught how to cope with unstructured problems." Counterinsurgency wars, like those in Iraq and Afghanistan, are all about unstructured problems. The junior and field-grade officers, who command at the battalion level and below, deal with unstructured problems—adapting to the insurgents' ever-changing tactics—as a matter of course. Many generals don't, and never had to, deal with such problems, either in war or in their training drills. Many of them may not fully recognize just how distinct and difficult these problems are.

Speaking by phone from his home outside Fort Leavenworth, Wass de Czege emphasized that he was impressed with most of today's senior officers. Compared with those of his time, they are more capable, open and intelligent (most officers today, junior and senior, have college degrees, for instance). "You're not seeing any of the gross incompetence that was common in my day," he said. He added, however, that today's generals are still too slow to change. "The Army tends to be consensus-driven at the top," he said. "There's a good side to that. We're steady as a rock. You call us to arms, we'll be there. But when you roll a lot of changes at us, it takes a while. The young guys have to drive us to it."

The day after his talk at Fort Knox, General Cody, back at his office in the Pentagon, reiterated his "faith in the leadership of the general officers." Asked about complaints that junior officers are forced to follow narrow paths to promotion, he said, "We're trying to do just the opposite." In the works are new incentives to retain officers, including not just higher bonuses but free graduate school and the right to choose which branch of the Army to serve in. "I don't want everybody to think there's one road map to colonel or general," he said. He denied that promotion boards picked candidates in their own image. This year, he said, he was on the board that picked new brigadier generals, and one of them, Jeffrey Buchanan, had never commanded a combat brigade; his last assignment was training Iraqi security forces. One colonel, interviewed later, said: "That's a good sign. They've never picked anybody like that before. But that's just one out of thirty-eight brigadier generals they picked. It's still very much the exception."

There is a specter haunting the debate over Yingling's article—the specter of General Douglas MacArthur. During World War II, General Dwight D. Eisenhower threatened to resign if the civilian commanders didn't order air support for the invasion of Normandy. President Franklin D. Roosevelt and Prime Minister Winston Churchill acceded. But during the Korean War, MacArthur—at the time, perhaps the most popular public figure in America—demanded that President Truman let him attack China. Truman fired him. History has redeemed both presidents' decisions. But in terms of the issues that Yingling, McMaster and others have raised, was there really a distinction? Weren't both generals speaking what they regarded as "truth to power"?

The very discussion of these issues discomforts many senior officers because they take very seriously the principle of civilian control. They believe it is not their place to challenge the president or his duly appointed secretary of defense, certainly not in public, especially not in wartime. The ethical codes are ambiguous on how firmly an officer can press an argument without crossing the line. So, many generals prefer to keep a substantial distance from that line—to keep the prospect of a constitutional crisis from even remotely arising.

On a blog Yingling maintains at the Web site of *Small Wars Journal,* an independent journal of military theory, he has acknowledged these dilemmas, but he hasn't disentangled them. For example, if generals do speak up, and the president ignores their advice, what should they do then—salute and follow orders, resign en masse or criticize the president publicly? At this level of discussion, the junior and midlevel officers feel uncomfortable, too.

Yingling's concern is more narrowly professional, but it should matter greatly to future policy makers who want to consult their military advisers. The challenge is how to ensure that generals possess the experience and analytical prowess to formulate sound military advice and the "moral courage," as Yingling put it, to take responsibility for that advice and for its resulting successes or failures. The worry is that too few generals today possess either set of qualities—and that the promotional system impedes the rise of officers who do.

As today's captains and majors come up through the ranks, the culture may change. One question is how long that will take. Another question is whether the most innovative of those junior officers will still be in the Army by the time the top brass decides reform is necessary. As Colonel Wilson, the West Point instructor, put it, "When that moment comes, will there be enough of the right folks in the right slots to make the necessary changes happen?"

19

Bush and the Generals

Michael C. Desch

I T   I S   N O   S E C R E T   T H A T the relationship between the US military and civilians in the Bush administration has deteriorated markedly since the start of the Iraq War. In 2006, according to a *Military Times* poll, almost 60 percent of servicemen and servicewomen did not believe that civilians in the Pentagon had their "best interests at heart." In its December 2006 report, the bipartisan Iraq Study Group—of which Robert Gates was a member until President George W. Bush tapped him to replace Donald Rumsfeld as secretary of defense last year (2006)—explicitly recommended that "the new Secretary of Defense should make every effort to build healthy civil-military relations, by creating an environment in which the senior military feel free to offer independent advice not only to the civilian leadership in the Pentagon but also to the President and the National Security Council."

But the tensions in civil-military relations hardly started with Iraq; the quagmire there has simply exposed a rift that has existed for decades. During the Vietnam War, many military officers came to believe that their unquestioning obedience to civilian leaders had contributed to the debacle—and that, in the future, senior military leaders should not quietly acquiesce when the civilians in Washington start leading them into strategic blunders.

For a time after Vietnam, civilian and military elites avoided a direct confrontation as military leaders focused on rebuilding the armed forces to fight a conventional war against the Warsaw Pact and civilian officials were largely content to defer to them on how to do so. But the end of the Cold War uncovered deep fissures over whether to use the military for operations other than foreign wars and how to adapt military institutions to changing social mores.

The Bush administration arrived in Washington resolved to reassert civilian control over the military—a desire that became even more pronounced after September 11, 2001. Rumsfeld vowed to "transform" the military and to use it to wage the global war on terrorism. When they thought military leaders were too timid in planning for the Iraq campaign, Bush administration officials did not hesitate to overrule them on the number of troops to be sent and the timing of their deployment. And when the situation in Iraq deteriorated after the fall of Baghdad, tensions flared again. Retired generals called for Rumsfeld's resignation; there is reportedly such deep concern among the Joint Chiefs of Staff (JCS) about the Bush administration's plans to use nuclear weapons in a preemptive attack against Iran's nuclear infrastructure that some of them have threatened to resign in protest; and the Bush administration's "surge" now has tens of thousands more troops going to Iraq against the advice of much of the military.

The new secretary of defense therefore has a lot on his plate. In the short term, Gates must play out the endgame of a war in Iraq that he admits the United States is "not winning" but that he and the president do not want to "lose" either. He must continue the efforts to transform the US military while repairing a ground force that has been nearly "broken" by almost four years of continuous combat in Afghanistan and Iraq. But Gates can hope to succeed at those tasks only if he manages to rebuild a cooperative relationship between civilian leaders and the US military. He must both rethink how civilian officials oversee the military and clarify the boundaries of legitimate military dissent from civilian authority.

The key is that Gates needs to recognize that Rumsfeld's meddling approach contributed in significant measure to the problems in Iraq and elsewhere. The best solution is to return to an old division of labor: civilians give due deference to military professional advice in the tactical and operational realms in return for complete military subordination in the grand strategic and political realms. The success of Gates' tenure in the Pentagon will hinge on his reestablishing that proper civil-military balance.

Salute and Obey?

There is an inherent tension between senior military leaders and their civilian overseers. Debates about using force, contrary to popular perception, tend to pit reluctant warriors against hawkish civilians. The current civil-military breach actually began with the Vietnam War. The decision to intervene in Vietnam was driven largely by civilian leaders: Presidents John F. Kennedy and Lyndon Johnson, Secretary of Defense Robert McNamara, Secretary of State Dean Rusk, National Security Adviser McGeorge Bundy, and a supporting cast of lower-ranking officials. From the start, the senior military leadership was unenthusiastic about committing US ground forces to Southeast Asia. Even after civilian officials persuaded them that vital national interests were at stake, they had serious reservations about Washington's strategies for the ground and air wars. By the summer of 1967, military discontent had reached such a level that the JCS reportedly considered resigning en masse. They did not, but the damage done by the military leadership's willingness to salute and obey as the debacle in Vietnam unfolded was not lost on junior officers.

In one of the most memorable passages in his memoir, former Secretary of State Colin Powell recalls that during Vietnam, "as a corporate entity, the military failed to talk straight to its political superiors or itself. The top leadership never went to the secretary of defense or the President and said, 'This war is unwinnable the way we are fighting it.'" Colonel H. R. McMaster's *Dereliction of Duty*—a book that was long featured on the chairman of the Joint Chiefs of Staff's reading list—demonstrates that this lesson of Vietnam has now been thoroughly internalized by the contemporary officer corps. The implicit message of McMaster's military bestseller is that unqualified allegiance to the commander in chief needs to be rethought.

The Vietnam experience was a ticking time bomb just waiting to explode civil-military relations. Only the Cold War kept it from going off. There was mutual agreement then that the military's primary mission was to prepare for a conventional war in Europe with the Warsaw Pact, and civilian leaders gave the military great latitude in determining how it did so. Still, Army Chief of Staff General Creighton Abrams consciously reconfigured active-component army divisions so that they could not go to war without Reserve or National Guard "round-out brigades," thus ensuring that future presidents would have to fully mobilize the country in order to fight a major war.

The post-Vietnam officer corps truly began to assert itself only after the inauguration of Bill Clinton, the first post–Cold War president and a man who came into office with an already difficult relationship with the military. Large cuts in the defense budget (27 percent between 1990 and 2000), significant personnel reductions (33 percent of the active component over the same period), and an ambitious social agenda (integrating gays into the military and allowing women to join the combat arms) placed civilian and military leaders in an openly adversarial relationship. A greatly accelerated operational tempo, as the armed forces were deployed to Somalia, Haiti, Bosnia, and other global trouble spots, only worsened the strain.

Clinton's tense relationship with the military hampered his ability to make good on a number of campaign promises. After criticizing the first Bush administration for not doing enough to end the bloodshed in the Bosnian civil war, Clinton promised a more assertive US policy of humanitarian intervention. In response, Powell (then chairman of the JCS) published an opinion piece in the *New York Times* and an essay in *Foreign Affairs* arguing against such a policy and on behalf of more restrictive criteria for the use of force, which became known as the Powell Doctrine. The military's reservations about intervening on the ground in Bosnia played an important role in limiting US military options to air strikes in August 1995.

Another of Clinton's early initiatives was to end the Pentagon's policy of excluding homosexuals from the military. This had also been an important campaign plank, one to which he was reportedly deeply committed on civil liberties grounds. When he tried to implement it, however, Clinton ran into a firestorm of military and congressional opposition. He had to back down and accept a face-saving compromise—"don't ask, don't tell"—which most analysts do not regard as a real change in policy.

The poor civil-military relations that plagued the early years of the Clinton administration continued to affect it right up to the end of Clinton's second term. By the spring of 1999, it was apparent that Serbian President Slobodan Milosevic would cease his ethnic cleansing in Kosovo only in response to military force. Clinton and his civilian advisers, such as Secretary of State Madeleine Albright and National Security Adviser Sandy Berger, advocated the use of limited air strikes and the threat of ground operations. The JCS, however, pushed for a more extensive air campaign while resisting any threat to use ground forces. Within days of the start of the war, a torrent of leaks sprang from the Pentagon about how the president had intervened in Kosovo against the better advice of the military. The JCS subsequently did as much to constrain the campaign in Kosovo as to facilitate it—to the point of dragging their feet on supplying certain forces to General Wesley Clark's NATO operation. While promising to provide Clark with everything he needed, the Pentagon delayed for weeks in sending him the Apache attack helicopters he had requested and then never allowed him to actually use them.

This military resistance to many of the Clinton administration's initiatives should not have been surprising. After all, the senior military leadership emerged from the Vietnam debacle believing that civilians could not be trusted with weighty decisions that affected both the military's internal organization and where and how the military was used. Powell boasted that he and his post-Vietnam military colleagues had "vowed that when [their] time came to call the shots, [they] would not quietly acquiesce in half-hearted warfare for half-baked reasons."

Even after Powell's military retirement in 1993, the Powell Doctrine remained alive and well in the Pentagon. Powell's successor as chairman of the JCS, General Hugh Shelton, remarked to me in a 1999 interview, "I firmly believe in [former Secretary of Defense Caspar] Weinberger's doctrine, amplified by General Powell, and I think that we followed that" in the Kosovo operation. Echoing Powell, Shelton argued that military force should be the tool of last resort and proposed what he called "the Dover test" for committing US forces to combat: "When bodies are brought back, will we still feel it is in US interests?"

The Civilians' Revolt

Many expected the 2000 election of George W. Bush to usher in a new golden age of civil-military amity and cooperation. After all, Bush campaigned for military votes with the promise that "help is on the way" after eight years of supposed neglect. In his speech accepting his party's nomination in August 2000, he warned, "Our military is low on parts, pay, and morale. If called by the commander in chief today, two entire divisions of the army would have to report . . . 'not ready for duty.' This administration had its moment. They had their chance. They have not led. We will." An administration that included two former secretaries of defense (Rumsfeld and Vice President Dick Cheney) and a former JCS chairman (Powell) ought to have had excellent relations with the senior military leadership.

But Bush also entered the White House with an ambitious defense policy agenda, which made continuation of the civil-military conflict all but inevitable. In a September 1999 speech at the Citadel, Bush had said that he intended to "force new thinking and hard choices" on the military. In the first few months of the new administration, Rumsfeld set out to transform the US military in line with what he and other civilians anticipated would be a "revolution in military affairs."

This brought immediate friction with military leaders (and their allies on Capitol Hill), who had deep reservations about both the style of the new secretary of defense and the substance of his policies. Rumsfeld dismissed these concerns. "If that disturbs people and their sensitivities are such that it bothers them, I'm sorry," he told the Pentagon press corps. "But that's life, because this stuff we're doing is important. We're going to get it done well. We're going to get it done right. The Constitution calls for civilian control of this department. And I'm a civilian. And believe me, this place is accomplishing enormous things. We have done so much in the last two years. And it doesn't happen by standing around with your finger in your ear hoping everyone thinks that that's nice." Some military visionaries, such as Admiral William Owens and Vice Admiral Arthur Cebrowski, hopped aboard the transformation bandwagon. But Rumsfeld did not trust even those in the uniformed services who seemed to support his revolution. Transformation, he believed, would take place only with considerable civilian prodding and guidance. By the fall of 2001, as a result, Rumsfeld's relations with the senior military and congressional leaderships could not have been much worse. Many observers predicted that he would be the first cabinet-level casualty of the Bush administration.

The attacks of September 11, 2001, and the early stages of the global war on terrorism in Afghanistan imposed a temporary truce between Rumsfeld and senior military leaders. But as the Bush administration made clear that it considered Iraq the next front—a view most military professionals did not share—this truce broke down. In the face of what they saw as military intransigence, Rumsfeld and Deputy Secretary of Defense Paul Wolfowitz showed little compunction about meddling in such issues as the number of troops required and the phasing of their deployments for Operation Iraqi Freedom. The clearest display of civilian willingness to override the professional military on tactical and operational matters was Wolfowitz's cavalier dismissal of troop-requirement estimates by General Eric Shinseki, the army chief of staff. In congressional testimony in February 2003, Wolfowitz dismissed Shinseki's assessment that the United States would need in excess of "several hundred thousand troops" for postwar stability operations as "wildly off the mark." Wolfowitz got his way.

When those "postwar" operations ran into trouble, finger-pointing and mutual recriminations between recently retired generals and civilian leaders in the Bush administration brought the persistent fault lines in US civil-military relations to the fore. Lieutenant General Gregory Newbold, former JCS director of operations, wrote, in a searing piece in *Time,* that it was his "sincere view . . . that the commitment of [US] forces to this fight was done with a casualness and swagger that are the special province of those who have never had to execute these missions—or bury the results." Newbold joined a raft of other recently retired generals—including General Anthony Zinni (former head of Central Command), Major General Paul Eaton (former head of the Iraqi training mission), Major General John Riggs (former head of the army's transformation task force), and Major Generals Charles Swannack and John Batiste (former division commanders in Iraq)—in calling for Rumsfeld's resignation. According to a *Military Times* poll, 42 percent of US troops disapprove of President Bush's handling of the war in Iraq.

In the fall of 2006, the White House and influential hawks outside of the administration finally conceded that the United States did not have the troop strength to secure contested areas in Iraq. But by then, senior US military commanders in Iraq had come to believe that US forces were part of the problem, rather than the solution, as the insurgency had morphed into an interconfessional civil war. So instead of asking for more troops, as they did in the run-up to the war, many senior commanders in Iraq began to argue that the United States needed to lower its profile and reduce its footprint. Less than 40 percent of troops supported an increase in force levels, the *Military Times* found. General John Abizaid, the current head of Central Command, told the Senate Armed Services Committee in November that he did "not believe that more American troops right now is the solution to the problem" in Iraq. In response to prodding from Senator John McCain (R-Ariz.), Abizaid explained that he had "met with every division commander, General [George] Casey, the corps commander, General [Martin] Dempsey [head of the Multi-National Security Transition Command in Iraq]. . . . And I said, 'In your professional opinion, if we were to bring in more American troops now, does it add considerably to our ability to achieve success in Iraq?' And they all said no."

Abizaid and other senior US commanders believed increasing the number of US forces in Iraq would be counterproductive. As Abizaid explained on *60 Minutes,* "There's always been this tension between what we could do and what the Iraqis do. If we want to do everything in Iraq we could do that, but that's not the way that Iraq is going to stabilize." In congressional testimony, he noted, "We can put in 20,000 more Americans tomorrow and achieve a temporary effect . . . [but] when you look at the overall American force pool that's available out there, the ability to sustain that commitment is simply not something that we have right now with the size of the army and the Marine Corps." But despite such protests, the military leadership was once again overruled by civilians in Washington—leading to the "surge" taking place right now.

Armchair Generals

Why did civil-military relations become so frayed in the Bush administration? James Mann recounts in his book *Rise of the Vulcans* that key civilian figures on Bush's national security team believed that the Clinton administration had failed to "keep a tight rein" on the military. Rumsfeld famously thought of civilian control of the military as the secretary of defense's primary responsibility, and he, along with Wolfowitz and other top administration figures, came into office convinced that they would have to resort to more intrusive civilian involvement to overcome service parochialism and bureaucratic inertia. After 9/11, Rumsfeld and other civilian proponents of a war for regime change in Iraq realized that the key obstacle to launching such a war—and waging it with minimal forces, in line with Rumsfeld's vision of military transformation—would be the senior leadership of the US Army. Instead of listening to the warnings of military professionals, they resolved to overcome both widespread military skepticism about the war and, in their view, the bureaucratic inertia dictating how the services thought about the size and the mix of forces necessary to accomplish the mission. The fact that Wolfowitz, rather than Shinseki, prevailed in the debate about the force size necessary for the Iraq War shows just how successful the Bush administration was in asserting civilian authority over the military.

In their determination to reassert civilian control, administration officials were even willing to immerse themselves in operational issues such as determining force sizes and scheduling deployments. As former Secretary of the Army Thomas White recalled, Rumsfeld wanted to "show everybody in the structure that he was in charge and that he was going to manage things perhaps in more detail than previous secretaries of defense, and he was going to involve himself in operational details." Such an intrusive form of civilian oversight was bound to exacerbate friction with the military.

In his seminal treatise on civil-military relations, *The Soldier and the State*, Samuel Huntington proposed a system he called "objective control" to balance military expertise with overall civilian political supremacy. Huntington recommended that civilian leaders cede substantial autonomy to military professionals in the tactical and operational realms in return for complete and unquestioning military subordination to civilian control of politics and grand strategy. Although not always reflected in practice, this system has shaped thinking about how civilians ought to exercise their oversight of the US military for fifty years. When followed, it has generally been conducive to good civil-military relations as well as to sound policy decisions.

The Bush administration embraced a fundamentally different approach to civilian control. Administration officials worried that without aggressive and relentless civilian questioning of military policies and decisions at every level, they would not be able to accomplish their objective of radically transforming the military and using it in a completely different way. Former Defense Policy Board member Eliot Cohen—recently named by Secretary of State Condoleezza Rice as counselor for the State Department—provided the intellectual rationale for this more intrusive regime. His book *Supreme Command* was read widely by senior members of the Bush national security team, reportedly even landing on the president's bedside table in Crawford, Texas.

Cohen's thesis was that civilian intervention at not only the strategic but also the tactical and operational levels was essential for military success. In order to overcome military resistance or incompetence, civilian leaders needed to be willing to "probe" deeply into military matters through an "unequal dialogue" with their professional military subordinates. Commenting in May 2003 on the Bush administration's performance, Cohen noted approvingly that "it appears that Rumsfeld is a very active secretary of defense, rather along the lines essential for a good civil-military dialogue: pushing, probing, querying. But not, I think, dictating in detail what the military should do. [On Iraq,] the Bush administration was engaged in what was a very intensive dialogue with senior military leadership, and I think that was right." As late as April of 2006, Cohen still thought that "one could say much to defend Secretary of Defense Donald Rumsfeld against the recent attacks of half a dozen retired generals" who criticized his (and his deputies') handling of the Iraq War.

Unfortunately, things did not go as planned, and, in retrospect, it would have been far better for the United States if Bush had read Huntington's *The Soldier and the State* rather than Cohen's *Supreme Command* over his 2002 summer vacation. Given the parlous situation in Iraq today—the direct result of willful disregard for military advice—Bush's legacy in civil-military relations is likely to be precisely the opposite of what his team expected: the discrediting of the whole notion of civilian control of the military.

Restoring the Balance

Defense Secretary Gates now faces a doubly difficult situation: Little real progress has been made in transforming the US military, and it is now embroiled in a conflict that not even he is optimistic about. Worse, he has to address these problems in a climate of distinct frostiness between civilians in the Bush administration and senior military leaders. Former Secretary of the Army White, summarizing the Bush and Rumsfeld legacy, noted, "By definition, [secretaries of defense] are civilians. Some of them might have had experiences in their younger years in the military, but their job, among other things, is to take the wise advice offered them by the military and think that over and give it some credence and then make a decision. The question is, have we lost the balance of that? I think they went too far." Gates's key challenge, therefore, is to reestablish that civil-military balance.

To be sure, Gates cannot and should not abdicate his responsibility to exercise civilian control of the military. In a democratic political system, decisions about war and peace should be made not by soldiers but by voters through their elected leaders. At the same time, however, Gates should encourage, rather than stifle, candid advice from the senior military leadership, even if it does not support administration policy. The military has a right and a duty to be heard. After all, soldiers are the experts in fighting wars—and it is their lives that are ultimately on the line. If senior officers feel that their advice is being ignored or that they are being asked to carry out immoral orders, they should resign. Indeed, had Shinseki or Newbold resigned in the run-up to the Iraq War, he would have sent a powerful message about the military's reservations about the war—one far more effective than protests after the fact. Threats of resignations among the Joint Chiefs may be influencing the Bush administration's Iran policy (including derailing plans to use nuclear weapons against hardened Iranian nuclear installations). Barring such extremely serious reservations, after senior military officers have had their say, they should salute and obey.

Ironically, General David Petraeus, the recently appointed commander of US-led forces in Iraq, has in the past written of the failure of the senior military leadership to talk straight about the Vietnam War and its impact on subsequent US civil-military relations. Petraeus is himself now in a position to advise both the administration and the new Democratic-controlled Congress. In his confirmation hearings before the Senate Armed Services Committee, Petraeus promised that he would give his "best professional military advice, and if people don't like it, then they can find someone else to give better professional military advice." Hopefully, he will speak candidly—and Gates will listen.

The proper balance would give civilian leaders authority over political decisions—such as whether the United States should stay in Iraq or use force against Iran—and the military wide leeway in making the operational and tactical decisions about how to complete a mission. The line between the two realms is not always perfectly clear, and sometimes military considerations affect political decisions, and vice versa. But the alternative—civilians meddling in matters of military expertise—is almost as bad as the military involving itself in politics. Whenever the civil-military balance is off-kilter in either direction, the country suffers as a result.

PART FOUR

THE FUTURE OF MILITARY LEADERSHIP

WE POSE A QUESTION ABOUT the future of military leadership because of contemporary events that have challenged the traditional image of military leaders. Senior officers are critiqued by the media in real time. Missions are mixed between war, reconstruction, and peacekeeping. Mistakes of significance and of little impact are communicated widely and both friend and enemy engage in assessments of leadership decisions. These military missions are more ambiguous and complex. Limited resources force downsizing, delays and cancellations of new weapons and supplies, long tours for active-duty and reserve personnel with concomitant social issues, and challenges to the retirement contracts for active-duty and retired service members.

As we consider the future, we come back to the concept of transactional and transformational leadership. With more complex environments, establishing a vision of the future military will be a continuing challenge. Identifying and building consensus for core values will be different as we recognize the increasing intellectual and cultural diversity of our constituents and followers. Culture, climate, and the environment of organizational life will be changed as the military services alter missions, respond to new tasks, and strive for efficiency.

The military must focus on operating in an environment that demands flexibility and responsiveness. The military that initially thought it would fight a global war after 9/11 now faces two regional conflicts. Frustrations over constantly changing expectations have challenged military leaders. Few of our senior political leaders in Washington have military experience. And although they will quickly tout the achievements and sacrifice of our armed services, few of them can truly empathize with the challenges facing those in uniform and their families.

Reserve and National Guard units increasingly engage in the ongoing wars in Iraq and Afghanistan. Clashes in culture within the part-time units, as well as differences within active-duty forces, test existing leadership paradigms. Military leadership is global in scope, and senior leaders must demonstrate multinational experience. A variety of multicultural and crosscultural issues is addressed each day, and this diversity adds complex dimensions to leadership effectiveness. Within the military, and with those who are friend as well as foe, appreciating the different contributions and perspectives of heritage, characteristics, values, and norms compounds the difficulties of executing leadership.

Military organizations must deal with constant social and technological change with effective processes that allow the adaptation of strategies and tactics to those changes. Despite the sophistication of our weapons, pinpoint targeting often results in ancillary damage to people and the environment. Military leaders must anticipate all consequences and be prepared to accept responsibility when technology fails. Information technology is both a resource and a constraint. Influence is based upon our ability to access, analyze, and disseminate information. We collect mountains of data but still cry out for better intelligence. Military leaders encounter the realities of too much information and, at the same time, delay decisions in the quest for more information. This is a paradox of modern-day leadership in general; the military happens to have access to leading technologies but the challenges remain.

Accepting and managing change are key aspects of effective leadership today. Focusing on short-run successes for unit efficacy often conflicts with taking a long view to ultimately accomplish a larger strategic goal. Leaders must pay attention to both and understand the balance required for effectiveness. How military leaders adapt is subject to close scrutiny, and as the performance expectations increase, so do the penalties for failure.

Intuition is a valuable guide for leadership. It is our education and experience—what we have learned. Synthesizing what we know is, at times, contrary to logic. The temptation is to go with the data because the logic is documented. Yet, effective leaders understand that creativity (challenging accepted logic) and listening to their "gut" are important aspects of how they lead. Intuition is based upon information that is not easily explained, and military history is replete with examples of leadership that succeeded as a result of decisions made based upon intuition. As captains and lieutenants in Iraq and Afghanistan are making decisions previously reserved for higher-ranking officers, understanding intuition as the sum of one's knowledge and experience is important—*knowing* when to use intuition is critical.

We need to ask whether the risk associated with intuition will be permitted in the future. If mistakes always result in failure and punishment, we will encourage leaders to minimize risk. Defense of a mistake becomes personal. Thus, we must examine our accountability measures carefully to ensure that we will not penalize taking risks in unimportant decisions and reinforce the intuitive self-confidence so that leaders are prepared to take the big risks when demanded by the situation and the stakes. At the same time, if we reduce the willingness to take risks, we will reduce leaders' ability to manage change. In the future, instantaneous communication and the reporting of events to the entire world through television, blogs, e-mail, and other media will expose military leaders' process and the outcome of their decisions. The challenge is whether the risk that makes a difference in effective leadership will be inhibited or maintained.

Followers' leadership expectations also are changing. In effective leadership, the climate of the military as well as the individual unit is expressed by how people treat each other and what they say compared to what they do. Often we can anticipate followers' responses to their leaders. This can be described as the organization's "personality." Units in trouble resonate fear and uncertainty. Effective organizations reflect confidence and optimism. Leadership style sets the tone and is the major influence on climate. Watch the leader and his or her behavior. Effective communicators are open and candid. Doing what one promises is integrity. Working hard and setting high standards through words and deeds create high expectations for superior results. Being loyal to those who make mistakes and learn from them encourages self-confidence and innovation. All of these are examples of how the leader establishes and sustains the climate of the unit or organization.

The generational differences between senior leaders and new recruits continue to be important to consider. The tenets of giving one's best, accepting any and all assignments out of duty, welcoming competition, and striving for promotion and advancement reflect more traditional generations. These people struggle with military members who seek to fulfill minimum standards of performance, look for assignments based upon the quality of life, prefer collaboration over competition, and might be content to stay in a favored job rather than seek advancement. Future leaders must consider melding these perspectives and attributes into a smoothly working force, which will be no easy task.

There is a unique culture in the military as well as in each of the armed forces. Characterized by tradition, mores, norms, and socialization, a unique set of social patterns emerges as both a strength and a shortcoming. Organizational culture is the shared assumptions, beliefs, and values that form the basis for individual and collective behavior. The phrase "duty, honor, and country" describes the nature of the organization's culture. Men and women coming into the military know it will be different from the lives they left. Those in the military know they are set apart from the rest of society. The culture is promulgated thorough history, stories, rituals, and symbols.

Subcultures exist in the military. Special Forces, Seabees, and other groups develop cultures that reflect their training and missions. Reserve and National Guard members have cultures different from their active-duty counterparts. Many of these subcultures reflect cultures that are counter to the larger military organization. The values of the subcultures may conflict or complement those of the larger organization. What appears to be the trend is an increasing inability to predict personal values, making leadership more challenging. So talk with people, observe them working, and sense the spirit and energy that comes from discussions about their work and their aspirations.

Despite the obvious importance of leadership in combat, too few scholars devote attention to strategic leadership at the tactical level. More than five years into the war in Iraq, for example, nearly all analysis of wartime leadership has focused on senior-level general officers or policy-makers in the Pentagon. In their piece, "How the West Was Won: Strategic Leadership in Tal Afar" (Chapter 20), Eric B. Rosenbach and John Tien, an active-duty colonel who recently commanded a battalion in Iraq, examine how Army field-grade officers serving in the Iraqi town of Tal Afar demonstrated a unique brand of strategic leadership that they believe transformed the war's trajectory.

Michael Flowers presents his view of the Contemporary Operation Environment in "Improving Strategic Leadership" (Chapter 21) by describing the environment in which future leaders must work. "Complex," "unpredictable," and "ambiguous" are how he describes the military landscape of the future. He suggests that the current cultures of the military restrict the development of strategic leaders. Communication, flexible perspective-taking, and leadership development are the tools to ensure strategic leadership.

"The Gettysburg Experience: Learning, Leading, and Following" (Chapter 22) is a unique leadership development program created by Lawrence Taylor and William Rosenbach. Using the Gettysburg battlefield as the "classroom," they describe this process as one that uses history as a metaphor for enduring leadership issues. Using case studies, experiential exercises, and other learning tools, Taylor and Rosenbach use experts on the battlefield to help the participants understand the context of the case studies. The emphasis is on appreciating the power of transformational leadership.

The noncommissioned officer (NCO) is the heart and soul of the military. Major General Robert Scales provides a passionate and concise update on this reality in "The Sergeant Solution" (Chapter 23). This piece shows how US forces started rebuilding Iraqi military forces by concentrating on developing first-rate NCOs. Training these individuals must be in the context of their culture rather than a US model, and Scales notes that this will come only with the ability to create a strong corps of noncommissioned officers.

A fascinating view of leadership in the Russian forces is presented in Brigadier General Kevin Ryan's piece, "Leadership in the 'City of Exiles'" (Chapter 24). Ryan reports that Chita and the Siberian region was known as the "City of Exiles" and was closed off to the world until recently. He had the opportunity to travel to the headquarters of the Siberian Military District and observe leadership in this unit of the Russian military. The challenges of an isolated command, social conditions, and tradition are being challenged as new expectations and values are being developed. This piece is one look at another military organization and, at the same time, an opportunity to think about American forces in similar situations and how those situations call for varying levels of transactional and transformational leadership.

Commandant Paul Whelan of the Irish Defense Forces explores the notion that today's professionals embrace different values, attributes, and aspirations for their working lives than did previous generations, in his article, "Generational Change: Implications for the Development of Future Military Leaders" (Chapter 25). Interestingly, Whelan refers to the military's "corporate environment." He observes that new generations question and challenge seniors, and they want feedback and attention. Comparisons of the Silent Generation, Baby Boomers, Generation X, and Generation Y show a consistent questioning of authority. Future leaders should understand the practical implications and benefits of questioning if they are to be effective with the new generations.

Finally, Bernard Bass's paper, "Leading in the Army After Next" (Chapter 26), looks at the leadership requirements for future military forces. This piece was part of an Army project that focused on winning and maintaining peace and included a scenario of effective warfighting leadership in 2025. In his paper, Bass outlines leadership characteristics and attributes as they relate to unit cohesiveness. He prescribes the key elements for assessing and training future military leaders.

All of these articles help to outline the changing environments and guide us in the changes we must face in developing future military leaders. From the senior commanders to the newly minted junior officers, the issues here are tentative and, thus, we allow the leader to answer the question, "What is the future of military leadership?"

20

How the West Was Won

Strategic Leadership in Tal Afar

Eric B. Rosenbach and Colonel John Tien

Leaders and their followers, not policies or tactics, decide the outcome of wars. Despite the obvious importance of leadership in combat, the military has devoted too little attention to leadership lessons learned on the battlefields of Iraq. More than five years into the war in Iraq, nearly all analysis of wartime leadership has focused on senior-level general officers or policy-makers in the Pentagon. After-action reviews from Iraq focus almost exclusively on evaluating the implementation of various operational tactics. These narrow, if not myopic, analyses of military leadership have missed an important learning point: Army field-grade officers serving in the northwest Iraq town of Tal Afar demonstrated an unusual brand of leadership that transformed the war's trajectory. These officers exhibited not only the classic aspects of strategic leadership but also the unique characteristics of outstanding transformational leaders.

The Colonels' War and Tal Afar

Multiple investigations and studies have illustrated in detail that during the initial occupation of Iraq the United States suffered from poor strategic leadership at the highest levels of the military and Department of Defense.[1] In 2007, Army Lieutenant Colonel Paul Yingling sparked an intense debate about the competence of general officers' leadership. The military's strategic leaders, Yingling argued, "repeated the mistakes of Vietnam" in Iraq by failing to anticipate the future of warfare, miscalculating the means to secure post-conflict Iraq, and not accurately reflecting the complexity and difficulty of the situation in Iraq to the American public. We disagree that an entire genera-tion of general officers failed.

The debate about generals' leadership has clouded observation and study of field-grade leadership in Iraq. Too few military officers have noted the sig-nificant impact of leaders on the ground in Iraq and recognized that localized security dynamics and national-level resource constraints turned Iraq into a "colonels' war."[2] The "colonels' war" moniker is more than just a flashy head-line; it reflects the reality of the complex environment and the devolution of strategic decision-making from echelon-level central headquarters to brigades and battalions. Since the security environment in Iraq varied greatly from lo-cation to location, brigade and battalion commanders often developed a rel-atively unique strategy for their specific area of operations. Colonel H. R. McMaster, who served in Tal Afar as commander of the 3rd Armored Cavalry Regiment, explained that Iraq should be considered a "colonels' war because it's important to understand the very complex ethnic, tribal, and sectarian dy-namics within a particular region, and then to craft a strategy that is mindful of those dynamics."[3]

The most instructive case studies of leadership clearly illuminate lessons learned in a way that will apply to the future challenges facing other leaders. With that as a goal, studying the two brigade commanders—Colonels H. R. McMaster and Sean B. MacFarland—who served in Tal Afar from mid-2005 to mid-2006, provides an excellent opportunity to derive widely applicable lessons about strategic and transformational leadership.

For the duration of Operation Iraqi Freedom, the situation in Tal Afar, a volatile multiethnic city located along major lines of communication in northwestern Iraq, has represented one of the most complex security envi-ronments the American military has faced. One former commander who served in Tal Afar noted, "If you take all the complexities of Iraq and com-pressed it into one city, it is Tal Afar."[4] Clearly, the environment's complexity demanded leaders to push the limits of their leadership skills. Many of the skills they demonstrated mirror what Army doctrine extols in general officers who strategize in the nation's capital, and this strategic leadership made the difference in Tal Afar. In the words of the city's mayor, Najim Abdullah Al-Jibouri, "Tal Afar is the first place Iraqis and the Americans were able to get it right."[5]

Getting it right in Tal Afar from mid-2005 to mid-2006 set the stage for the dramatic shift in momentum that occurred for American forces in all of western Iraq, particularly Ramadi, in 2007. Thus, the ultimate impact of strategic leadership in Tal Afar warrants study.

Strategic Leadership

What is a strategic leader in the military? Army doctrine asserts that strategic leaders exist almost exclusively at the military's highest levels. To succeed, these senior-level officers have to be "comfortable in the departmental and political environments of the nation's decision making."[6] According to Army doctrine, strategic leadership is characterized by the long-term planning and interagency coordination of national-level policy that occurs in Washington. Not surprisingly, this doctrine places a heavy emphasis on the significance of hierarchy: Strategic leaders are by definition general officers.

In Iraq, strategic leadership at the tactical level has taken on an entirely different, and more important, role than the Army has ever formally recognized. The paradigm of the strategic leader has evolved mostly due to the complexity of the security environment in Iraq. An Army general back at the Pentagon and the sergeant holding a strategic bridge are still important. But Iraq has forced leaders on the ground to actually craft the *strategy* necessary to win the war on a city-by-city or regional basis. Thus, successful commanders in Tal Afar demonstrated a brand of strategic leadership that differs, and perhaps even redefines, the Army's current doctrine on the topic.

The Makings of a Strategic Leader

In the past, most reviews of field-grade leadership have focused on commanders' implementation of certain tactics or operational strategies. For example, common lessons-learned studies explain how a unit conducts a cordon-and-search operation or how a unit establishes forward combat outposts. Gleaning important lessons from tactical operations is certainly important and represents one of the crucial bedrock aspects of the American military's ability to improve and adapt over time.

But these studies most often skip a crucial step: They neglect to begin the lessons-learned process by assessing both the leadership and thinking that produced the broader strategies encompassing those operations. The ability to think strategically allows leaders in the field to adjust their plans and actions during ongoing operations. In an ideal world, Army field-grade leaders should first focus on learning how to think and analyze problems strategically, then move on to assimilate all the specific tactical lessons from past commanders.

The colonels who exhibited strategic leadership in western Iraq share several characteristics. Extraordinary vision allowed these leaders to see beyond the tactical elements of a complex security environment. Strategic leaders in western Iraq also demonstrated the ability to craft "smart power" strategies that utilized nonkinetic aspects of American military power. Empathy allowed these leaders to adjust their strategies to win the support of the local population and tribal leaders. And the best strategic leaders in Tal Afar complemented these traits with a deep creative streak that allowed them to cope with limited resources and derive solutions to complex problems.

Vision

A commander with authority can issue a plan; a strategic leader promotes a vision. More than any other quality, vision differentiates the strategic leader from the average Army commander. Vision, after all, allows a leader to recognize that accomplishing complex objectives requires more than a plan or operations order. When first conceptualizing the vision's ultimate larger objectives, a leader likely will not even consider the type of tactics that would be necessary to achieve it. In Tal Afar, Army leaders recognized that their units needed a longer-term strategy that weaved together all of their plans into a comprehensive approach that addressed as many of the environment's flashpoints as possible.

A coherent and compelling vision begins with the explicit recognition of the problem. During the initial years after the invasion of Iraq, some policymakers in Washington were reluctant to label the violence an insurgency. Military leaders on the ground in Tal Afar, however, recognized relatively quickly that they faced an insurgency. As McMaster noted, it was extremely important to identify the presence of an insurgency in Tal Afar because then he and other strategic leaders could study the history of counterinsurgencies "in breadth and then in depth ... [to] understand the complex causality of events."[7]

After recognizing the significance of burgeoning insurgency, Army leaders developed a vision for Tal Afar's future. The vision was holistic. It required a new perspective on security, the cornerstones of which would be a competent police force, a functioning economy, and a viable local government. Colonel Sean MacFarland served as the brigade commander for 1st Brigade, 1st Armored Division in Tal Afar immediately following McMaster. Later, he and his unit transferred from Tal Afar to the town of Ramadi in Al Anbar province. Reflecting on the success his unit achieved in Ramadi, MacFarland noted that "Tal Afar taught us that competent local police forces were vital for long-term success."[8]

Smart Power

Strategic leaders often recognize that military power alone rarely establishes the lasting and durable security necessary to quell an insurgency. As Secretary of Defense Robert Gates noted in 2007, the United States in general, and the military in particular, needs to better integrate soft power with hard power.[9] This balance and integration between the two is what Harvard professor Joseph Nye has labeled "smart power." Smart-power strategies, which are generally composed at the highest levels of government, attempt to harness the capacity of all relevant national-level agencies, such as the State, Agriculture, or Treasury departments.

Finding the appropriate balance of hard and soft power is a significant challenge for US military leaders in Iraq. In a traditional combat environment, the term "hard power" normally refers to the assertive use of force with military (or "kinetic") operations. For example, a leader may need to establish initial security in an area where an entrenched enemy dominates the environment by launching offensive operations to hunt and eliminate foes. Yet, leaders on the ground in Tal Afar realized that after initial aggressive military operations they needed to leverage nonkinetic "soft power" tools to promote more lasting security and stability. As noted in a recent high-profile report from the Center for Strategic and International Studies, "Soft power is the ability to attract people to our side without coercion. Legitimacy is central to soft power. Soft power is essential to winning the peace."[10] Soft-power tools include the ability of military leaders to win the "hearts and minds" of the local population by engaging in local public relations efforts or providing infrastructure development projects. Simply put, winning an insurgency requires leaders to recognize the importance of soft power.

In Tal Afar, Army leaders recognized that the smartest application of power was in bolstering Iraqis' belief in the rule of law. After years of repressive rule under Saddam Hussein, most Iraqis had little appreciation for an objective system of justice and governance. Unfortunately, Abu Ghraib and other highly publicized failings greatly diminished the legitimacy with which the US military promoted the ideals of the rule of law.

Army leaders in Tal Afar recognized that Abu Ghraib and other events far beyond their area of operations significantly influenced the locals' perception about the United States' application of the rule of law. Without confidence in the legal and judicial systems in Tal Afar, the local population would be unlikely to provide support that would result in lasting security frameworks. Army leaders therefore wisely crafted a strategy that transmitted the message that democratic regimes must respect the rule of law and justly treat prisoners. They then backed up this message with action. Recognizing the need to leverage for all elements of US capacity, they turned to Army lawyers to help provide professional role-modeling to the Iraqi police, lawyers, and judges. Brigade commanders also provided a strong role model. Almost daily, MacFarland or his battalion commanders would inspect the various Iraqi detention facilities in Tal Afar to ensure that they met international legal standards. They did so as part of a joint inspection team with their Iraqi military or police counterparts to indicate the importance of rule of law in a democratic culture.

Empathy

The fall of the authoritarian government, and resulting power vacuum in many regions of Iraq, forced many Iraqis to fall back on local leaders and traditional tribal structures to survive. Unfortunately, too few of even the best analysts in the American military and intelligence communities recognized prior to the invasion just how important local leaders would be in stabilizing and securing the country. This oversight left tactical-level leaders like those in Tal Afar to recognize the strategic importance of this issue.

Leaders who recognized the importance of these local leadership dynamics possessed an unusual ability to empathize with the population and devise strategies based on their needs. In some cases, this knowledge was derived from extensive professional readings about counterinsurgencies and complex security environments. In other cases, military leaders simply recognized that local leaders and tribal structures held the key to improving security because they devoted extensive time to speaking and listening to locals.

Leaders with empathy also recognized the strategic importance of winning support among local Iraqis. Inevitably, military operations in the region would sometimes result in damage to local infrastructure, such as walls, fences, or individuals' houses. In a true show of empathy and strategic leadership, commanders in Tal Afar instructed their legal officers to literally "mend fences" with Iraqis by establishing a transparent process of compensation for damages. Tal Afar's mayor, Najim Abdullah Al Jabouri, commented on the program's impact: "You are the most powerful force in Tal Afar, you don't ever have to say sorry, but we respect that you do."

MacFarland, the brigade commander who initially served in Tal Afar before moving on to Al Anbar province, recalled, "One of the keys to success in Tal Afar was the establishment of a credible local government with a mayor respected by the populace."[11]

Local engagements were far from ad-hoc or tactical in nature. The best leaders on the ground created a formal engagement process that identified the most appropriate individuals, assessed their motivations and interests, and made a strategic plan.[12] The best commanders in Tal Afar stepped back, surveyed the landscape of individual local Iraqi leaders, and then proceeded to leverage their expertise and influence in a targeted fashion.

The impact of American military units cooperating with local and tribal leaders in Al Anbar province has been well documented and assessed. Most experts agree that the "awakening" changed the strategic direction of Iraq's security environment. As stated, prior to repositioning from Tal Afar to Ramadi in June 2006, MacFarland and his followers saw firsthand the successful strategies implemented in Tal Afar. MacFarland had 20 percent fewer troops and tanks than the previous commander. Rather than worry about the lack of resources, however, he crafted a clear and compelling strategy: Win the people, win the war. He recognized the integral need to maintain personal relations with Iraqi leaders, develop the local security forces, and improve the economic day-to-day life of the average Iraqi citizen. MacFarland later implemented this same strategy with great success in Ramadi.

Creativity

In his classic text, *Generalship,* Major General J. F. C. Fuller emphasized that creativity was a key virtue for a strategic leader at the general-officer level. Fuller believed that the mental capacity to "do something that the enemy does not expect" and the intellect to think creatively allowed leaders to succeed in the most difficult battlefield scenarios.[13] Fuller would be proud of the tactical leaders who devised creative strategies that allowed the American military to secure Tal Afar.

In 2005, nearly two years before similar efforts emerged in Al Anbar province, Army leaders in Tal Afar clearly demonstrated strategic leadership by adapting normal standard operating procedures and tactics to address the region's unique environment. The now extremely well-known strategy in Iraq of "clear, hold, and build" was still a novel concept at the time, but such leaders as McMaster and MacFarland recognized the need for creative, outside-the-box thinking. In the words of the *New York Times,* Tal Afar "is becoming something of a test case for a strategy to break the cycle: using battle hardened American forces working in conjunction with tribal leaders to clear out the insurgents and then leave behind Iraqi forces to try to keep the peace."[14]

Transformational Leaders

Too often, analysis of strategic leadership overlooks the importance of a leader's active involvement in implementing a vision. The most effective military leaders, whom scholars normally label as transformational leaders, are those who move their followers beyond the mechanical transactions of standard operating procedures. Transformational leaders articulate the importance of the strategy so that followers transcend tactical and operational constraints to achieve broad objectives. Transformational leaders who commanded in Tal Afar ensured the implementation of the strategy by pushing strategic decision-making to even lower levels of the organization.

Confidence is a trait common in most transformational leaders. Leaders in an environment like Tal Afar, however, possessed confidence in two distinct ways. First, confidence allowed them to push forward a unique security strategy that had not yet been tested or advocated in other parts of Iraq. This confidence extended beyond their personal decision-making: Strategic leaders in Tal Afar also empowered their subordinates to devise the most effective methods for implementing the larger strategy and vision. Transformational leaders enable followers to perform beyond expectations by sharing power and authority. By underscoring that subordinates could attempt—and probably even fail—in devising creative solutions for nonlethal objectives, leaders pushed strategic decision-making to company-grade officers.

For example, in the spring of 2006 perhaps the most important officer in Tal Afar was neither MacFarland nor his subordinate lieutenant colonel battalion commander, but the US Army battalion civil-military operations officer, Captain Chad Pillai. He saw Tal Afar as a whole and recognized that agriculture should drive the city's economy. In his ten months in Tal Afar, Pillai brought the sheiks together to form an agriculture cooperative, developed a new transparent and efficient contractor bid system, and personally built, started, and maintained the Tal Afar small business center. When historians talk about the Iraq War, they will rightly reference General David Petraeus, Ambassador Ryan Crocker, McMaster, and MacFarland. But Pillai deserves a place in that dialogue as well.

Many scholars have noted the importance of "presence" in a transformative leader. Normally, leaders with presence have a unique type of gravitas, or ability to communicate. Presence essentially establishes the leader's seriousness and her or his command of the organization. In the complex security environment in Tal Afar, Army leaders redefined the concept of presence in two ways. First, leaders incorporated into their strategy the need for a security presence in the most volatile and dangerous parts of the region. For example, Army leaders in Tal Afar recognized that the United States could establish a strategic presence in areas controlled by insurgents or al Qaeda in Iraq by using combat outposts. This concept demonstrated strategic thought leadership, which served as a significant component of later operations in Al Anbar province.

Second, Army leaders demonstrated their commitment to the importance of a strategic security presence by providing a role model for implementation. The best Army leaders were not afraid to take the lead in formation when patrolling in dangerous neighborhoods or to sleep and eat with subordinates operating combat outposts. This type of presence clearly showed subordinates and Iraqis alike that the leaders believed in their strategy. More important, these actions facilitated followers' strong personal identification with both the leader and with the unit's overarching mission.

The words in this article describe the actions of Army officers in a small town in the northwest of Iraq. The article's true intent, however, is to show what a strategic leader can and should be for his subordinates and his country: visionary, holistic, creative, empathetic, transformative, empowering, and personally unafraid to take risks. McMaster and MacFarland were two leaders who demonstrated strategic leadership from mid-2005 to mid-2006 in the Iraqi city of Tal Afar. Building on what he learned in Tal Afar, MacFarland and his unit later succeeded in Al Anbar province. Together, McMaster and MacFarland changed the trajectory of the Iraq War. The ultimate future of Iraq remains unclear. But when historians look back at the progress made in western Iraq during a critical time of the conflict, they will almost certainly note the extraordinary performance of the strategic leaders who served in Tal Afar.

Notes

1. See, for example, Donald Wright and Timothy Reese, *On Point II: Transition to the New Campaign*, Army Combined Arms Center, July 2008.

2. The term "colonels' war" was used in a PBS *Frontline* documentary. This was also the title of a talk given by Lawrence Kaplan to the American Academy in Berlin after this article was completed in May 2008.

3. "A Colonels' War," PBS *Frontline* interview with H. R. McMaster, June 2007.

4. Richard Oppel, "Magnet for Iraq Insurgents Is Test for US Strategy," *New York Times*, June 16, 2006.

5. Samantha Stryker, "Iraqi Mayor Writes New Chapter of Success," US Army releases, November 14, 2006.

6. "Strategic Leadership," Army Field Manual 6-22, October 12, 2006, p. 12-1.

7. "A Colonels' War," PBS *Frontline*.

8. Niel Smith and Sean MacFarland, "Anbar Awakens: The Tipping Point," *Military Review*, March/April 2008, p. 44.

9. Excerpted from the Landon Lecture given by Secretary of Defense Robert Gates, Kansas State University, Manhattan, Kansas, November 26, 2007.

10. Joseph Nye and Richard Armitage, CSIS Commission on Smart Power, CSIS, 2007, p. 6.

11. Smith and MacFarland, "Anbar Awakens," p. 46.

12. Michael Eisenstadt, "Tribal Engagement Lessons Learned," *Military Review*, September/October 2007.

13. J. F. C. Fuller, *Generalship* (CITY: Military Service Publishing Co., 1936), p. 32.

14. Oppel, "Magnet for Iraq Insurgents."

$$\star\ \star\ \star\quad \mathbf{21}\quad \star\ \star\ \star$$

Improving Strategic Leadership

Brigadier General Michael Flowers

THE CONTEMPORARY OPERATIONAL ENVIRONMENT (COE); force design; political and military complexity on the battlefield; joint and combined operations; and mission execution have caused changes that require leaders who can understand strategic implications earlier in their careers than has been required in the past. Therefore, the US Army must begin educating officers for strategic leadership positions earlier in the leader development process. The context within which the US Army executes its responsibility under US Code, Title 10, "Armed Forces," has expanded in an unprecedented fashion.[1]

The increase in the number, variety, and complexity of missions places a greater demand on the Army than ever before and creates great ambiguity in the methodology for successful mission accomplishment. Therefore, the Army must redefine its traditional paradigms of leader development associated with traditional echelons of execution. In fact, the boundaries between echelons of leadership have become so blurred that they overlap almost to the point of invisibility.

The need to develop tactical leaders into strategic leaders and to empower them to lead in such a challenging environment has never been more apparent. Strategic leaders responsible for large organizations, thousands of people, and vast resources cannot rely on lower-level leadership skills for future success.

Developing strategic leadership skills using a set of finite leader competencies with broad application as a foundation is necessary to provide a common direction that transcends all leadership levels. Broad competencies span boundaries and provide continuity for leaders when they must function at multiple levels simultaneously. The Army needs competent, confident, adaptive thinkers to exercise battle command. Senior leaders must develop the skills and confidence necessary to apply military means in a strategic environment of global economies and instant communications.

Leaders must acquire operational- and strategic-level skills earlier in their careers to successfully meet future challenges. The Army must begin strategic leader development sooner to prepare leaders to understand and execute successful strategic leadership and to accomplish the mission.

The COE is now more complex and unpredictable, and the future operational environment (FOE) promises to be equally so. The ambiguity of contemporary crises and military events demands that the Army begin developing officers early in their careers who can—

- Predict second- and third-order effects.
- Negotiate.
- Understand globalization.
- Build consensus.
- Analyze complex and ambiguous situations.
- Think innovatively and critically.
- Communicate effectively.

The COE has been becoming more complex and unpredictable for some time. An asymmetrical environment or a noncontiguous battlespace was as much an experience during the Vietnam War as it is in the post–11 September 2001 world. The Army needs an officer corps that can operate in any environment, not just the current one. The Army must prepare for future environments as well. General officers clearly need such skills, but company commanders and field grade officers must also be aware of the strategic implications of their actions in a complex COE.

Former Chief of Staff of the Army (CSA) General Eric K. Shinseki's comment about the NATO Stabilization Force (SFOR) in Bosnia applies as well to the need for better professional development in strategic skills. He said that being SFOR commander is "the most difficult leadership experience I have ever had. Nothing quite prepares you for this."[2] In Bosnia and other peace operations, even junior officers face challenges in which their tactical decisions are likely to have immediate strategic consequences. Therefore, they need to develop strategic awareness that lower levels of institutional education and training do not offer.

Army leadership research is consistent with Shinseki's observation; it must do more to improve how it develops strategic leaders, thus improving strategic leadership. Studies, reports, and analyses of Army leaders corroborate that there is room for improvement at all levels of leadership, especially at the strategic level.[3] Improvement is essential for the success of Army Transformation.

Managing revolutionary change in a transforming Army and commanding soldiers in an ambiguous, noncontiguous battlespace requires strategic leadership skills, such as envisioning and consensus-building, and key leadership competencies, such as self-awareness and adaptability. To develop these skills, the Army must introduce broad-based, doctrinal competencies during accession and precommissioning.

Why Change Is Required

Army culture contains many challenges and obstacles that hamper the development of strategic leaders and can sometimes be a double-edged sword—facilitating efficient tactical military operations while stifling the communication necessary to operate effectively at the strategic level. The traditional hierarchy often teaches officers to protect their turf and to stovepipe, filter, and control information.

At the strategic level, communication requires:
- Sharing information, not controlling it.
- Open dialogue, not rank-determined discussions.
- Flexible perspective-taking, not turf protection.

The Army's leadership training for preparing officers for tactical or operational roles is generally sound, but its training for preparing leaders for their strategic role is incomplete at best. Some leaders consider it unsoldierly to have a strategic focus.[4]

Many officers who attend senior service colleges never emerge from the realm of tactics. Some never develop leadership skills other than direct ones. Division commanders and assistant division commanders supervise the tactical operations of the commands in which they serve on a daily basis. Developing strategic awareness does not become a top priority until late in an officer's career. Few, if any, quality exercises exist in the Army's curricula that involve strategic issues for company and field grade officers.

The Army's rapid operational pace provides few opportunities for improvement in subjects that are not of immediate utility, but the COE requires unit leaders to shift rapidly from a tactical context into a strategic context and employ their units with equal skill. Can we afford to continue this pattern when we know future doctrine will require this ability earlier?

Strategic leadership requires understanding all three levels of war and how the military functions as part of a larger whole. Consider the current Global War on Terrorism. CSA General Peter J. Schoomaker reinforced the idea of transcending military boundaries when he said, "We have harvested the opposition [to the Taliban] to do our will in Afghanistan."[5] His concept is a keen insight into the environment—one that far exceeds what is taught at any war college.

The ambiguity that characterizes recent conflicts demonstrates the need for skills that far exceed simple tactical-level leadership. Given the far-reaching military, economic, political, and diplomatic implications of the operations, no military center of gravity exists that requires leaders to operate at all levels while simultaneously maintaining a strategic perspective.

The Army generally promotes and selects for senior command those who succeed at the direct level of leadership. The implicit and somewhat tenuous assumption of this selection process is that those who are successful at the direct level of leadership will acquire, as they rise to higher echelons of command, the requisite skills and experiences for strategic leadership.

A review of general officers' résumés reveals that they often have little time for assignments that provide opportunities for quality reflection and study. Operational assignments are the norm. Many who become generals have only one nonoperational assignment, which allows little time for reflection and assimilation of skills. Brigadier General David Huntoon said, "We are rushing officers through promotion gates too fast to ensure they are amassing the experience and expertise necessary to be able to summon up the instincts, insights, foresight, and wisdom essential to success in a complex battlespace."[6] Most colonels serving as executive officers, as well as general officers serving on the Army staff, do not gain the perspective that colonels on the joint staff or in the Department of Defense gain. Officers whose duties take them into daily contact with people from the Department of State, National Security Council, CIA, and NATO develop broader perspectives and a nuanced understanding of strategic issues.

Coupled with education, experience in the interagency process is increasingly useful for senior leaders. Operations with increased strategic and political implications, as well as joint, interagency, and multinational execution early in an officer's career, will become the norm. This suggests the need to change how to manage midlevel assignments. The Army must provide experiences to those officers most likely to rise to positions of strategic responsibility. The Army might also reconsider what assignments are nominative and how much latitude branches have in assignments to develop future strategic leaders.[7]

Clearly the Army must carefully manage the assignment process to ensure the development of requisite strategic leadership skills. The Army can improve the assignment process by identifying and carefully managing worthwhile assignments during appropriate windows of opportunity. Developing higher-level skills places increased importance on educating Army leaders at all levels in both the institutional and operational Army in subjects that augment strategic leadership skills.

Improving Army officers' strategic leadership skills should begin with accession and precommissioning and continue through the general officer level. Becoming a competent general officer takes a lifetime of education, training, and experience. The Army's goal should be to develop an officer corps that has the requisite skills and has learned to correctly perform actions crucial to strategic leadership.

Much anecdotal and systematic evidence suggests that some strategic leaders engage too readily in micromanagement, indicating over-reliance on the direct leadership mode. Micromanagement stifles creativity and can create an environment that rewards permission-seeking, relegating such maxims as "be bold" and "take risks" to mere rhetoric. Educating officers early on about strategic leadership will make the requisite transition to it more likely.

Improving Strategic Leadership

The Army's current officer education system begins the development of strategic leaders at the US Army War College (AWC) at Carlisle Barracks, Pennsylvania. The US Army Command and General Staff College at Fort Leavenworth, Kansas, has also added a track of study for strategists. Given the changing context within which the Army fulfills its responsibility to the Nation and the inherent requirements in this new operating environment, developing strategic leaders at the War College level comes too late.

The leader development process requires progressive training and education that produces leaders who possess appropriate skills at the appropriate time, and clearly, the sooner strategic leadership development begins, the better for the officer, the Army, and the Nation.

The Army currently does not have a concerted methodology to develop strategic leaders, although it does have some excellent institutional courses. Unfortunately, the courses are based on past paradigms that wait for leaders to achieve certain developmental gates before training them for the skills associated with the next level of performance and that rely on success at lower levels of performance to predict future success.

Filling the gap in education and training that exists today will require paradigm-breaking, multilevel leadership skill development. The Army can better use education to leverage skill development. The Army can require that officer assignments exercise and develop strategic leadership skills. The Army and the leader can use self-development to reinforce skill development.

Institutional Opportunities

The Army should strengthen strategic leadership instruction in Army schools and courses and not limit this effort to general officers or AWC courses. The Army should introduce elements of strategic-thinking skills during Intermediate Level Education and expand them at the Army War College. Curricula should be periodically reviewed based on feedback and on a changing operating environment. A review of the training available through the General Officer Management Office (GOMO) shows that there is useful, focused tactical- and operational-level training but little strategic-level work. The current GOMO training message offers eleven courses, but only three touch on strategic leadership issues:

- The Brigadier General Training Course (BGTC) introduces new general officers to the general officer experience, but discussions about strategic leadership skills are anecdotal. Three days is not enough time to train a strategic leader. BGTC could easily add a session focused on strategic leadership.
- The Capstone Course is six weeks long, but much of that time is spent visiting commands worldwide. The course offers no true strategic-level leadership training other than a three-day exercise at the Joint Warfighting Center at Suffolk, Virginia. Any strategic wisdom general officers gain from their fifteen days of overseas travel is serendipitous

at best and depends on the senior mentor and the balance struck between tourism and concentrated study time.

- The Army Strategic Leadership Course is a giant step toward developing strategic leaders who can effectively manage change. The course could expand its current target audience of brigadier and major generals to include former brigade commanders, division chiefs of staff, corps G3s, and other senior colonels.

Other opportunities.   General officers can also acquire knowledge by participating in strategic-level programs at the Kennedy School of Government or the Fletcher Conference. Joint, multinational, and interagency war games also provide useful education and training. The Army should expand opportunities to participate in these programs where possible. The Center for Creative Leadership seminars, a mandatory program for all brigadier generals, concentrates on strategic-level issues. Most attendees are direct- and organizational-level leaders in civilian industry.

Opportunities to partner with academic institutions that offer strategic educational programs have increased since 11 September 2001. The links to Georgetown, American, George Washington, and other universities, and to the think tanks in Washington, D.C., also provide useful opportunities. GOMO's partnership with Syracuse and Johns Hopkins Universities through the National Security Leadership Course is a good example of collaborative efforts. Quality distance-education technology allows users similar opportunities, to a greater or lesser extent, worldwide. Still, opportunities for senior officers to attend such courses in the face of the extraordinary operational pace in every command are difficult to arrange.

In the past, fellowships offered opportunities for select officers to gain a strategic perspective. The contemporary operating environment requires that strategic leaders understand the many instruments of national power and the asymmetrical nature of current and future threats. The Army must overcome a bias against education in both teaching and learning in order to make quality time for reflection. The Army should consider increasing the quantity and quality of officers in educational positions and in its schools and allow a select few to serve for extended periods as master educators. According to Huntoon, "There is also a need to provide greater opportunity for our field grade officers to complete a focused master's- to doctorate-level education. The latter can be provided by either the Army's senior institutional centers or through quality civilian graduate centers, through resident, distance-learning, or a hybrid means."[8] If the Army is going to develop more and better strategic leaders, it must invest and commit to changing Army culture. The institutional Army plays a critical role in preparing strategic leaders.

Operational Opportunities

Operational opportunities should include strategic staff rides and strategic training and evaluation, such as a Battle Command Training Program (BCTP) evaluation for nondivisional unit or corps commanding generals. BCTPs and the combat training centers could include a strategic planning phase for division and assistant division commanders. The forum, which would be a general officer-level forum run by senior retired officers, Senior Executive Service members, or other subject matter experts, would compel participants to learn strategic thought well in advance of warfighting and mission-rehearsal exercises for operational deployments.

General officer-level workshops on strategic and operational challenges around the world could become a norm. We can do this in the new general officer pre-command course (PCC) at Fort Leavenworth. Staff rides that include a consideration of the strategic dimension of such operations as Normandy or the Ardennes would also be beneficial. Officers could also do some strategic-level work during battalion and brigade command PCCs as well.

To expose leaders to the strategic environment, we can leverage internships, fellowships, and assignments to joint staffs or the National Security Council staff. Such assignments would allow officers some time to study and reflect in a strategic environment. For this to work, the Army must make a cultural shift to balance such assignments with traditional operational assignments. The Army must also reward or recognize those who serve in positions that cultivate the broad perspectives that are necessary to acquire strategic leadership skills.

Self-Developmental Opportunities

Self-developmental opportunities should include directed readings or functional modules delivered by distance or distributed learning. Self-development is a critical foundation for lifelong learning. Self-development is a primary means to complement institutional or operational opportunities and to develop critical, creative thinkers who can serve as leaders managing strategic change.

Current military professional reading lists include few books about strategic leadership. Strategic leaders should refine their reading lists to include the best available material on the strategic environment and leadership as well as books that discuss the moral dimension at the strategic level.[9] Army leaders should encourage dialogue by publishing articles or writing books on strategic leadership.

Given the complexity of strategic leadership, a holistic approach for improving how we develop strategic leaders is important. We must also include joint, interagency, and multinational perspectives. Generals Tommy Franks and Schoomaker believe we should give more value to joint assignments. Huntoon said, "We must break the Army-centric view. Army strategic leaders need to think asymmetrically. Future missions are dynamic; sometimes the threat of force is more useful, other times it is not."[10]

The Army needs leaders who understand this vision and can convey it to their subordinates, to the American people, and to the US Congress, the Secretary of Defense, and the President. Schoomaker recommends changes in operational assignments and education that will change the Army culture and "allow for subordinates to be creative."[11]

Developing an officer corps capable of strategic leadership involves accepting a shift to skill development complemented by experience and reflection and to acquiring strategic leadership skills through the education and experiences gained from specific career patterns. Developing enduring competencies rather than teaching perishable skills is the key. To develop officers capable of strategic leadership, the "first of the critical areas to be examined is the identification of strategic leader skill sets."[12] Developing these skills will produce officers who are confident, doctrinally competent, cognitively resilient, and comfortable with ambiguity. After fully identifying leadership competencies, many of which already exist in leadership doctrine, the next step is to institute ways to develop them, such as embedding skill-development programs throughout the officer education system and in the operational Army.

Officers need to know that the Army expects them to develop strategic-leadership skills early in their careers. The value of the broad-based competency approach to skill development is that competency will transcend leadership levels. When the Army trains junior officers to be conceptually competent, they will understand that the Army expects them to display conceptual competency throughout their careers.

Long-term solutions might focus on providing appropriate educational opportunities throughout an officer's time in service. Educational opportunities that allow officers to reflect on past experiences are valuable and might include teaching as well as student assignments.[13]

Serving the Nation

The COE/FOE and the future Army will need doctrinally competent leaders who possess conceptual as well as interpersonal competence. Effective strategic leaders realized this long ago. George C. Marshall, reflecting on his appointment as the Chief of Staff of the Army, wrote, "It became clear to me that at the age of 58, I would have to learn new tricks that were not taught in the military manuals or on the battlefield. In this position I am a political soldier and will have to put my training in rapping out orders and making snap decisions on the back burner, and have to learn the arts of persuasion and guile. I must become an expert in a whole new set of skills."[14]

One aspect of skill acquisition that many agree on is that waiting until one becomes a general officer to acquire strategic leadership skills might be too late. Indeed, developing conceptual and interpersonal competence must begin much earlier. However, assignments that include broadening educational opportunities and providing time for reflective thinking are key to strategic leader development; developing strategic leaders for tomorrow will require change.

To transform and succeed in the COE/FOE, the Army must be adaptive. To improve strategic leadership, Army leaders must venture forward boldly. Leading change is always difficult, but the Army's success depends on moving forward. The Army must challenge and change part of its culture.

The Army must view strategic leadership as a subject worth studying, learning, understanding, and applying. It must embark on a path that includes developing strategic leadership skills throughout an officer's career. Army Transformation provides this opportunity. Now is the time, as the Army transforms the officer education system, to introduce strategic concepts and leadership competencies earlier in an officer's career and more frequently in the courses.

An officer corps whose education is based on developing confidence and enduring competencies will lead an Army able to win in any environment. These officers will provide a full complement of self-aware, adaptive strategic leaders who are constantly improving themselves and always ready to serve the Nation.

Notes

1. US Code, Title 10, "Armed Forces," online at www.access.gpo.gov/uscode/title10/title10 .html, accessed 11 March 2004.

2. Howard Olsen and John Davis, "Training US Army Officers for Peace Operations— Lessons from Bosnia," *US Institute of Peace Special Report,* 29 October 1999, 1.

3. John A. Spears, Emil K. Kleuver, William L. Lynch, Michael T. Matthies, and Thomas L. Owens, "Striking a Balance in Leader Development: A Case for Conceptual Competence," National Security Program Discussion Paper Series, no. 92–102, John F. Kennedy School of Government at Harvard University, Cambridge, Massachusetts, 1992; Stephen J. Zaccaro, "Models and Theories of Executive Leadership: A Conceptual/Empirical Review and Integration," US Army Research Institute for the Behavioral Sciences, Alexandria, Virginia, October 1996; Richard A. Gabriel and Paul L. Savage, *Crisis in Command: Mismanagement in the Army* (New York: Hill and Wang, 1978); Garry Wills, *Certain Trumpets: The Nature of Leadership* (New York: Simon & Schuster, 1994); *US Army Training and Doctrine Command,* The Army Training and Leader Development Panel (Officer Study) (Washington, DC: US Government Printing Office, 2001).

4. Michael D. Pearlman, in *Warmaking and American Democracy* (Lawrence: University Press of Kansas, 1999), 20, says, "At best, said the commandant of the National War College in 1990, the Armed Forces 'presume there is something unsoldierly about an officer who grows to intellectual stature in the business of military strategy.'"

5. Interview with Gen. Peter J. Schoomaker, Frontier Conference Center, Fort Leavenworth, Kansas, 29 November 2001.

6. Gen. David Huntoon, "General Officer Strategic Development," Information paper, 4 October 2001. Few officers have spent significant time in joint and multinational assignments that could broaden their perspective and give them the opportunity to learn how the Department of Defense, the Executive branch, and foreign militaries operate. The Army does not always consider officers who have spent considerable time in joint assignments as being as "competitive" as officers who remain in Army billets. The Army must value their experiences in tangible ways.

7. Col. James Greer to Lt. Gen. James C. Riley, e-mail, "Tng (Training) strategic leaders," 12 July 2002.

8. Huntoon.

9. Ibid.; Joseph Gerard Brennan and Admiral James Bond Stockdale gave a series of lectures known as the Stockdale Course for senior military leaders at the Naval War College, Annapolis, Maryland. The result was "The Foundations of Moral Obligation," a useful work on ethics and morality for strategic leaders. Two other notable, relevant titles include Michael Walzer's *Just and Unjust Wars: A Moral Argument with Historical Illustrations* (New York: Basic Books, 2000) and Paul Christopher's *The Ethics of War and Peace: An Introduction to Legal and Moral Issues* (Paramus, NJ: Prentice Hall, 1998), which deal directly with moral issues related to the Army's public charter—the ethics of killing.

10. Huntoon.

11. Schoomaker, 29 November 2001. The idea that we need to provide more educational as well as training experiences has broad support.

12. Memorandum Thru Vice Chief of Staff, Army, for Maj. Gen. Robert R. Ivany, Commandant, US Army War College (USAWC), Carlisle Barracks, Pennsylvania, "Charter Guidance—USAWC Student Studies on Strategic Leader Skill Sets and Future War, Future Battlefield," 1.

13. Gen. Dwight D. Eisenhower often noted that his experiences as a teacher helped him prepare for high levels of leadership. Generals Tommy Franks, Eric K. Shinseki, Creighton Abrams, John M. Keane, and Montgomery C. Meigs had similar educational teaching assignments. Many others have had broadening educational experiences—with opportunities for quality reflection—that have helped them develop the requisite skills for successful strategic leadership.

14. US Army Field Manual 6-22 (formerly 22-100), *Army Leadership* (Washington, DC: US Government Printing Office, 31 August 1999), 7-1.

22

The Gettysburg Leadership Experience

Learning, Leading, and Following

Lawrence P. Taylor and William E. Rosenbach

THE GETTYSBURG BATTLEFIELD HAS BEEN called "the finest classroom in America," and not just for the study of history and military tactics, but also for contemporary leadership development. We believe that classrooms for leadership development are best understood as places of learning rather than teaching. The Gettysburg Leadership Experience (GLE) is a fresh, unique approach to leadership development that is designed to use history as a metaphor for contemporary leadership issues. The program incorporates an assortment of learning styles, including large- and small-group interaction. Our diversity of learning experiences includes in-depth case studies, a variety of experiential learning activities, and creative use of video as an auxiliary dimension of historical case studies that define transformational leadership, the common thread of our entire program. The keystone of the program's learning experiences is visits with expert facilitators to sites on the battlefield where focal events of the case studies occurred in July 1863.

The Conceptual Framework

The distinctive character of *The Gettysburg Leadership Experience* is based on eight pillars of learning. These are:

We treat every participant as an adult professional. We seek to engage each participant in a variety of learning experiences, many of which are action-based, that recognize her or his unique potential for professional growth and development.

We design the program to incorporate diverse learning experiences, ranging from classroom discussions to experiential team activities and visits to the historic Gettysburg Battlefield, that synergistically reinforce the core leadership concepts.

There are literally dozens of leadership concepts; our core leadership concepts are transactional and transformational leadership. The emphasis is on developing participants' transformational leadership skills and capabilities so they may direct organizational change and lead people at the strategic level.

We deliberately decided not to be "an expert knowledge transfer program"—in fact, we are not sure leadership can be taught, but we know that it can be learned and developed. We deal with that paradox by putting our expertise into the program's design. Through a variety of learning techniques we facilitate and encourage participants to *think*, think differently, more seriously, more creatively, and more critically as they develop a higher level of understanding of the conceptual framework of strategic thinking and action.

We use the history of Gettysburg as the foundation for our uniquely designed case studies and stories that illustrate timeless leadership principles in action, principles that were present in 1863 and are equally present in today's professional and organizational lives. Through these case studies we identify leadership metaphors that allow participants to learn emotionally as well as intellectually. The Gettysburg Battlefield becomes a leadership laboratory that includes a specific emphasis on understanding the important role of followership in organizational performance and how to develop followers as partners in building effective, high-performing teams.

We believe in and practice continuous improvement and over time have incorporated participant feedback and our own reflection in ways that have deepened and enriched the program. We are proud of this program and we know it is not perfect. We strive to learn from each program, and we apply our learning to improve future programs.

We deliberately incorporate sustainability elements to encourage participants to engage in ongoing development after the Gettysburg portion of the program ends. These elements include the creative use of historical metaphors that act as mental bookmarks, the commonsense application of the transactional and transformational leadership concepts to leader responsibilities, the emotional staying power of Gettysburg, its history, and a special emphasis on the value and use of proactive reflection as an important tool for continuous growth and self-awareness.

We do not offer a "one size fits all" program. We discuss each group's purposes, objectives, and priorities, and, within the limits of our capabilities, we design and deliver a program tailored to their special needs.

The Case Study as Archetype

Though all eight pillars are important components of the program, the GLE case studies have become the program's signature elements for most of the participants, and as such merit special mention. We have developed ten case studies, with two others under development. Each emphasizes different aspects of leadership, followership, or organizational dynamics.

All of the case studies differ in terms of content; however, they all take about a half day to fully unfold, and all have a common design template as follows:

- discussion of the leadership concepts to be explored
- video portion of case study based on an event in the Battle of Gettysburg
- visit to Gettysburg Battlefield, where events in video transpired
- return to classroom for wrap-up small-group/large-group discussion.

These four structural parts of the case study correspond to the underlying four-step learning design that is common to each regardless of the content:

- clarity of concept(s) in the initial discussion
- visualization of the concept(s) in behaviors in the video portion
- reflection on the various possible meanings of the issues using the battlefield visit as stimulus
- application of meanings to the participants' contemporary professional situations during the small-group/large-group discussions.

Given this design, the key to learning is in the reflection and application phases of the case studies, where participants use parallel or lateral thinking to apply insights from historical events to their current professional challenges and opportunities. When that process is explained carefully to groups, with concrete examples of how other participants have actually done it, they tend to embrace the process and use it creatively. It is their own engagement at this stage that defines each program's outcomes. Our experience has been that most exceed their own expectations.

Metaphors and Meaning at Gettysburg

Each GLE case study has a metaphor attached to it. For example, for the case of Union General John Buford, whose actions on the first day positioned his army with a strategic advantage, our metaphor is the High Ground. For the case study of Joshua Chamberlain, regimental commander of the 20th Maine, who defended the left flank of Little Round Top, the metaphor for a real or potential organizational vulnerability that requires risking one's assets to protect is the Left Flank. The metaphors function as mental bookmarks in the minds of the participants, enabling them to easily recall the full case study in the future; they also serve as a common vocabulary for the participants, and groups use these metaphors to communicate among themselves for years after the program. Yet the metaphors serve even more powerful purposes: A CEO told us recently that it was the shared experience of the GLE case study of Union Fifth Corps Commander General Daniel Sickles's behavior at Gettysburg that enabled him to work out a serious disagreement with a senior subordinate and keep him on the team; he said that one outcome alone justified the cost of the program to his company. In this case, the subordinate realized that the CEO had interpreted his behavior as insubordinate rather than constructive initiative.

Our case studies are designed and facilitated to avoid cookie-cutter thinking or outcomes to complicated issues. We probe, test, and challenge all ideas that tend toward rigid, one-right-answer judgments, in a belief that the complexity of the issues under discussion justifies this continuous questioning and that effective use of the Socratic process in decision-making is itself a valuable tool for participants to learn. In practice it is not unusual for our case studies to conclude with differences of opinion among the participants regarding the interpretation of the contemporary meaning of historical events or the application to current circumstances. But whatever their opinion, all believe they were thinking more clearly and critically.

A potential vulnerability to history-based development programs is the tendency to reason backward, instead of thinking forward. Since the participants are aware of the historical outcomes, it is easy for them to engage in types of "Monday-morning quarterbacking" that then pass for leadership lessons. We try to reduce the risk of this occurring in our early preparation phases of the program, which include a discussion of "learning traps," really logical fallacies associated with prior knowledge of outcomes. We identify three of these traps to specifically avoid as we process the case studies: (1) the error of backward causation, in which the outcome alone is taken as proof of the efficacy of the leadership inputs; (2) the "myth of inevitability," in which past events are assumed to have been inevitable and thereby it is possible to miss the ambiguity and complexity of the times, and the leadership issues inherent in that complexity; (3) and the tendency to pick and choose only those parts of the historical experience that reinforce preconceived attitudes and biases, and to reject new perspectives. Discussing learning traps has proven valuable for keeping these errors of reasoning out of the program, but it has become a minilesson in itself as participants recognize that these fallacies are commonly used as persuasion techniques in current organizational and political processes.

Thus in the case study on Robert E. Lee's order to General Richard Ewell to "take that hill if practicable," participants usually conclude with several new thoughts regarding effective communication within organizations, appropriate delegation of authority to subordinates, and leader/follower dynamics that have overtaken a common initial assumption that Lee should not have added "if practicable" to his message to Ewell. Similarly in the case study on Pickett's Charge, participants usually conclude with many new thoughts as to how organizations might more effectively manage disagreement over policy issues, and have long since discarded the initial idea that a key lesson is that Lee should have followed Longstreet's advice, and instead are focusing on thinking about why Lee, and they in similar circumstances, might not have followed such advice.

Like many programs here we often conclude with a walk across the fields of Pickett's Charge, always a powerful emotional and reflective journey, and say our farewells to the group at the Angle on Cemetery Ridge, near the high-water mark of the Confederacy. One point we stress for further thought is contrary to conventional wisdom: The repulse of Pickett's charge was not the "end." The battle may have been over, but the Gettysburg Campaign and the Civil War were not, so the defeat may be better understood as the beginning of a new reality for both the Army of the Potomac and the Army of Northern Virginia in which new leadership demands were placed on both organizations. Indeed, we have a case study on Lee's retreat from Gettysburg and Meade's pursuit that examines organizational crisis management and how skillful leadership in the face of adversity might prevent a major tactical failure from becoming a strategic failure for the organization.

The Dual Role of Leader and Follower

A noteworthy characteristic of the GLE, from its inception, has been an emphasis on the importance of effective followership in determining organizational performance. We designed three Gettysburg case studies devoted to examining followership and developed a sound conceptual model to support the studies. The followership focus has always received strong positive feedback from participants, most of whom said they had never been exposed to a professional assessment of the concept and that it accurately described their organizational experiences. The followership case study has become one of the most requested by participants.

Our followership focus was transformed in 2005, when General Michael Mosley, then Air Force vice chief of staff, brought his team of general officers to the program. Their contribution to the richness of the case studies' reflection and application phases was extraordinary; many of their insights have been incorporated into the program, enabling new groups to benefit from their perspectives as well. Perhaps more important, their presence led to an ongoing relationship with the US Air Force in which we designed a new program for Air Force chief master sergeants; in "The Dual Role of Leader and Follower," concepts of followership are a central theme.

In their professional responsibilities, the chiefs are near-perfect examples of the need to simultaneously perform effectively in both leader and follower roles. Their contributions in discussion and feedback based on the realities of their own experiences in both roles have led to a continuous strengthening in the followership portion of the GLE. As a result, a specialized instrument to measure follower styles, the Performance and Relationship Questionnaire (PRQ), was developed. The followership case studies, the followership model, and the PRQ now form a substantial stand-alone component of the program increasingly requested by clients who have completed the leadership portion of the program.

The Whole Is Greater Than the Sum

Though the eight pillars define the program and the case study has become its signature element in the minds of the participants, it is the careful sequencing and blending of these with other important learning initiatives that together provide the power of the learning experience in influencing participants to take the Gettysburg Experience and translate it into enhanced job performance.

Proactive reflection.   We begin each program with a short presentation on the importance and power of proactive reflection as a primary tool of continuous learning and personal growth and development. We then begin each subsequent day of the program with a session of reflection, in which participants discuss the meaning of the previous day's activities in terms of their own personal and professional lives. We encourage participants to continue this process of proactive reflection after they return home and provide examples of how they might comfortably do so. In a strategic sense, the proactive reflection is the glue that ties together the entire program for its duration and can continue the experience indefinitely into the future.

Expertise vs. experts.   We aim to have real expertise in all phases of the program, minimizing the use of experts. GLE is about the participants, their needs, their leadership, their followership, and their goals and objectives. Our expertise is designing and delivering a set of experiences that enables them to learn and grow. We do not lecture or try to shape discussions to influence them to think as we do. We do try to answer all questions accurately but also in ways that stimulate critical thought. There is always more to learn, and experience shows that over time we learn much from the participants and then incorporate that insight into the program through our commitment to continuous improvement. The participants are the "experts" in applying the insights and lessons learned in the context of their professional lives.

History.   We are not a history program or a military strategy program. Gettysburg's history is seductive, and, therefore, we continually pay attention to ensure that the program doesn't drift into more and more history. The historians in us tend to want to ask whether the story is true and to go ever deeper into factual discovery, spending more time on the battlefield. Instead, we ask participants to seek the leadership issues in the story much as we would in reflecting on Shakespeare's insights into human nature. We allow the program's reflection and application phases to play out to their full potential, so the battlefield experience may serve as an inspirational catalyst for those processes and not be permitted to become the program's focus. Participants have identified the battlefield experience as an emotional component that lends power and credibility to the program.

Transactional and transformational leadership.   One of our eight pillars, yet here the issue is the enormous benefit of having a core proven leadership concept with a solid research base to serve as an anchoring theme. There are just too many concepts of leadership to float among them, and the word *leadership* itself is so loosely used that it can lose any actionable meaning. Of course, it does not have to be transactional/transformational leadership, but choosing the right one for the material has provided this program with power and conceptual legitimacy.

Diversity. The GLE is committed to the value of cognitive diversity both as a learning technique and as a serious dimension influencing organizational performance. That commitment is designed into the case studies and is reinforced in facilitating the program, in which Americans of all ethnic, gender, and religious groups or affiliations are made comfortable, productive participants. The outcomes of the reflection and application phases of the case studies continuously demonstrate how important this is to our learning model.

Preparation, preparation, and preparation. Our programs range between two days and five days in length depending on the objectives of participants, who ideally number about twenty and who mostly are unfamiliar with the history of Gettysburg. We depend on appropriate preparation to have all group members ready from day one to fully participate in all aspects of the experience. To accomplish this we assign a preseminar reading of Michael Shaara's book *Killer Angels* (New York: Ballantine Books, 1987), which functions as a common starting point for our case studies, as well as selected readings on transactional and transformational leadership. Whenever possible, we meet with group members for about an hour before they come to Gettysburg to orient them to the program's philosophy and flow, to introduce ourselves to them, and to hear from them directly about any concerns or issues regarding their upcoming participation. We hold an opening reception and dinner event to set the stage for the program. Finally, by opening the program with proactive reflection, we bring them directly into the conversation by concluding the preparation phase and smoothly transitioning into the case studies.

Conclusion

On the bottom line, the key to the GLE case-study methodology is facilitation that engages, excites, and delights the participants by enabling them to feel that this experience is connected to new ideas, new information, new perspectives, and new insights about issues that are important to them. Leadership is a choice! The essence of leadership is a fervent willingness to accept responsibility for influencing the future. It involves the heart and mind of the one who commits and the hearts and minds of those followers who willingly are influenced by the leader. Thus, groups and organizations are transformed one person at a time. That reality is the spirit of *The Gettysburg Leadership Experience.*

23

The Sergeant Solution

Major General Robert H. Scales

Today [April 8, 2008] General David Petraeus testifies in front of Congress. He will note the progress being made in Iraq thanks to his new counterinsurgency strategy and the "surge." He will also remind everyone that much remains to be done, as the recent battle in Basra demonstrated.

But no matter what he says, it is clear that the writing is on the wall. The bulk of American ground forces will be leaving Iraq. The only question is how many and how fast.

The first group of soldiers from the new Iraqi army prepare to graduate in 2003. After we leave, the Iraqis will have to shoulder the burden of maintaining stability in their country. How well prepared they are for this task will depend on how strong the Iraqi army's noncommissioned officer (NCO) corps is when we leave. NCOs, sergeants and corporals provide a center of gravity for effective fighting forces and often lead small units. They will be vital to sustaining the Iraqi army through the battles ahead.

As a flurry of facts and figures buzz through the air on Capitol Hill today, keep in mind the Army adage that armies are best built from the bottom up, squad by squad, platoon by platoon. Winning wars is not a test of numbers or matériel so much as it is a test of will. The side that wins is the side that wants most to win, and has young soldiers willing to die to secure victory. In good armies, the will to win is set by example, by junior leaders, sergeants and lieutenants, who lead from the front.

The most encouraging news from the battlefield recently is that Iraqi leadership at the small-unit level is improving. Sadly, finding effective young officers in wartime is a brutal process, as it requires testing them in action. The American Army in the Civil War experienced a similar baptism of fire, at a cost of more than half a million dead.

NCOs are the backbone of the American Army. But strong NCOs, who take a leadership role, are an alien concept in areas of the world ruled by strict hierarchies. The Iraqi army is no exception.

In Saddam's military, sergeants were only expected to hold formations, account for equipment and march soldiers from one place to another. Officers made all of the decisions. That's why Saddam had so many of them—and why his army was not as flexible as it needed to be. General Petraeus is trying to change the old-Iraqi-army culture, and he must if the Iraqis are to have a robust military with depth and staying power on the battlefield.

At General Petraeus's urging, last year the Iraqis started divisional schools for NCOs. About 10 percent of each basic training class is sent to three additional weeks of instruction to learn to be corporals, the first rung of the NCO leadership ladder. Successful corporals attend a five-week course, where they learn how to take care of soldiers and the details of leading small units in close combat.

The most senior course teaches sergeants to lead platoons, learning skills formerly reserved for captains and majors. Many newly minted NCOs depart from these schools directly into combat, where they learn to get better in the harsh classroom of real war.

This process of "on the job training" among small units in combat has been made more efficient with the addition of American military training teams. These are squad-sized units embedded in Iraqi combat battalions and brigades.

Experience has shown that the surest way to quickly increase the competency of small-unit leaders and their men is to have direct, hands-on instruction in the field by American NCOs. In such a setting, our NCOs demonstrate professionalism and a "take charge" attitude while fighting side by side with their Iraqi counterparts. Our NCOs teach by doing.

Today there are only 5,000 of these embedded trainers in the field. As the Iraqis head into combat without American partner units, they will probably need more training teams to embed with them. How many? That is a decision that has not yet been made. But a consensus among senior officers engaged in this program suggests that the number of trainers must be doubled, perhaps even tripled if the new Iraqi army is to be successful.

The postsurge strategy should not be focused solely on creating an Iraqi army in the image of our own. The Iraqis only have to be better than their enemies. And there is a danger in committing the blood, treasure and time necessary to train a large Iraqi army. Wars are not won by the bigger force, but by intangibles. Leadership, courage, adaptability, integrity, intellectual agility and allegiance ultimately determine who wins wars.

$\star$ $\star$ $\star$ **24** $\star$ $\star$ $\star$

Leadership in
the "City of Exiles"

Brigadier General Kevin Ryan

THE RUSSIAN CITY OF CHITA and the Siberian region around it are isolated. Known as the "city of exiles," Chita was long closed to foreigners—a place the czarist and later Soviet regimes sent people to "disappear." Today Chita is a city of 300,000, connected to the rest of Russia by an airport and the Trans-Siberian Railway, but it still sits six time zones east of Moscow on the fringe of Russian economic resurgence.

Chita is also home to the headquarters of the Siberian Military District. In the summer of 2002, as the US defense attaché to Russia, I visited the district with the commanding general of US ground troops in Europe as part of an exchange to familiarize our leaders with each other's armies. At the time, those two armies were in vastly different conditions. The Russian military was embroiled in its second Chechen war, which was going badly. About two hundred soldiers a month were dying in the Caucasus. The United States had just completed an invasion and overthrow of the Taliban government in Afghanistan, at a cost of half what Russia was losing monthly in its battle in Chechnya. The US military was at the top of its game. The Russian military was in its worst condition since the First World War.

As a longtime observer of the Russian military, I was interested to see how leadership would be manifested among the officers in this difficult time and "God-forgotten place" (as the Russian saying goes). In my twenty years observing, and sometimes working with, the Russian military, from the unit level to the Ministry of Defense, I have found that its leadership challenges, solutions, and styles are much like ours. To be sure, there are differences, but the similarities are far greater. Good leadership stands out anywhere; bad leadership—the same. And almost always, I agreed with my Russian counterparts about which was which. What I found in Chita was that the leadership required to keep an army together when it is in deplorable condition is at least as great as that required to lead an army that is well-funded and well-manned.

At the Siberian District Headquarters we were greeted by the deputy commanding general who was responsible for a territory greater than all the US states east of the Rockies. During the Cold War, tens of thousands of Soviet soldiers assigned to the district guarded against an invasion by millions of Chinese living across the border. Today, with trade and people flowing freely across the border daily, the district command struggles to convince Moscow of its importance in protecting the country. When we arrived, the command was grappling with a shortage of junior officers. The volunteer-based US Army turned away recruits without high school diplomas and officer candidates without college degrees, but the Russian army could not meet recruiting goals even with mandatory service. There was no hope that Moscow would send any reinforcements to Chita, and the officers there knew this very well. The first site we visited was an attempt by the district to solve this challenge: a local academy set up by the district to train second-year soldiers to be lieutenants and warrant officers.

In the Siberian District's academy, we watched a captain lead prospective officers, *Kadety,* in training on electronics and radio communications; drilling them on nomenclature and function of various circuits and devices. Uniforms were sharp, and the room, though spartan, was tidy and in good order. The *Kadety* rose when spoken to and rendered the salutes and courtesies associated by all military leaders with disciplined troops. They were well fed, athletic, and motivated. Most of all, they exhibited a pride in their work and their country—a pride that was in contrast to the support they got in return from their government in wages and resources. In all, they appeared well cared for.

The district's decision to identify its best second-year soldiers and train them to fill the vacant junior officer slots was logical given the lack of other personnel resources. I remembered doing a similar thing in the 1970s, moving enlisted specialists into "acting jack" sergeant slots. The benefit of the practice is that it helps fill vacant junior leadership positions, but the risk is that it will assign too much responsibility too quickly to improperly prepared leaders.

Success requires developing in those subordinates the talent to think and make decisions on their own. In my experience that meant emphasizing instruction on critical thinking and leadership. The American Army has found this especially important in the current wars with operations dispersed at company and even squad level. As we watched the Russian instruction, though, I began to doubt they would be successful. In the electronics class, the *Kadety* drilled on memorizing descriptions of circuits and how they worked. The methodology was repeated in the next class, where students gathered around an armored personnel carrier with its inner mechanics revealed by cutouts in the vehicle's side. The focus of their entire curriculum was memorization of equipment components when it seemed they should be studying leadership and command techniques. I left the classrooms convinced that their leader training system was outdated for the challenges facing today's officers and would fail to develop the necessary leadership skills. It wasn't until several weeks later in a Moscow diner that I learned the wisdom in the Russian approach to training and understood how it fit into their system of leadership—but more on that later.

Before we traveled to Chita, I had prepared a report about the Russian army's readiness and how uniformed leaders everywhere were battling critical budget and personnel shortages. The obstacles the Siberian District deputy commander was facing made the problems of his visiting US counterpart seem small by comparison. Russian commanders and their troops operated their own farms in the summer to ensure fresh food was available for everyone and their families, and in the winter, troops shoveled coal from railcars to army trucks to provide heat to barracks, offices, and apartments. During the winter before our visit, newly privatized Russian electric companies routinely shut off electrical power to government agencies in Siberia, including the military, because they were unable to pay their bills. When utility companies turned off power to missile and nuclear sites, it raised the objections of not only Russian commanders but also officials in Washington, who were concerned that disgruntled troops in nuclear units might respond by selling off their weapons or abandoning them—a terrorism nightmare. As a result, power was quickly restored to missile and nuclear units. But less strategic units like infantry and tank divisions in the district had no advocates beyond their commanders and sometimes languished for weeks without power. In some cases local military commanders raided electric plants and occupied the buildings until power was restored.

I recalled a visit to Moscow three months earlier by the chief of the American Army, General Eric Shinseki, to his Russian counterpart, General Nikolai

Kormiltsev. Shinseki asked Kormiltsev what his biggest problems were as leader of the Russian army. Trying to put a good face on a dire situation, Kormiltsev said, "Well, we're okay, really, except I could use a little more money and a few more troops." I wondered what Shinseki thought of Kormiltsev's assessment, because those were almost the same words he had used to describe the US Army's condition to his own generals the same year. But the two armies could not have been in more different situations with respect to resources. Kormiltsev was leading a force that was hemorrhaging junior officers and privates on a budget of less than $5 billion, while Shinseki was in charge of an army with nearly 100 percent manning on a budget of over $80 billion.

From the academy classrooms, the deputy commander led our group on foot to a briefing room at the nearby headquarters building, where he confirmed what we already knew about his situation. As we sat through an orientation briefing, it was clear that the once-proud Siberian Command was now relegated to the bottom tier of units, behind the volatile North Caucasus and Western commands, which could claim priority against threats from terrorists and the West. Despite this reality, the commander and his staff continued to plan and execute combat training where it could be afforded. That summer of 2002, the district had managed to raise the level of exercises from company to battalion for the first time in several years. But the officers were upset they still could not afford to maneuver at brigade or division level.

Later that day we also visited one of the troop barracks. The three-story building was 1950s cinder-block construction with open sleeping bays quartering up to fifty soldiers each. Each of the barracks buildings had an arms room with an iron door and large padlocks securing AK-47 rifles and other small-caliber weapons. Each floor had a soldier standing watch against misconduct, theft, or other dangers. In many ways they reminded me of buildings I inherited as a young lieutenant in the mid-1970s at the end of the Vietnam War and the beginning of our switch to a volunteer army. The care and attention to keeping floors polished and walls painted could not completely hide the underlying deterioration of the structures. I felt a kinship with the officers who were saddled with keeping up standards under such advancing conditions. The problem in the US Army was eventually solved by tearing down the structures in the 1980s—either to be rebuilt or left flattened. I imagined that the same solution would be required in Russia's case, if the government would ever commit the funds necessary to fix the problems. Until then, the command would be patching holes as quickly as they could find them.

The realities in this isolated command made me wonder what initiatives American officers would take under similar circumstances. There were many parallels to my first days in our army thirty years earlier. In 1976, we had little money for training or upgrading our 1940s-era barracks, so we often invested in paint where lumber was called for. Duty officers carried loaded weapons for their own security on the weekends because of the indiscipline among troops caused by drugs and racial tension. Pay and morale were low, and it was difficult to imagine that things could improve. Yet, some officers found ingenious ways to motivate and train their troops on little more than the money they could pool among themselves. Most of us at least made the best of what we had and muddled through. Under such conditions, initiative is highly valued, and I am convinced that the initiative required in an army of few means is greater than that required for a well-resourced army.

The situation reminded me of another meeting I had on a train with a Russian lieutenant colonel who had commanded a unit in the troublesome Caucasus before the breakup of the Soviet Union. "I know that you Americans think we Russian officers lack initiative," he told me in Russian as we sat across from each other talking on the train. "Let me tell you what initiative is," he said. "After I arrived to the Caucasus to take command of my tank regiment, I discovered that the supply officer had sold all of my regiment's ammunition on the black market. I had inherited an unarmed unit, and my first inspection was scheduled in thirty days. When the inspectors showed up thirty days later, they found a complete and certified ammunition stockpile. That's initiative."

The colonel's story revealed much about the challenges Russian military leaders face. Corruption, a staple of any society, was exacerbated in Russia after the Cold War by the extreme poverty in which military officers found themselves. In the 1990s, general staff officers in Moscow, who went months without pay, would routinely take days off from their official jobs to earn money as salesmen or taxi drivers to support their families. This still goes on in the more remote regions, such as Siberia. It was inevitable that some officials would also take advantage of their positions to sell off any state property they could get their hands on. I remember that in Berlin after the end of the Soviet Union, American servicemen could buy Russian gas masks, uniforms, and even missile components at German flea markets. Officers, like the tank commander above, who violate regulations to remedy crimes by others or take care of troops seem almost virtuous by comparison.

In the two days we spent with the Siberian deputy commander and his staff, it seemed to me that they were more like us than not. They dealt with the same basic problems confronting American military leaders—infrastructure repair, personnel shortages, training and equipment issues, and others—just on a different scale. The leadership we saw under those hardships was generally what one would expect and hope for from American officers.

What we were not shown, however, but has been openly reported in the Russian press, were the situations where officers had succumbed to the pressures of low pay and underresourcing and misused their leadership positions for personal gain. Anna Politkovskaya, a Russian journalist gunned down in 2006 for reporting abuses in the military, wrote a book filled with examples of soldier abuse. The practice is so widespread that it has a name in Russia— *dedovshchina,* which roughly means "grandfathering." But this is far from a nurturing or mentoring grandfatherly relationship. Largely associated with second-year soldiers hazing first-year recruits, it can be brutal. In a particularly egregious case, an officer fighting in Chechnya loaded up his Russian troops in a truck for a work detail but delivered them to Chechen guerrillas in exchange for money. Soldiers who did not then agree to fight for the Chechens were executed by the rebels. According to the Russian Army's chief military prosecutor, soldier abuse continues to thrive in the army. In 2005, over 6,000 soldiers were reported injured as a result of hazing.

The great eighteenth-century Russian general Alexander Suvorov wrote, "There is nothing more precious than a drop of a soldier's blood." How is it that some twenty-first-century Russian army leaders could be guilty of such contrary conduct as *dedovshchina*? The reasons are a combination of harsh living conditions, greed, and human frailty. It may seem impossible to American officers that such abuse could ever arise in our army, but there is no genetic or cultural immunization against human misbehavior. If in Chita I could see similarities between good leadership in both Russia and America, I should not be surprised to someday find common examples of bad leadership. The lesson for American leaders is that the Russians are as capable of good leadership as we are, and we are as capable as they are of bad. Our officers' traditions, training, and responsibilities are similar enough that such choices are not impossible, and American leaders must remain vigilant against them.

A few weeks after the visit to Siberia, I had the opportunity to correct my earlier negative assessment of the training of the young Russian *Kadety* in

Chita. Eating lunch with a visiting US astronaut who was training at Star City, the Russian space complex outside Moscow, I told him I was disappointed with the Russian way of training junior leaders. It seemed too focused on memorization and not enough on the knowledge needed to make good leadership decisions. I asked him what he thought of the Russian training provided to astronauts at Star City. His answer helped me understand the "why" behind leader training in the Russian army.

My friend explained that I needed to see Russian training in the context of the broader Russian environment. When something on a US space shuttle breaks or malfunctions, he said, US astronauts call NASA, report the problem, and NASA tells them what to do. When a Russian cosmonaut discovers a problem in his *Soyuz* capsule, he calls Star City, reports the problem, and tells them what he is doing to fix it. No one in the Russian system knows the equipment or the problem better than the cosmonaut. Through memorization and repetition, he has learned every nut and bolt of his spacecraft. In an emergency in space, when seconds could mean the difference between life and death, the Russian approach to fixing a problem could save lives. The closest analogy in the American military might be the knowledge required of a nuclear submarine commander.

It's acceptable that American Army officers do not know why a radio malfunctions or why an armored vehicle is running poorly, because in our army, which is supported by the world's greatest logistics tail, we don't have to. We simply replace the underperforming "equipment" and drive on. The training we provide our leaders, which focuses more on critical thinking and decision-making than equipment, works for us because of the whole system in which it works. The same reasoning applies to the Russian approach. Working with a logistics tail that is suspect and unreliable, a Russian officer must be able to understand and fix problems without outside help. What is superfluous knowledge to an American officer is vital to a Russian.

The Russian army today is ill-equipped, underpaid, and poorly resourced. And yet, in a second-tier unit, in a remote district, good leadership exists. Maybe it is because of the stark challenges to leaders there that good leadership stands out so noticeably. Russian army officers strive to provide their soldiers with what they need to accomplish their mission and to survive: functioning equipment, fuel, shelter, food, weapons, training, etc. Faced with a lack of support from the center, those officers build their own schools and provide the leadership training that will develop junior leaders out of their own ranks. There are failures and abuses. But many leaders are committed to the mission and aspire to the standard Suvorov set two centuries ago in caring for soldiers.

Perhaps we should have expected as much in the "city of exiles," because it was the Decembrists, rebellious Russian army officers exiled there by the czar in 1826, who established the first schools and transformed the small outpost into a thriving city. Their initiative and leadership is still evident today in the officers serving there.

25

Generational Change

Implications for the Development
of Future Military Leaders

Commandant Paul Whelan

IN THE LAST DECADE, THE raison d'être of the international military environment has experienced a transition in scope and perspective. These changes in military perspective have an impact on the way the military interacts with both the professional and nonprofessional world within which it operates. Employee aspirations and attributes are evolving too. Today's employees exhibit values and aspirations different from their older generational counterparts. Both of these factors conspire to paint an altered and challenging landscape for the practice of leadership and management in the military in future years.

This paper will address the future of military leadership and management within the context of generational change among its management employees. It will outline this future in the context of the new and wider purpose of the Irish Defense Force. It will present current evidence gathered from the science of organizational behavior and management, and contrast this evidence with the model of training and socialization processes that the Irish military currently applies to cadets and newly commissioned officers, or, more appropriately, the military managers of the future.

The Corporate Military

S. C. Sarkesian, a scholar of organization and management, has written that "all professions are corporate in nature."[1] Sarkesian, a former US Army officer, argues that all corporations employ a system of bureaucracy and adhere to specific rules and regulations. He suggests that all professions embrace certain values, ethics, and ideals in the conduct of their business that are unique to each profession. They maintain standards of performance by which they gauge progress. Professions employ and mold their members to share in the common corporate goal of achieving legitimacy of purpose. Sarkesian posits that the modern military, as a profession, is substantially similar in concept to a corporation.[2] The models of practice outlined above could equally apply to the military as they do to a profession such as law or business. However, the understood role of the international military has changed dramatically from the roles that had been defined for it in previous decades. These changes are currently reflected in the international security strategies of both the United States and Europe.[3] These changes have also been acknowledged in the Irish Defense Forces: "One thing that comes up in every discussion is the transformation process that seems to be ongoing in all forces today, and the fact that as transformation is ongoing, the operational demands are increasing and becoming more diverse and complex in nature."[4]

Essentially, the modifications of military purpose have had the effect of moving the military model even closer to that of a professional corporation.[5] For military formations internationally, the possibility and probability of participation in total war has declined. Instead, the prospect of involvement in total war has been replaced by a higher likelihood of joint participation in counterterrorism efforts, low-intensity conflicts, limited wars, high technology information warfare, and a diverse array of peace operations. This new range of missions has brought about a necessary shift in focus for today's military organization. "The emphasis on technology and scientific knowledge has transformed the military from a parochial, inbred instrument of land battle to a highly sophisticated, multifunctional organization closely linked to society."[6] Aligned with these changes of purpose, the military today are working in increasingly active cooperation with an ever-widening range of other military, nonmilitary, and professional organizations. These circles may be political, civil, corporate, or nongovernmental.

The Military's New Professional

A corollary of the organizational changes that are sweeping the cultures of both the corporation and the military is the idea that "employees are changing too."[7] Today's professionals embrace different values, attributes, and aspirations for their working lives when compared to their counterparts in earlier generations. They view the world differently from the way their parents might have viewed it. From an early age, today's generation of young and aspiring employees has recognized and mentally registered the trials and traumas confronted by their parents in an era when economies, politics, employment values, and employment rules were vastly different from today's.[8] They have grown up alongside technology and innovation and, having been exposed to computer technology from a young age, they are comfortable with change and motivated by technological advancement. They are inquisitive. They are generally well traveled.

Through modern approaches to parenting, and through more open and conscientious schooling, today's generation possesses a better understanding and a better acceptance of different cultures, nations, and societies.[9] They therefore possess attributes and values that distinguish them from previous generations. This generation represents the newest entrants to the workplace, and is popularly referred to as "Generation Y."[10]

Personal Perspective

Since my commissioning in early 1991, I have held varied levels of responsibility for the selection, employment, and training of military cadets. I have spent the vast majority of my career training cadets and young officers in both the academic study of flight and in the skilled discipline of military flying itself. In that time I have witnessed a tangible transition in the type of person I am educating. During my early days of instructorship, when training someone to fly, I would always imagine myself in the student's place. By doing so, and by taking due cognizance of his or her capability, personality, and attitude, I felt able to deliver more considered, relevant, and effective instruction. I became more aware of the student's possible reactions, and the fact that these reactions would probably and usually coincide with my adopted position. I therefore became more capable of providing an appropriate response or reaction to situations or problems presented by the student.

As my experience as an instructor progressed, however, I found this process increasingly difficult to apply. I felt that a disconnection was taking place between my students and myself, and that this disparity, at least to me, was based on personality. On mature reflection, the student and I were on diverging paths. I, fixed in my methods and responses, was moving further away from the student as the years passed and the faces changed. The student's attributes, attitudes, aspirations, and outlooks were becoming increasingly different from mine. The younger students were changing, and I remained firmly fixed in my generation, and therefore wedded to my methods of instruction.

The members of this younger generation are different people. They question and challenge professional direction more frequently. They actively seek considered and honest guidance, and despair when none is forthcoming. I learned that newer employees' initial career expectations could be thwarted by meaningless direction from their superiors. I also learned that the psychological contract that exists between employer and employee requires constant and considered attention at the employment entry phase and thereafter. Active and considered employee socialization processes, or "onboarding" efforts, on behalf of the new employer can serve to successfully guide the new employee toward a clearer and more considered approach to their new career.

What Is "Generational Change"?

Generations are defined not by a formal process, but rather by demographers, popular culture, the press and media, and even by the generations themselves. The differences in personality experienced and recognized by organizations in their managers, both young and old, are categorized as "generational." The majority of literature emanating from the discipline of organizational behavior dealing with this topic of generational change is American in origin, and thus applies its focus to a Western style of organizational behavior. While slight discrepancies exist in the identification and categorization of the various generations, delineations have nevertheless been made in the literature that delineates the various generational cohort groups for the purposes of study.

In order to enable clarity of definition, I will begin with the "Silent Generation," as the portrayal of this generation allows more clearly definitive comparisons to be drawn when examining today's generation, Generation Y. Examining the two generations that reside between these extremities allows an appreciation of the evolution of the values attributed to Generation Y.

The Silent Generation
Most analysts date the birth of members of the Silent Generation between 1925 and 1942. Despite some debate about the exact dates, virtually all authors broadly agree on the attributes and values of this cohort group, as its members were influenced by the historical and social conditions of their time.

Essentially, this generation is approaching or has already concluded its working life in the professional world. Some scholars have posited that the Silent Generation was the product of families that lived through the Great Depression, and that they were influenced by the difficulties that their parents faced to treasure employment and to be loyal employees, and by their parents' generation's service in the military during the Second World War to be command-oriented in the way that they managed their employees. The Silent Generation spent their early management careers in a postwar world that rarely, if ever, questioned authority, adhered to rather rigid chains of command, and observed a system of honor, subservience, and reverence for seniority. They are disciplined in that they are willing to accept poor direction, even when they know it to be flawed, and tend to tolerate it silently. They believe resolutely in law and order and are conservative by their nature.

The Baby Boomers

The birth years of the next generational cohort, known as the Baby Boomers, are usually held to be between 1943 and 1964. Particularly in the case of the United States, this generation was born into an era of rebellion and postwar national wealth, and their views were shaped by the emergence of the counterculture in the 1960s, the Vietnam War, and the Watergate scandal, all of which served to call into question established forms of authority. These trends would be mirrored in much of Europe, as in the 1968 student uprising in Paris. For this generation, authority appeared increasingly unreliable, an object of suspicion. They were further influenced by the styles of idealism proffered by emerging leaders such as Martin Luther King Jr. and John F. Kennedy.

According to one group of scholars, this cohort group believes in growth and expansion, take great pride in themselves as professionals, are optimists, are oriented towards teamwork, and have "pursued their own personal gratification uncompromisingly, and often at a high price to themselves and others."[11]

Generation X

The next generational cohort, which has been dubbed Generation X, was born between 1960 and 1980. This generation lacked the experience of growing up through "real" wars that the two generations discussed above experienced. Members of Generation X are described by Zemke as being self-reliant, seeking a work-life balance and placing greater importance on family. Their approach to authority is casual and sometimes skeptical. They also possess a greater level of comfort with technology, having grown up in the computer age. Personal sacrifice for professional work advancement, which was so well practiced by older generations, has relatively little appeal for members of Generation X. "In a nutshell, they distrust hierarchy. They prefer more informal arrangements. They prefer to judge on merit rather than on status. They are far less loyal to their companies."[12]

Generation Y

A fourth group is now in evidence—Generation Y, or the "Millennials," a cohort made up of those born after 1980. This group is now making its presence felt within the professional world. Members of Generation Y are relative newcomers to the workforce, but early indications are that they are highly motivated and actively seek to improve their skills and abilities. They are not averse to questioning authority and, like the members of Generation X, lack permanent affiliation or commitment to their job. Martin et al. describe this generation as one possessed with much aplomb. They are a "generation of new confidence, upbeat and full of self-esteem," perhaps not surprising as they "grew up basking in the 'decade of the child,' a time when humanistic theories of childhood psychology permeated counseling, education and parenting."[13] They state that this period of psychological parenting has taken place under the cloud of isolation brought about by absentee double-income parents, often being raised by nannies or other nonparental caregivers. Generation Y has been brought up in environments that advocate that career-minded parents pursue their professional ambitions, while their children reside within a care environment or fend for themselves, independent of sustained parental presence and interest. By way of replacement, through access to vastly more information than was available to previous cohorts, this generation learns of the world's ills through the proliferation of electronic media.

These four generational dimensions, distinct and complete, are each products of the eras in which they grew up. Their values have been shaped and oriented according to the various political, environmental, and social backdrops to which they were exposed and against which they were raised; in turn, they defend and promote these virtues throughout their working lives. Generations are delineated by major world-historical events, such as the period of the Great Depression, the World Wars, Vietnam, cultural rebellion in the 1960s, the attacks of 9/11, etc. These events redefine ideology and social behavior; they are true "paradigm shifts," in that they reshape and alter people's intellectual approaches to the world.

Questioning Authority

The subject of generational value differences is important in the context of organizational behavior in that it raises questions about generational conflict in management, management employee permanence, socialization processes, and a host of other issues. Sarkesian, writing of the civilianization of the military profession, remarks that it has "taken on the characteristics of a civilian profession, and in doing so has opened itself not only to reassessment and criticism by its own members but also by outsiders."[14] He refers to the organizational conflict that can arise between the older, more traditionalist officer and his younger subordinate. He states: "Traditionalists have a tendency to perpetuate the heroic role of the military, while the more modern and liberal professionals feel that the military must do more than manage violence."[15] Sarkesian highlighted this internal conflict in 1975, at a time when US military focus was still centered on the Cold War.

More recently, an article written by Walter F. Ulmer Jr. for the journal *Parameters* in the United States highlighted the issue again: "A survey sponsored by the Army Command and General Staff College in 1995 found some concerns about leadership and the command climate strikingly similar to those reported in the 1970 Army War College *Study on Military Professionalism*."[16] Ulmer continues, "Many senior service college students in recent classes seem to display more than typical student skepticism about the quality of senior leaders they have observed. Anecdotes about poor leadership, particularly at the field grade and general officer levels, are too persistent to ignore."[17]

In addition to highlighting various levels of dissent regarding elements of seniority, Ulmer in his article suggests that the increase in questioning of authority is linked to organizational changes associated with the modern military. He highlights the organizational qualities required in the officer ranks of today, in addition to the traditional traits and characteristics of leadership. He also notes the civilianization of the military, and calls for more effective work in the management of organizational change.

What both Sarkesian and Ulmer present, albeit only as part of their overall work, is evidence of the increasing tendency to question the viability of leadership and authority by military juniors or subordinates in the modern era. The time of unquestionable honor and reverence for leadership, as described by Conger in his appraisal of the Silent Generation, has passed. The new generations (both X and Y) do not simply accept direction out of obligation, and feel justified in seeking qualification, clarification, and justification for the orders they are given.

This questioning tendency is further developed in an article by Catherine Loughlin and Julian Barling. They suggest that "Many young workers do not attach the same status to authority as previous generations, and there is now a pervasive cynicism about leadership and leaders."[18] It could be contended that "cynicism" in this context is a little harsh. It is possible that, through questioning, conflict and contradiction may emerge in the authority figure's qualifications, which in turn may disappoint the expectations of the questioner.

Practical Implications for Organizations

Kakabadse et al. state: "The idea of a lifelong career in one company, quite common in the past, seems increasingly remote today." Today's new employees "develop new competencies and stay with an organization only as long as they find it challenging."[19] So what acknowledgement should organizations today make in recognition of the newer generational employee?

In his research paper and case study written on the generational implications of organizational behavior for the Australian Defense Forces (ADF), Bradley Jorgensen takes a critical look at the aspects of generational change. He tests the applicability of the hypothesis that generational issues should be accounted for in the design of workplace policy for the ADF. He acknowledges the differing approach to careers taken by Generations X and Y, paying particular attention to their inquisitive nature, their independence, their loyalty, and their skills and expertise in technology. He notes "that intention to leave increases markedly in line with educational attainment."[20] He notes in particular an attribute of the newest generation, in that the Generation Y cohort "values skill development and thrives on [the socialization aspect of] mentoring/coaching" and that, "like the Generation X cohort, they are motivated to do work but seek more direction and meaning in their work. They are not afraid to question authority, and will challenge management decisions that they deem unreasonable."[21]

This particular study by Jorgensen concludes: "The claims put forward by generational writers regarding the need to manage workforce through generationally-targeted mechanisms lack the necessary rigor on which to base workforce policy decisions. Rather, academic literature appears to support the notion of individualization and tailored measures rather than bulk or generic workforce policy approaches."[22] The recommendations proffered by Jor-gensen, in my opinion, offer sound and qualified judgment.

However, the recommendations may have been made in the knowledge that existing training, management, and socialization techniques in the ADF already calculate to a large extent for generational difference. The reference to "individualization" is important, as it raises the issue of the socialization and mentoring of employees both on and after initial employment. This is the pe-riod during which notional expectations of employment on the part of both the employer and the employee are either confirmed or undermined, and may present a valuable tool toward determining employee career dedication and career permanence.

Ulmer states that, in relation to the US military, there presently are "no highly visible, heavily resourced efforts to define, inculcate and monitor the creation and sustainment of organizational climates that challenge, inspire, and motivate all ranks."[23] According to Ulmer, the practice of mentoring in the military is restricted to the annual "Officer Efficiency Report," which he finds to be insufficient. Organizational best practices in the area of "develop-mental feedback and monitoring," he concludes, have left the military behind.[24]

The Socialization Process

In essence, the aforementioned body of literature provides an overview of the change in the military's approach to the newer generations (X and Y) and their employment. These generational cohorts utilize a different approach to authority than their predecessors, the Silent Generation and, to a lesser ex-tent, the Baby Boomers. Issues of generational conflict are highlighted in the wish by newer generations to constantly seek direction, qualification, and purpose from their employers. This quest, from my own experience, is con-ducted unashamedly and with ample merit.

One method of guiding new employees through the mist of the first stages of a new position is through the utilization of considered socialization tech-niques. Socialization, whether consciously or not, is a method used by the Irish Defense Forces to extend the training acquired through the Cadet School and apply this training to employment practice. While socialization within the Irish military is not currently a discretely identified process after a cadet's commissioning—that is, it is not monitored or controlled by any training or management body—it can and does form a vital component of the individual's induction into the organization. It also makes a definite and lasting impression upon the employee.

As stated at the beginning of this paper, military employees are involved now more than ever with a widening circle of military, non-military, and civilian organizations.[25] The emphasis of such contact has shifted away from one directed toward purely military objectives. This diversification of professional contact requires that military officers and personnel be equipped professionally with the wider relationship skills required for such associations. Effective socialization processes through peer or superior mentoring can serve to foster and develop appreciation of the skilled requirements of diplomacy.

Through socialization, the initial expectations of the employee are tested against the reality of the job, and a tentative adjustment in attitude and behavior can then take place.[26] Initial military training falls under the category of "divestiture" in socialization terms.[27] Through divestiture, one tries to deny and/or change the identity of the newcomer. There follow, then, two methods of socialization, as proposed by Ardts et al.:

- Institutionalized socialization and personnel instruments
- Individualized socialization and personnel instruments

Institutionalized methods of socialization are selected "when one wants conformist newcomers that have little intention to leave the company, that are loyal and emotionally committed to the organization."[28] This is a method of formalized socialization. The method or program makes use of a mentor or role model, and aims toward the affirmation of the new employee's own identity and quality.

Individualized methods of socialization are selected "when one wants innovative newcomers, and does not want to offer them a job for life, and if one is less concerned about newcomers that are loyal and that feel emotionally attached to the organization."[29] This method does not employ a mentor to facilitate the process. It may be done on an ad hoc basis, without clearly defined steps and without a predetermined time frame.

Allowing that there is no clearly established method or framework of socialization recognized and undertaken by the Irish military after commissioning (with the exception of the AF451, the Officer's Annual Performance Appraisal), it follows that the IDF utilizes individualized socialization methods after the period of initial military training. In theory, then, the employee is allowed to construct their own understanding of the organization based on their own immediate experience, which in an organization as diverse as a nation's military can serve to undermine the previous beliefs and/or career expectations of the employee and thwart their potential for self-actualization.

Indications

The need for a high level of intellectual capability within the military will not diminish. In order to maintain and embellish both its self-image and its image with respect to society—especially while cooperation with society increases in response to a widening of the military's roles—education must be high on the military agenda. The forces of history and societal evolution have presented a new variant of generational cohort who will fulfill the duties of management well into the future. However, Generations X and Y are somewhat fickle cohorts. The psychological requirement for self-improvement exhibited by these generations reflects the motivational theories of Maslow, but qualifies even further the "needs" theories of Alderfer, in that, "If a need is consistently frustrated, an individual 'regresses' to being motivated by lower-order needs that are already being fulfilled to a sufficient degree."[30]

Studies in organizational psychology and behavior have identified the aspirations and values of the new employee/managers of the future, Generation Y. They are an impressive generation. They symbolize the progressive, inquisitive qualities that qualify general evolutionary thought. They require honest and meaningful direction, and they seek it voraciously.

Generation Y's inquisitive nature, however, is amplified by a marked reluctance to simply adhere to direction and authority without question. Direction and authority must be both qualified and justified. This questioning of leadership is readily identified in youth society today, and is equally apparent within the military environment. New generations of employees, while lacking the kind of career permanence that their Silent Generation predecessors possessed, will nevertheless relish organizational systems of training and socialization that serve to satisfy the intangibility of career expectation. Effective and meaningful socialization techniques can serve to assist development processes while diminishing career apathy and unmet expectations among newer employees.

Is it possible, however, that older generations will always view younger generations as being "difficult to deal with," "argumentative," and as "having no persistence," not just in relation to their careers but to all undertakings? The quality of an even, consistent pace has always been associated with older generations, who are thought to prefer to control, manage, and maintain their affairs carefully and deliberately. The converse has always been imputed to younger generations, with the assumption being that they prefer to take risks and seize opportunities as they arise. Criticisms relating to younger generations are not a new phenomenon, and can be traced back (at least) to ancient Egyptian manuscripts. Is it possible, though, that the theories that define generational change are simply an attempt to psychologically categorize what has been known throughout history? Jorgensen posits this possibility in his assessment of generational change effects and their implications for the ADF. In any assessment of generational change, however, credence must be given to the societal and historical background from which the different generations grew. Today's new employees are the products of a society that possesses values that are markedly different from those of their parents.

The previous focus within military organizations on roles that are purely focused on military tasks, narrowly defined, is being quickly replaced by new and widening liaisons that require new levels of professionalism. The lines of demarcation are being rewritten, and as the military diversifies into its new roles, the training and socialization of new employees needs to reflect the levels of managerial professionalism required to meet the military's new missions. Examining the motivations and future expectations of these new employees may provide a valuable insight into the aspirations of the military manager of the future.

The theory of generational change holds that today's employee, a member of Generation Y, displays different aspirations and attitudes in his/her approach to work and life than did members of earlier generations. Do the Irish Defense Forces therefore need to alter their approach to accommodate this difference, in terms of its methods of training and its practices of socialization?

Square Pegs and Round Holes

When reflecting on the lives of past generations, one tends to reflect on the qualities, the characteristics, and the tempo of the era in question. Life almost always appears to have been simpler in the past compared to the present. This simple reflective practice applies to all generations. When I began this thesis, I did so in the assured knowledge that the cohort I had identified, Generation Y, was somehow removed from me psychologically, and that their lives certainly reflected complicated influences that were unknown to me in my own formative years. Would it be feasible or even possible, however, to use an American model of generational delineation as a framework within which to evaluate an Irish generational equivalent in terms of chronological placement, attitudes, and traits? In my journey through the construction of this thesis, I have learned that the practice of attaching concrete rules and codes of behavior to an identified group of people can quickly become problematic. In many ways, deeply demographic studies amplify modern values in teaching us that no single, definitive scientific truth may be applied in its totality to the study of a complete generation. As Ryder summarizes, "It is invalid to transform a proposition about populations into a proposition about individuals."[31] The application, however, of a "simplification of values" that encompasses the expected attributes of a given generation, a generality of traits that distinguish one generation from another, can be constructive in the evaluation of predicted impacts upon society and, through more focused application, upon organizations.

Messages That Motivate

The Irish Defense Forces today coexists with a highly competitive corporate environment in which the institution of human resource management has emerged as an element of critical organizational importance. Human resource management recognizes that today's generation of employees exhibits fundamentally different values and attitudes to those of predecessor generations, and that they bring with them clear and unambiguous intentions for their future. If the IDF has an advantage over corporate career alternatives, it resides in the fact that today's cadet/employee chooses to serve their country in a career that promises and advocates continual challenge. It becomes evident from my research that this challenge is met during cadet training, as exhibited by the assured confidence of cadet participant responses. Developments demonstrated within the cadet training environment and within the socialization methods employed by the Human Resources Section of the Defense Forces, whether intentional or not, have served to meet the needs of Generation Y. The expectation of continued challenge by new cadets is also evident, and it is quietly assumed that the IDF will continuously provide meaning and direction in the form of active and considered socialization processes that will define, support, and nurture these expectations. The Irish military, much like its corporate peers, exists in an environment of changing visions, policies, and objectives. This is particularly true not just in the aims of the organization, but also in the conditions under which it employs and maintains its employees.

The effective propagation of the policies and purposes of the Irish Defense Forces relies on the continued effectiveness of its employees. An enlightened productivity may be achieved if employee potential is considerately nurtured right from the beginning: "The more effective and efficient the socialization, the sooner a newcomer can be productive for the organization."[32] The individualized socialization method currently adopted by the IDF post commissioning does not effectively embrace the dynamism of Generation Y in a way that inculcates and encourages the possibilities that this generation brings to bear. Members of Generation Y require qualified direction that enables the expectations of the organization to be set unambiguously. Once the expectations are set, the organizational goal is clarified, and the ability to measure performance is heightened. If the expectations of the new employee are not frequently clarified and qualified, the resultant ambiguity will disappoint and disillusion the cohort. Members of Generation Y embrace the prospect of challenge in a way that distinguishes them from previous generations, and underpins their choice of career path. According to Grainne Cullen, the attraction towards personal challenge appears more prevalent through interviews among those members of Generation Y who aspire to a career in the military as opposed to a career outside the military.[33] Cullen highlights a surprising statistic from her research, in which she asked sixty cadet applicants what other career path they would pursue if they failed to achieve a cadetship. Almost 50 percent responded that they would pursue an entrepreneurial career path over the more stable and possibly expected civil, security, or banking environments.[34]

Why? The Benefits of Questioning

Members of Generation Y will question everything. This is a natural progression from an upbringing that permits and encourages such inquisitiveness. It is a method through which clarity of purpose is identified and security of purpose is ensured. It is a quality, though, that in an organization such as the military may serve to undermine older views of obedience and respect for authority. However, it is a practice that for this generation assures continued and unabridged application to task. If the ability to openly question orders is removed, so too is the confidence and assuredness of the employee. Through questioning authority, the ability of the employee to confidently dispel ambiguity preserves the motivation to complete the task at hand and confidently justify the resultant product. This questioning trait is not something limited to Generation Y, but rather is a quality that has naturally evolved with society. Older generations may have been more capable of tempering the desire to question, based on the situation and on the audience. Hence, this questioning phenomenon is reasonably new to the military. To Generation Y, however, questioning is a quality that is ingrained within the person, something that life has taught them should be practiced regardless of the weight or authority of the recipient. It is not done out of malice, but rather is well-intentioned and whole-heartedly justified in the eyes of the questioner.

The encouragement of questioning within the military can only serve to improve the transparency and legitimacy of what has traditionally been a hierarchical and bureaucratic structure. It cannot be ignored, though, that the latitude and flexibility that allow such a trait to openly express itself do not survive within the rigid chains of command that embody the military ethos. The military is possibly one of the last remaining organizational structures in which flexibility with regard to the questioning of authority cannot apply through all levels of the hierarchy. One aspect of a changing military, however, resides within the remit of operational planning processes for crisis management operations, in which the active encouragement of questioning ensures that all potential military responses are rigorously tested for every eventuality. The value of questioning in an open environment cannot be underestimated, and creating latitude for its productive employment within the confines of the employee's immediate environment should be embraced. Again, to cite Cullen, it is through questioning authority that one questions the organization, and it is only through questioning the organization that you enable organizational change. A future study based on this generation's progression might allow an evaluation of any correlation that might exist between rapid organizational change and the openness of that organization to employee inquisitiveness. Certainly, organizations today have achieved great success through open promotion of "flatter," less hierarchical management structures that actively encourage such a practice.

It follows that the questioning tendency inherent in Generation Y will be a byproduct of the new employee's attempts to proactively influence their own adjustment to their new work environment. Questioning is a method of self-socialization, which serves to elicit information about the new employee's environment. Studies show that "newcomers who frequently seek information and ask for feedback have more knowledge of the job and of the organization, and are more socially integrated."[35] The employee's formative years within any organization are a hugely important period of adjustment, in which the initial promises of the career are either fulfilled or belied. In organizations that have adopted institutionalized methods of socialization, this is the period where mentoring or coaching is deployed and aimed at "the affirmation of the newcomer's own identity and quality."[36] The indicated expectancy of some form of coaching on and after job commencement by the researched cadet group highlights a desire for methods of socialization that the IDF does not undertake as a formal practice. Coaching and/or mentoring is not a recognized pursuit within the Irish military, and when it is performed, while beneficial, it is entirely unregulated and informal. The annual performance appraisal system remains the sole mechanism whereby employees gain an insight into the level of their own performance against what is required or expected. Coaching and mentoring as a recognized organizational practice can serve to nurture this confident generation's aspirations, dispel ambiguities, and promote the levels of professionalism so strenuously demanded by today's changing military. The practice may serve to bridge the apparent disconnection between older military generations and the new cohort. It will serve to satisfy the insatiable questioning trait, and ultimately promote the career perseverance of members of Generation Y.

Parallel Study Possibilities

A factor that cannot be overlooked when debating the implications of generational change for organizations is whether or not work values remain constant throughout employment, or if in fact they change as employees mature into their chosen careers. Every employee will commence their career with preplanned priorities and aspirations, but do these values change in consonance or dissonance with their employment? Are these values more influenced by generational experiences, or by age and maturation? Does the issue of work-life balance, so important to newer generations, imply that this factor alone will dictate employment values in future years? The issue of the achievement of a balanced lifestyle permeates Irish society today, and has become a necessary focus for the continued viability of commercial organizations. Given the nature and necessarily unique culture of the Irish Defense Forces, what adjustments (if any) can be made to accommodate the future requirements of the IDF's employees?

Conclusion

The Irish Defense Forces places great emphasis on the procedures and mechanisms employed in the recruitment and selection of prospective officers. The selection process is both rigorous and demanding, and is designed to identify those persons who possess the myriad qualities that define the ethos of military leadership and management. The process produces that small percentage of those persons who display the desired requirements, the "cream of the crop," as it were. The career motivations of today's generation are generally more focused and calculated than those of previous generations. The successful lure resides within the career that offers diversity and consistency of challenge. The attraction is not the safe and secure pensionable job that provides a reasonably comfortable refuge in less economically prosperous times. The problem now for the military consists in the maintenance of that challenge on and after commissioning. Career permanence is not as powerful a value as it once was. Thus, it is the retention of the engagement of the employee that now more than ever defines the challenge for the Irish Defense Forces.

It can be argued that youthful exuberance and motivation will always indicate a desire to change occupational course when occupational challenges fail to materialize. Certainly, as generations progress and mature, and their familial and financial responsibilities increase, their values may change, and occupational security can become paramount. Today's society, however, advocates occupational change as a natural matter of course. The robust state of the Irish economy has allowed the employee to become a valuable commodity, to be traded and upgraded across the spectrum of career opportunities that present themselves. Furthermore, previous studies have illustrated that "work values are more influenced by generational experiences than by age and maturation."[37]

As one generation learns from its mistakes, these lessons are passed on to the next generation. The ideal for all generations, though, is to ultimately achieve the "life fully worth living."[38] The members of Generation Y represent the workforce of the future. As modern progressive organizations embrace the use of psychological evaluation to assess and understand the motivations of their employees, and then seek to exceed them throughout their careers, so too should the military. In an age where the challenges facing the Irish Defense Forces are diversifying, the requirement to embrace employee values that in turn thrive on challenge is paramount to the successful achievement of organizational vision. Generation Y will meet and even exceed these challenges in an environment that recognizes, respects, and accedes to its needs.

Notes

1. S. C. Sarkesian, *The Professional Army Officer in a Changing Society* (Chicago: Nelson Hall Publishers, 1975), 9.

2. Ibid., 10.

3. See George W. Bush, *The National Security Strategy of the United States of America* (Washington, D.C.: The White House, 2002), 13; and *European Security Strategy* (2002), 3.

4. Lt. Gen. J. Sreenan, transcript of speech presented to the 62nd Command and Staff Course, The Curragh, County Kildare, Ireland (24 February 2006), 1.

5. Walter F. Ulmer Jr., "Military Leadership into the 21st Century: 'Another Bridge Too Far?'" *Parameters* (Spring 1998): 6.

6. Sarkesian, *Professional Army Officer*, 8.

7. A. Kakabadse, J. Bank, and S. Vinnicombe, *Working in Organisations, The Essential Guide for Managers in Today's Workplace*, 2nd ed. (London: Penguin, 2005), 47.

8. Catherine Loughlin and Julian Barling, "Young Workers' Work Values, Attitudes, and Behaviors," *Journal of Occupational and Organizational Psychology* 74:4 (2001): 545.

9. Ron Zemke, Claire Raines, and Bob Filipczak, *Generations at Work* (New York: AMACOM, 2000), 137.

10. Bruce Tulgan and Carolyn Martin, *Managing Generation Y: Global Citizens Born in the Late Seventies and Early Eighties* (Boston: HRD Press Inc., 2001), xi.

11. Ron Zemke, Claire Raines, and Bob Filipczak, *Generations at Work: Managing the Clash of Veterans, Boomers, Xers, and Nexters in Your Workplace* (New York: American Management Association, 1999), 67.

12. Jay A. Conger, *Winning 'Em Over: A New Model for Management in the Age of Persuasion* (New York: Simon & Schuster, 2001), 9.

13. Tulgan and Martin, *Managing Generation Y*, 4.

14. Sarkesian, *Professional Army Officer*, 14.

15. Ibid.

16. Ulmer, "Military Leadership into the 21st Century," 2.

17. Ibid.

18. Loughlin and Barling, "Young Workers' Work Values, Attitudes, and Behaviors," 551–552.

19. Kakabadse et al., *Working in Organisations*, 46–47.

20. Bradley Jorgensen, "Baby Boomers, Generation X, and Generation Y: Policy Implications for Defence Forces in the Modern Era," *Foresight* 5:4 (2003).

21. Ibid., 4; Tulgan and Martin, cited in Jorgensen.

22. Jorgensen, "Baby Boomers."

23. Ulmer, "Military Leadership into the 21st Century," 6.

24. Ibid.

25. See Sarkesian, *Professional Army Officer*; Ulmer, "Military Leadership into the 21st Century"; and M. Vlachova and L. Halberstat, "A Casual View into the Future: Reform of Military

Education in the Czech Republic," Geneva Centre for the Democratic Control of Armed Forces, Working Paper No. 105 (2003).

26. See Kakabadse, et al., *Working in Organisations.*

27. J. Ardts, P. Jansen, and M. van der Velde, "The Breaking In of New Employees," *Journal of Management Development* 20:2 (2001): 159–167.

28. Ibid., 163.

29. Ibid.

30. See A. H. Maslow, *Motivation of Personality* (New York: Harper and Row, 1954); and C. P. Alderfer, *Existence, Relatedness and Growth: Human Needs in Organizational Settings* (Boston: Free Press, 1972). Quote from Alderfer, cited in M. Morley, S. Moore, N. Heraty, M. Linehan, and S. MacCurtain, *Principles of Organisational Behaviour: An Irish Text,* 2nd ed. (Dublin: Gill & Macmillan, 2004).

31. N. Ryder, "Notes on the Concept of a Population," *American Journal of Sociology* 69 (1964): 459.

32. Ardts et al., "The Breaking In of New Employees."

33. Grainne Cullen, a psychologist working with the Irish Defense Forces, was interviewed by the author. All quotations here and below are taken from the author's records and notes from the interview.

34. Twenty-eight prospective Cadets chose an entrepreneurial career path as their preference should they be unsuccessful in their attempt to join the IDF. The choice of entrepreneur was not listed among the career alternative options, but rather was independently written in under the option "Other Careers."

35. Ardts et al., "The Breaking In of New Employees."

36. Ibid.

37. K. W. Smola and C. D. Sutton, "Generational Differences: Revisiting Generational Work Values for the New Millennium," *Journal of Organizational Behavior* 23 (2002): 379.

38. H. A. Shepherd, "On the Realization of Human Potential: A Path with a Heart," in the *Organizational Behavior Reader,* 7th ed. (Englewood Cliffs, NJ: Prentice Hall, 2001), 146.

26

Leading in the Army After Next

Bernard M. Bass

As the US Army celebrates its 223rd birthday this year [1998], senior Army leaders are already focusing on how the Army After Next might look in the year 2025. As we move into the twenty-first century's "high-tech," information-laden world, leadership principles and practices must be clearly defined and differentiated for junior, senior and strategic leaders. As the author posits, "the principles of leadership do not change; only the conditions in which they are applied." Therefore, "the first priority should be increasing the match between leadership behavior and leadership doctrine."

In discussing leadership requirements for the Army of 2025, I will take into account expectations about the geostrategic setting in 2025 of the Army After Next (AAN), its technology and art, as well as the human and organizational issues it will face. In doing so, I will look at the leadership requirements for AAN readiness for warfighting peer competitors, regional conflicts and low-intensity conflicts (LICs). Then I will attempt to predict leadership requirements of the AAN in winning and maintaining peace.

Several assumptions underlie what I have to say:

The principles of leadership do not change; only the conditions in which they are applied. Over time, we gain a better and more accurate understanding of the concepts and principles, but they were in effect as Initiation and Consideration when Julius Caesar exhorted his troops before storming Alesia— although it took us 1,900 years to refine and measure the concepts.[1]

US Army doctrine has attempted to fit with these principles, changing over time, mainly in interpretations and applications.

Although the principles are the same at all levels, the practices need to be differentiated for junior, senior and strategic leaders.

US Army doctrine has been espousing these principles for more than 220 years of trusting subordinates and earning their trust, respecting them and "engaging their voluntary commitment to the mission by giving them honest and complete information," but the behavior of leaders in the Army has "deviated sharply from policy."[2] For instance, although mentoring of junior officers by senior officers is a well-established principle, 85 percent of junior officers report they only receive their support form for such counseling less than one week before the Officer Evaluation Report is due.[3] So whatever we say about the requirements for leadership in 2025, the first priority should be increasing the match between leadership behavior and leadership doctrine.

The Full Range of Leadership

For discussion purposes, I will use a theory and leadership model that has accounted for effective leadership in the military and elsewhere.[4] However, I will focus on how practices in its application will fit with the needs for leadership in the AAN.

The theory is that of transformational and transactional leadership, and the model of their relationships is the Full Range of Leadership.[5] The theory explains that leaders must mobilize their followers to go beyond their self-interests for the good of the group, organization and society, while building the self-esteem of the followers and keeping in mind their self-interests. The most recent confirmatory factor analysis of 360-degree behavioral assessments of platoon leaders and platoon sergeants suggests that the best fitting model includes the following transformational factors:[6]

Inspirational leadership: Trusted, valued leaders provide meaning and challenge, set examples and envision and articulate attractive goals and futures.

Intellectual stimulation: Leaders help followers become more innovative where appropriate.

Individualized consideration: Leaders attend to the individual needs of their followers as well as the needs of their units.

The transactional factors are as follows:

Contingent reward: Leaders reward followers in exchange for followers carrying out their assignments.

Active management by exception: Leaders monitor followers for deviations and errors and take corrective and disciplinary actions as needed.

Passive leadership: Leaders wait for problems to emerge before correcting, or they avoid taking action.

Effective Warfighting Leadership in 2025

Consistent with previous meta-analyses of military as well as civilian investigations, the profiles of the platoon leaders and platoon sergeants who subsequently lead more effective platoons in Joint Readiness Training Center exercises reveal behaviors earlier in garrison that are more transformational and less transactional or passive.[7] Commanders who are seen as more transformational and less transactional have more constructive self-images, create more feelings of empowerment in their subordinates and higher productivity in their units.[8]

I expect that the same will be true in 2025, although much can be said about how this will be played out in practice in the AAN. It is expected to be an Army which will deploy extremely quickly, be logistically self-sufficient, be intelligence-rich and facile, with instant information about its own and enemy forces and conditions. Personnel will be widely dispersed in the battle— contested ground, air and space above. Units will be small and linked mainly by information to one another and to higher command. Organizations will be flatter than today's. These fast-moving, highly maneuverable units will have great firepower.[9]

Given the changing nature of information technology, I suspect that today we are likely to greatly underestimate the state of the art in 2025. The flow of information upward, sideways and downward is likely to be timely, precise, accurate and open to immediate feedback with computerized support for prioritizing and analyzing. Much of the information flow will be by voice input and output and secure against enemy penetration and viruses. It would be expected that all combatants will be briefed on objectives, goals and expectations on a continuing basis. They would be part of, and be participants in, information processing, tactical thinking and mission accomplishment. Individualized consideration would be at a premium in the need to be ready for instant feedback from above, laterally and below. Information overload and enemy infiltration would be problems for leaders to monitor and control. Risk of our soldiers being captured with too much information to be squeezed out beyond rank, name and serial number would also be a problem to be resolved. Leaders would need to know ways around system disruptions and glitches. They would also have to be able to quickly adjust minion plans and orders to maintain progress toward mission achievement in a dynamic, tactical environment. These are just a few examples of the overriding need for individualization in leadership.

In 2025, the Army will be in transition from the legacy of Army XXI to AAN, and integration will call for individualized consideration. Such consideration would also be needed in integrating efforts in the joint service environment and with allied forces. In general, individualized consideration, as well as transformational leadership, would be important in establishing and maintaining the cohesiveness needed for success.[10]

Leadership and Unit Cohesiveness

Cohesiveness encompasses both horizontal social bonding among peers and vertical social bonding of superior and subordinates based on the development of trust and interdependence.[11] Strong evidence points to the contribution of all three factors of transformational leadership to such cohesion. Within the cohesive team, inspirational members set examples for others and foster acceptance of mutual goals. Intellectually stimulating members build on one another's ideas and develop a sense of ownership in solutions to problems. Team cohesion is further strengthened when members are individually considerate and show they care for one another.

Just as team cohesion depends upon the leadership displayed within the team by the different team members, so we see a strong connection between the leadership displayed by the formal group leader and the loyalty, involvement, commitment and attraction to the unit of its members. By providing meaning, challenge and a role model of confidence and determination, inspirational leaders help to promote identification and internalization of cohesive values and beliefs in their unit. Intellectually stimulating leaders encourage better use of resources and contributions to solutions to problems, thereby increasing feelings of worth and confidence in the unit led. Individually considerate leaders likewise increase subordinates' sense of self-worth, enhancing positive feelings toward the unit and its leaders.

Researchers P. T. Bartone and Faris R. Kirkland have shown how the critical leadership required for developing unit cohesiveness can be seen in stages from the new unit to the fully developed one.[12] Leaders should be commended for the extent they are able to develop such cohesiveness in their units and supported by personnel policies that avoid unnecessary transfers and replacements. The effective orientation and integration of new members into old teams is an important, individually considerate leadership competence.

Cohesion is a double-edged sword. It is a strong predictor of unit effectiveness when there is an alignment of the goals of the unit and the goals of the organization. But it can also be a strong predictor of the opposite. When the goals of a cohesive unit are opposite to those of the organization, the stage is set for sabotaging the organization. Effective leaders attend to the positive alignment of unit and organization goals. The seamless flow envisaged of arrival into the theater of war of forward-presence forces, early-arriving light forces and later-arriving heavy forces requires such positive alignment of all involved. It goes without saying that the AAN will require cohesive units and mature leadership.[13]

Decentralization

In industry, we have seen a sharp increase in decentralization that, at the extreme end, has produced the self-managed team. Such decentralized operations are envisioned for AAN to provide the tactical speed and agility to win battles. "Professional trust and confidence between leaders and led" will be essential.[14] At the organizational level, flexible architectures will need to be designed of self-contained units that can be detached for missions in isolation, then re-formed quickly and reintegrated into larger units. The speed and tempo of future battle will require flattened organizations with fewer echelons in the chains of command. This in turn will move leaders at the different echelons to rely more on active "managing by exception" to accommodate the larger number of direct reports. They will be helped by computerized decision support systems for situational analyses, coordination, communication, command and control. But it will also mean that they should be increasing the authority, flexibility and freedom of action they delegate to subordinates who, in turn, will keep their leaders fully informed about discretionary actions.

Delegation from one echelon to the next one below it is 100 percent when those at the lower level are organized into self-managing teams. It is totally absent when all actions at the lower echelon require orders from higher authority. A central theme for future AAN research should be "to what extent could every individual become involved in leadership functions?" Does shared responsibility mean that no one is responsible? Can every soldier be trained and ready to take on one or more of his leader's roles when he sees the role is needed but missing? What would the roles be for doing so? How much could current leader roles be delegated? How much self-management could be introduced into the squad, platoon or company? There is an evident trend in the Army to push decision making downward. For example, a tube-launched, optically tracked, wire-guided (TOW) team leader, a junior noncommissioned officer, now makes decisions that a captain made in World War II.[15]

In all our wars, the American soldier's individualism has been both a curse and a blessing to their leaders. There has always been a pervasive suspicion of authority and a resultant resistance to discipline.[16] But as S. L. A. Marshall pointed out, our European Allies in World War I could not believe how rapidly we could train and supply our own platoon leaders with "thirty-day wonders" because of the trait of initiative built into the American culture.[17] Researchers R. Ernest and Trevor N. Dupuy added that our soldiers were self-reliant and combined imagination with intelligence, often making it difficult for their leaders to stay one "mental jump" ahead of them.[18]

Teleteams

We are already seeing the teleteam in operation. The teams are connected by electronic mail (E-mail), facsimile (FAX) and telephone and do not meet face-to-face. We know little about how to lead such teams. As someone trying to do so, I can list some of the questions I have had in the process: How confident and certain should I be before sending out a controversial E-mail message that is irretrievable and about which I can only guess at the reactions? How much can I and should I encourage all-channel networking? How do I ensure as much two-way communication as possible and avoid too much one-way communication? How do I decide who needs to know what? How often am I kept out of the loop when team members interact with one another? What is the best mix of E-mail, FAX and telephone? How do I deal with the fact that some members respond immediately to questions, while others take a week or more?

Teleteams can be combined with group decision support systems (GDSS) to give teleteam leaders rapid collection and merging of proposals and consensus about priorities and evaluations. Teleteams and GDSS are likely to provide the necessary linkages among the isolated, logistically self-contained AAN units and individuals on future battlefields. All echelons will need to be trained and experienced in using GDSS and given practice in simulation exercises.

Conceptual Skills

Based on his analyses of cognitive and personality data of generals, D. P. Campbell noted that as a group they were in the 95th percentile in intelligence compared with the population as a whole.[19] They were extremely dependable, socially mature, alert to moral issues, competitive and action-oriented. At the same time, they were more conventional and less innovative than civilian executives in dealing with problems. If this is commonly true for other ranks as well, the Army should place a high priority on leadership that is intellectually stimulating and on selection and training of cognitive skills promoting innovative thinking.

Subordinates will need to be able to follow orders with "intelligent compliance." The union of knowledge and speed will obviously increase the demand for decisive, transformational leadership, highly coordinated communications, keen diagnostic abilities and a buildup of intuition based on attention to and recall of a variety of relevant past learnings and experiences. A balance will need to be sought between the purely rational approach to problem solving and the intuitive. The emotional will need to be factored into intellectual solutions as well.

Martin Van Creveld has argued that postgraduate military education does not necessarily enhance command ability.[20] Perhaps some of what is missing is the education in how to balance the rational and the intuitive.

Increasingly, team effort is sought—requiring leaders with the cognitive skills to develop their subordinates into teams. To do this, the leaders need the cognitive skills required to function effectively as good team players.

The technological availability of instant information suggests that research is needed on how more open communications could be made across echelons in the chain of command without jeopardizing coordination or introducing conflicts in messages and threats to authority and responsibility. Strengthened feedback loops, coupled with computerization to deal with overload, would be required. With the greatly increased use of manned and unmanned aerial vehicles for intelligence, firepower, logistics and communications, the spatial visualization of the 3-D battlefield will become as important a cognitive skill to the tactical commander as it is to the engineer. "Quickening" enables the underwater "flying" of submarines by presenting the pilot with a computerized display of what lies ahead to permit advance maneuvering of the submarine. Analogously, I would expect that some form of such quickening will be provided tactical commanders to assist rapid decision making and communication of decisions.

Assessment and Training for AAN Leadership

"The mature leaders leading cohesive groups" envisaged in the AAN call for assessment and training that increases transformation leadership and reduces passive management by exception and laissez-faire leadership among leaders and teams.[21] Already developed are online 360-degree interactive feedback systems that could be tailored for use by leaders at all command echelons. Online feedback could also be added for senior leaders about the platoons, companies and battalions under their command. Strategic leaders could also receive online feedback about the units under their command. They could also receive online feedback from civilian "clients," civilian peers and politicians.

Although technology such as the MILES program at the National Training Center, Fort Irwin, California, can provide objective data about the hits, misses and "casualties" sustained by platoons, companies and battalions, research is needed on the conditions under which the data could be used convincingly as criteria to evaluate assessment and training.

Researchers B. Shamir and E. Ben-Ari have already laid out many aspects of leadership for Army XXI that will continue to be true for the AAN: tele-leadership, telemedicine, cultural pluralism, flattened organizations, loosely coupled structures, professionalism and teamwork, just to name a few.[22] They expect that respect, loyalty, identification, competence, self-control, inspiration and personal example will be as important tomorrow as it is today.

Shamir and Ben-Ari argue for a generalized theory of leadership that transcends contingencies.[23] They presaged that, as I previously proposed in 1997, the concepts and principles of the Full Range of Leadership are universal, although they may be expressed in differing ways across organizational and national boundaries.[24]

Leaders are born and made. A strong genetic component has been unearthed in a number of personality traits, such as the absence of shyness, which correlate with leader behavior. Even more significant is finding that as much as half the variance in the components of self-assessed transformational and transactional leadership can be accounted for by heredity according to a private communication from Tony Vernon. A large-scale analysis was proposed of a 360-degree study of leaders.[25]

On the one hand, genetic profiling will be commonplace by 2025. On the other hand, its application to selection will remain an ethical question. It will be seen as discriminatory against some individuals, for such screening will deny them opportunities as victims of "unmodifiable characteristics." But this is already done with individuals who are shorter than minimum height, which, unlike an individual's weight, is unmodifiable. It is expected that such standards, which cannot be met through development, will have to be reexamined periodically. For instance, chronological age limitations may need to be raised to fit the increasing size and physical fitness of our aging population.

Other Ethical and Moral Issues

Shortening the time available for decisions will increase the difficulties of ensuring that the ethics and morality of decisions are maintained. M. O. Wheeler, writing about current conditions, suggested that "in combat environments, there is usually some reasonable delay between the giving and the carrying out of an order."[26] This interval allows some time for reflection upon the order, and reflection may produce a concern for the order's rationale. Why was the order given? "What purpose does the order seek to obtain?"[27] Because of the dramatic speed of action on the AAN battlefield, decisions may be made and orders carried out that, after the fact, may be regretted as immoral. It will help if soldiers' information processing and response skills, including ethical aspects, are developed and internalized for engagement in the hyperbattle environment.

Author L. S. Sorley suggests that younger officers often have more of an ethical sense than their seniors because seniors are more likely to have been affected by corruption in the system.[28] If this is true, then attention must be paid to remedial work on the systematic sources of unethical behavior. Moral beliefs in the value of life may be sorely tested in the AAN when going up against suicide bombers or ten-year-old children armed with assault rifles. Enemy forces that refuse to surrender, even when in hopeless situations, will have to be dealt with firmly.

AAN personnel at all echelons will be reasonably well educated and may balk at involvement in LICs or regional conflicts in which no vital US interests are at risk. As with Vietnam, their reluctance may also be reinforced by the media and the unpopularity of US involvement. Our AAN military leaders may need to be prepared to deal with conducting actions in which AAN personnel find it unjustifiable.[29]

Multiple Goals

Charles C. Moskos and J. Burk listed the varied missions of US forces during just a twenty-one-month period between April 1991 and December 1992. They included refugee relief in Kurdistan, flood relief in Bangladesh, volcano rescues in the Philippines, observer forces in the western Sahara, rescue of foreign nationals in Zaire, Haitian refugee relief, food relief in Russia, volcano rescues in Sicily, restoring order in south central Los Angeles, famine relief in Somalia, hurricane disaster relief in Florida, surveillance in Iraq, hurricane disaster relief in Hawaii and peace-keeping (PK) in Somalia.[30] Since then, we have seen the Army engaged in such varied missions as combating the drug cartels of Colombia, patrolling the border with Mexico to reduce illegal immigration, and PK in Bosnia, as we continue to do in the Sinai.

It is clear that in 2025, Army units are likely to be employed much more in such varied work than in combat. Nevertheless, the units must be kept ready through training and retraining as the world's most powerful deterrent force and for rapid entry into combat when necessary.[31]

Winning the Peace

The goal of warfighting is usually couched in terms of bringing force, or the fear of it, to bear on the enemy so that its will to resist is broken. But this can be seen as intermediate to the ultimate goal of establishing a lasting peace with the former enemy—be they rogue governments or illegitimate terrorist organizations. Although such a peace will depend much on the new relations that are established between the previously warring enemies, it will also depend on the military forces' behavior during the conflict. As they bring force and fear to break the will to resist, they can also bring the promise of a just peace that is more attractive than continued fighting.

At the start of the Mexican War in 1846, Brigadier General Stephen W. Kearny was ordered to lead his Army of the West of 300 regulars and 2,400 militia from Fort Leavenworth, Kansas, south to seize what is now New Mexico and then move on to take California. He faced 3,000 Mexican troops waiting for him en route to Santa Fe. Kearny sent an emissary ahead who convinced the Mexicans that he was coming down with an overwhelming larger force, so they moved out without a battle.

Kearny was determined to win the peace with a people he had just conquered. They were of a different language, traditions and religion, who had been living in the territory for almost 250 years. The figure is an excerpt from what he proclaimed to the assembled populace in Las Vegas, New Mexico.

Kearny won popular support by a promise of democratic government. The Kearny Code, based on translation and codification of Mexican provincial laws, became the basis of law in New Mexico. He left a supportive populace behind when his expedition moved on to take California. If he had concentrated on only destroying the will to resist, he could readily have alienated the population and set back the integration of Hispanic New Mexico into the United States for many years. Kearny clearly kept his eye on using his force to win the peace. He exhibited the political sensitivity, intellectual awareness and familiarity with the norms, mores and culture of the environment in which he was operating, characteristics which Shamir and Ben-Ari see as needed by military leaders who must span the boundaries from their organization to negotiate effectively with civilian populations in their midst.[32]

The Mexican War provides an even better example in the contrast between the actions of General Zachary Taylor and General Winfield Scott. One alienated the local populace, hardening the fighting, while the other attracted their support, smoothing the path to victory and peace.

The transformational/transactional profile of the most effective leaders in warfighting does not necessarily match the profile of the most effective leaders in "peace winning." Although transformational leadership will still be more effective than contingent reward, and active managing by exception will be more effective than passive leadership in both warfighting and peace winning, peace winning may call for more intellectual stimulation and individualized consideration; warfighting may place a greater premium on inspirational leadership and idealized influence. Contingent reward and management by exception may be reflected in different behaviors in warfighting and peace winning.

Individualized consideration is involved in taking special actions to deal with local feelings. Given wide media coverage, the actions may become the basis of a change of attitudes in a whole population. Kearny's promises of religious freedom and maintaining support of local authority are examples.

Contingent reward occurs in peace-winning negotiation of rewards for compliance. Thus, Kearny promised protection for allegiance to him.

Management by exception is required to win the peace. Order must be reestablished. Discipline must be maintained, but peace winning works best when it emphasizes the positive as in contingent reward and transformational leadership, but Kearny's threat to hang secret armed opposition emphasizes that disciplinary cautions have their place.

Laissez-faire leadership and passive management by exception remain contraindicated in both warfighting and peace winning.

As PK competes with warfighting for the AAN's services, preparation will be needed at all echelons for the different, sometimes opposite roles required. Instead of keeping one's head down and concealing one's presence in military conflicts, it will be necessary to learn to keep one's head up and to advertise one's presence as a peacekeeper. Overlearning these opposite skills will be required for the appropriate rapid reaction in either war or peace conditions.

When called upon to pacify a population, AAN will need to be prepared to work with police to seek out local rabble-rousers. Equally important will be the need for the AAN to learn how to convert enemies into friends. The reemergence of Japan and Germany after World War II as US allies contrasts sharply with the call for revenge by the French for forty-five years after the Franco-Prussian War. The Japanese, the Germans and the French all had been subjected to humiliating defeat, but the different outcomes following victory were partly due to the differences in behavior of the military victors. It is partly a matter of how US military leaders at all levels contrasted with their German counterparts, particularly as occupying forces. Villages all over Serbia have museums displaying the photographs of their civilians massacred by the Germans and Croats during World War II. The Croats and Serbs remain at each other's throats. While the US Army brought about peace in the American West with our Native Americans by almost destroying them, in recent confrontations and occupations, the record is mixed. Historical research may be useful in showing how American service personnel and the Army as a system behave in ways that contribute to winning the peace.

Currently, there is one Active Component civil affairs (CA) battalion and four Reserve Component battalions. The AAN would need to attach increased importance to the CA role, particularly in joint training exercises with combat units. CA will need to be in a position to perform joint operations with combat units, for instance, to provide both the "carrots and sticks" in counterterrorism missions. Such joint efforts characterized the British and Australian success in defeating the guerrillas in Malaysia in the 1950s.

When warfighting's objective is eliminating the enemy's will to resist, spreading in advance fear and a sense of hopelessness among the enemy will remain important to AAN's arsenal, although fear can often result in unpredictable consequences. If the ultimate objective is winning the peace, it makes sense to spread in advance among the enemy the benefits of avoiding battle and joining rather than fighting US forces. Psychological operations and CA will need to be expanded in resources, planning, scope and readiness, with more complete integration training and operations with combat units. The power of television, radio, the Internet and communication forms yet to be invented will need to be exploited much more than is possible today. More local culture specialists will need to be trained and ready to serve in the world's perceived hotspots. Relations between combat and CA personnel at all levels of command will need to be practiced to make for seamless operations. Warfighting and peace winning will need to be factored into strategies and tactics. AAN must avoid winning the war but losing the peace, but at the same time not incurring additional costs and casualties in doing so.

Priorities

In looking ahead to 2025, we certainly are not preparing for the last war. However, particularly in an era of stable or declining budgets, we have to take care in how we allocate our resources to preparations for LICs, regional conflicts and the threat from a newly emerging belligerent power. The probabilities are high for future LICs, intermediate for regional conflicts and low for the emergence of a peer power. Even at the height of the Soviet Union's perceived power in 1984 to engage us in a war, 88 percent of 257 US generals and admirals thought such a war was most unlikely to occur. But the threats to our national security of LIC, regional, or "great" power conflicts is in reverse of their probabilities of occurrence.

Taking into account both the probability and severity of the threat to security, it would seem that we need to give about equal priority to be ready for all three possibilities. We should seek ways to develop multipurpose tools, techniques, training and organizations. An example would be highly trained, easily transported light infantry with air support and CA capability to combat the high probability of future banditry and terrorists as well as the lower probability of regional and global conflicts. Such infantry could also be the backbone of diplomatic and economic missions to peacefully settle disputes within and between nations. These active force units would provide the "roots on which to graft: mobilization forces" and would be targeted against predictable threats. They could be combined rapidly into larger units as needed. Reserve Component units would be readied for unforeseen contingencies. Leaders and their units will need to be as flexible, adaptive, innovative and intellectually agile as transformational leaders and transformational teams would be.

To conserve our own forces, we should continue supporting alternatives to using our own troops to intervene in conflicts, particularly when their outcomes are not vital to our national interests. For instance, we should continue to help train a pan-African force for such interventions in the disruptions that plague the continent. At the same time, such training must avoid the creation of antidemocratic military elites such as occurred in El Salvador. High priority will have to be given to working with allied forces in joint actions. AAN will need to be ready to learn from its allies as it shares its skills with them.

Diversity

With the continued movement toward sex equality and the continued increase in the percentage of persons of color in the US population, women will engage in more diverse roles than they do today, and units will be more multiethnic and multiracial than today. Advances in tools, training and technologies, as well as further social change, may see women in the infantry. We are likely to see women in combat roles and in a variety of additional combat support services such as flying reconnaissance aerial vehicles.

The entry of large numbers of Asian Americans into higher education, particularly "high-tech" education, may result in an increasing number entering the officer corps and technical career specialties within the military. Similarly, by 2025, Hispanics will be the largest US minority. We should see larger numbers in the Army if they, constituting the largest per capita Medal of Honor winners for an ethic group, continue their tradition of seeing military service as consistent with their macho values and as the way out of the barrios. The Army should remain attractive to African Americans, and we should see more at higher officer levels.

In all, AAN is likely to be less white in 2025, mirroring what will have occurred in the general US population. Learning to lead and work in multiethnic, multiracial and mixed-sex groups will be of great significance to AAN readiness. Similarly, mandatory retirement ages may be raised to accommodate the increasing numbers and better health of older citizens.

Whatever elitism the service academies might introduce into the AAN officer corps is likely to be diminished further, either with the possible abandonment of the academies or the increasing roles of the universities in providing the corps with more broadly educated leaders with more diverse developmental and community experiences.

In looking ahead twenty-seven years, other questions remain. Are we tending to solve today's problems, not the problems of 2025? For instance, twenty-seven years hence, will we find that the antiheroism featured in so much of the media enterprise has eroded many of the values important to leadership? Can leadership as we now know it, with its recognition of the importance of respect, decisiveness and direction, be sustained in a world dominated by glorification of underclass values? Will our future development of leaders be handicapped by less devotion to our civil duties than to our civil rights? How much will self-management take root in civilian life, and how will it affect military organization? What will be the effects of the world's rapidly growing urbanization on the AAN? How will recruiting be affected by the sharply rising obesity and "junk food" nutrition of today's American children? What will be the effect of the movement by more women and minorities into positions of senior and strategic leadership in the AAN? Will we see strong mainstream backlashes?

As we approach the millennium, we are transiting rapidly into the postindustrial information age. Information is expandable, compressible, substitutable, transportable, diffusible and shareable. It is not necessarily a scarce resource. As a consequence, it will affect leader-follower relations in ways yet unseen. Leader-follower relations will become increasingly fluid rather than fixed in a person or position, making it difficult to capture what lies ahead for the leaders and the led.

PROCLAMATION OF BRIGADIER GENERAL STEPHEN W. KEARNY
TO THE PEOPLE OF LAS VEGAS, 15 AUGUST 1846

Mr. Acalde, and people of New Mexico I have come amongst you by the orders of my government to take possession of your country. . . . We come as friends—not as enemies; as protectors, not as conquerors. We come among you for your benefit not for your injury. Henceforth, I absolve you from all allegiance to the Mexican government, and from all obedience to General Armijo. He is no longer your governor. I am your governor. I shall not expect you to take up arms and follow me to fight your own people, who may oppose me; but I now tell you that those of you who remain peaceably at home, tending to their crops and herds, shall be protected by me in their property, their persons and their religion. Not a pepper nor an onion shall be disturbed or taken by my troops without pay or by the consent of the owner. But listen! He who promises to be quiet and is found in arms against me, I will hang.

From the Mexican government you have never received protection. The Apaches and Navajos come down from the mountain and carry off your sheep, and even your women, whenever they please. My government will correct all this. It will keep off the Indians, protect you and your persons and property and, I repeat again, will protect you in your religion. I know you are all great Catholics; that some of your priests have told you all sorts of stories that we would mistreat your women and brand them on the cheek as you do your mules on the hip.

It is all false.

My government respects your religion as much as the Protestant religion, and allows each man to worship his Creator as his heart tells him best. The laws protect the Catholic as well as the Protestant, the weak as well as the strong, the poor as well as the rich. I am not a Catholic myself; but at least one-third of my army are Catholics. I respect a good Catholic as much as a good Protestant.

There goes my Army—you see but a small portion of it; there are many more behind; resistance is useless. Mr. Acalde and your two captains of militia, the laws of my country require that all men who take office under me shall take the oath of allegiance. I do not wish, for the present, until affairs become more settled, to disturb your form of government. If you are prepared to take oaths of allegiance I shall continue you in office and support your authority.

Notes

1. B. M. Bass, *Leadership, Psychology and Organizational Behavior* (New York: Harper, 1960).

2. F. R. Kirkland, "Leadership Policy and Leadership Practice: Two Centuries of Foot-shooting in the US Army," *Journal of Psychohistory* 13 (1991): 317.

3. Lt. Gen. T. G. Stroup Jr., "Leadership and Organizational Culture: Actions Speak Louder Than Words," *Military Review* 76, no. 1 (January/February 1996): 44–49.

4. Bass, *Transformational Leadership: Industrial, Military and Educational Impact* (Mahwah, NJ: Lawrence Erlbaum & Associates, 1998); Bass, "Does the Transactional/ Transformational Leadership Paradigm Transcend Organizational and National Boundaries?" *American Psychologist* 52 (1997): 130–139.

5. Ibid.; Bass, *Leadership and Performance Beyond Expectations* (New York: Free Press, 1985).

6. Bass and B. J. Avolio, *Platoon Readiness as a Function of Transformational Transactional Leadership, Squad Mores and Platoon Cultures* (Alexandria, VA: US Army Research Institute for the Behavioral Sciences, contract DASWOI-96K-008, 1997).

7. K. Lowe, K. G. Kroeck, and N. Sivasubramaniam, "Effectiveness Correlates of Transformational and Transactional Leadership: A Meta-Analytic Review," *Leadership Quarterly* 7 (1996): 385–425; Avolio and Bass.

8. R. J. Masi, "Transformational Leadership and Its Roles in Empowerment, Productivity, and Commitment to Quality" (PhD diss., University of Illinois at Chicago, 1994).

9. "Knowledge & Speed," annual report on the Army After Next Project to the Chief of Staff of the Army, Washington, DC, Department of the Army, July 1997.

10. Bass, *Transformational Leadership*.

11. P. T. Bartone and Kirkland, "Optimal Leadership in Small Army Units," in R. Gal and A. D. Mangelsdorff, eds., *Handbook of Military Psychology* (New York: John Wiley & Sons, 1991).

12. Ibid.

13. "Knowledge & Speed," p. 21.

14. Ibid.

15. R. E. Dupuy and T. N. Dupuy, *Brave Men and Great Captains* (New York: Harper & Row, 1959).

16. S. L. A. Marshall, *World War I* (New York: American Heritage, 1964).

17. D. P. Campbell, "The Psychological Test Profiles of Brigadier Generals: War Mongers or Decisive Warriors?" (invited address, American Psychological Association, New York, August 1987).

18. M. Van Creveld, *The Training of Officers: From Military Professionalism to Irrelevance* (New York: Free Press, 1990).

19. "Knowledge & Speed."

20. B. Shamir and E. Ben-Ari, "Leadership in an Open Army: Civilian Connections, Interorganizational Frameworks, and Changes in Military Leadership" (Wheaton, IL: Symposium on the Leadership Challenges of the Twenty-first Century, March 27–29, 1996).

21. Bass, *Transformational Leadership*.

22. Bass, "Leadership and Performance Beyond Expectations" (New York: Free Press, 1985).

23. M. O. Wheeler, "Loyalty, Honor, and the Modern Military," in M. W. Wakin, ed., *War, Morality and the Military Profession* (Boulder, CO: Westview Press, 1979), pp. 179–188.

24. L. S. Sorley III, "Duty, Honor, Country: Practice and Precept," in Wakin, *War, Morality and the Military Profession*, pp. 143–162.

25. Shamir and Ben-Ari, "Leadership in an Open Army."

26. C. C. Moskos and J. Burk, "The Postmodern Military," in J. Burk, ed., *The Military in New Times: Adapting Armed Forces to a Turbulent World* (Boulder, CO: Westview Press, 1995).

27. D. Segal and D. Eyre, *The US Army in Peace Operations at the Dawning of the Twenty-First Century* (Alexandria, VA: US Army Research Institute of the Behavioral and Social Sciences, May 1996).

28. Shamir and Ben-Ari, "Leadership in an Open Army."

29. S. Strasser et al., "Can We Fight a Modern War?" *Newsweek*, July 9, 1984, p. 37.

30. "Security in Focus," *Defense Monitor* 25 (December 1996).

31. J. J. Shanahan, "CDI and the Quadrennial Defense Review," *Defense Monitor* 26 (August 1997): 1–8.

32. H. Cleveland, *The Knowledge Executive: Leadership in an Information Society* (New York: Dutton, 1985).

CREDITS AND ACKNOWLEDGMENTS

Chapter 1

Reprinted from Chapter 4 of *Leadership and Military Training* by Brigadier General Lincoln C. Andrews (Philadelphia: J. B. Lippincott Company, 1918).

Chapter 2

Reprinted with permission from *The Armed Forces Officer* (Washington, DC: Government Printing Office, 1998), 76–82.

Chapter 3

Reprinted with permission of *Harvard Business Review* from Daniel Goleman, "What Makes a Leader," *Harvard Business Review,* November/December 1998, © 1998 by the Harvard Business School Publishing Corporation. All rights reserved.

Chapter 4

In James H. Buck and Lawrence J. Korb, eds., *Military Leadership* (Beverly Hills, CA: Sage, 1981). Reprinted with permission of the author.

Chapter 5

Reprinted with permission from *Air & Space Power Journal* 20, no. 4 (Winter 2006): 82–90, Maxwell AFB, AL.

Chapter 6

Reprinted with permission of the authors.

Chapter 7

Revised by the author from *Armed Forces International* (July 1986): 54–69. Reprinted with permission.

Chapter 8

Reprinted with permission from *Leadership Excellence* 22, no. 5 (May 2005), ©2005 by Executive Excellence.

Chapter 9

Reprinted with permission from *Fortune,* November 12, 2007, 48, ©2007 by Time Inc. All rights reserved.

Chapter 10

From the *New York Times*, January 24, 1998. Copyright © 1998 by the New York Times Company. Used by permission.

Chapter 11

Reprinted with permission of the author.

Chapter 12

Reprinted with permission from *Government Executive* 38, no. 17 (October 1, 2006): 68.

Chapter 13

Reprinted with permission from *Leadership in Action* 23, no. 4 (September/October 2003): 22–24, © 2003 by Wiley Publishing.

Chapter 14

Reprinted from *Generalship: The Diseases and Their Cure* (Harrisburg, PA: Military Service Publishing Company, 1936), 23–35, © 1936 by Military Service Publishing Company.

Chapter 15

Reprinted with permission from *Parameters* 31, no. 2 (Summer 2001): 4–18, ©2001 Superintendent of Documents.

Chapter 16

Reprinted with permission of the author.

Chapter 17

Chapter 18

Chapter 19

Chapter 20

Chapter 21

Chapter 22

Chapter 23

Chapter 24

Chapter 25

Chapter 26

INDEX